Communities

A Survey of Theories
and Methods of Research

Dennis E. Poplin
Murray State University

The Macmillan Company, New York
Collier-Macmillan Limited, London

To My Wife,
Kay Brandon Poplin

THE MACMILLAN COMPANY
866 THIRD AVENUE, NEW YORK, NEW YORK 10022
COLLIER-MACMILLAN CANADA, LTD., TORONTO, ONTARIO

Library of Congress catalog card number: 70–169979
Printing: 1 2 3 4 5 6 7 8   Year: 2 3 4 5 6 7 8

Preface

During the last few years I have had responsibility for teaching courses entitled "The Community" or "The Urban Community." Perhaps the thing which has bothered me most often is that it is extremely difficult to decide what approach to take in teaching these courses. One approach the writer has tried is essentially descriptive, i.e., the student is asked to familiarize himself with the basic characteristics of rural and urban communities, with the spatial organization of cities, and with a variety of other features of the modern community. This approach has some real merits, but it has one crucial drawback: it does not necessarily help the student to adopt the thought patterns of the professional sociologist. Today's sociologist is not content to engage in armchair description. Rather, he develops concepts, advances theories, and conducts research. It is the goal of this book to give the student an opportunity to follow the sociologist as he seeks knowledge about the community.

Thus, in Part I of this book the student is asked to think about the concept of community. This is one of the most confusing terms that sociologists use. If the student does not grasp some of the meanings we attach to it, he will gain little from our efforts to instruct him. His confusion will become even greater if he tries to distinguish among various types of communities. This is our fault. We use such terms as *village, city,* and *metropolitan area* with alacrity, but sometimes we fail to define them precisely.

Sociology has become both theory conscious and research oriented. The sociology of community life has not been exempted from this trend. Hence, Part II of this book draws together and

summarizes various theories of community. Specifically, consideration is given to social system theory and functionalism as they apply
to the study of communities, as well as to some of the more traditional types of community theory. Likewise, in Part III the student
is introduced to methods of community research. We do not attempt to teach him how to conduct a community study. Rather,
he is encouraged to think about the ways we gain knowledge about
community life.

One of the things which might be considered new about this book
is its organization. I have attempted to summarize and evaluate
some of the most significant contributions of those sociologists who
have seen the community as a worthy object of study. An undertaking of this type has its dangers. It is challenging enough to put
one's own thoughts into writing. To summarize and evaluate the
work of others is difficult indeed. Nonetheless, I have attempted to
deal fairly and accurately with the articles, books, and other publications considered in this text. If I have at times failed, those whom
I have slighted might bear one thing in mind: it is my fault, not
theirs!

To express my appreciation to everyone who has lent a hand in
the preparation of this manuscript is impossible. Nonetheless, a
special note of thanks must be extended to Professors Walter J.
Cartwright and John H. Watson, both of whom provided that kind
of encouragement which is so necessary if a project of this type is
to be completed. Likewise, I owe a heavy intellectual debt to Professors Therel R. Black and Evelyn H. Lewis of Utah State University and George A. Hillery, Jr., of Virginia Polytechnic Institute.
Only they can understand the nature of this debt. Many of my
colleagues and students have been kind enough to read portions of
the manuscript and to make a number of comments and suggestions. They include Francis B. Collins, Harry J. Hale, Jr., Harold
R. Hepler, George A. Hillery, Jr., David R. Rodnick, Jon P. Tyner,
John H. Watson, and Robert Whitten. Personnel of The Macmillan
Company, and especially Charles E. Smith, have been thoroughly
helpful and deserve much credit. Mrs. Joycelyn Graves and several
of her student assistants rendered invaluable help in typing a complete draft of the manuscript and in otherwise assisting me with
the details of its preparation. Finally, without my wife's encouragement, patience, and concrete assistance this manuscript would have
never reached completion. To all of these people I extend my
deepest gratitude.

D. E. P.

Contents

one   **The Concept of Community**   **1**

1 *The Concept of Community*   **3**

Community: A Word of Many Uses   3
Moral Communities and Mass Society   5
The Community in Sociological Perspective   9
Summary   25
Bibliography   27

2 *Major Community Types*   **29**

Rural and Urban Communities: A Survey of
   Differences   29
Major Community Types   41
A Further Look at the Metropolitan Community   50
Summary   58
Bibliography   59

two   **Theories of Community**   **63**

3 *Human Ecology*   **65**

Historical Development   66
Classical Ecology   67
Neo-orthodox Ecology   91
Sociocultural Ecology   96
Social Area Analysis   100
Summary   103
Bibliography   105

4 *Constructed Types and Community Theory*   **108**

Constructed Types   108
Ferdinand Tonnies   114
Communal Types: Major American Contributions   121
Robert Redfield: The Folk–Urban Continuum   125
Some Recent Innovations   133
Summary   143
Bibliography   146

5 Social System Theory, Functionalism, and Community **148**

The Community as a Social System 148
Functionalism and Community Analysis 163
Summary 175
Bibliography 178

6 Community Action and Community Leadership **180**

Community Action Theory 180
Leadership and Involvement 193
Summary 206
Bibliography 207

7 Community Change and Community Problems **210**

Types of Community Change 211
Unplanned Change and the Modern American
  Community 212
Type of Planned Community Change 220
Summary 239
Bibliography 240

three Research and Community Study **245**

8 Research on Community Life **247**

Research and Community Study 247
The Varieties of Community Research:
  A Review of Literature 257
Summary 271
Bibliography 272

9 Methods of Community Study **275**

Participant Observation 276
The Social Survey 287
Documents as Data 298
Summary 303
Bibliography 304

Index **305**

The Concept of Community

The purpose of this book is to present the reader with a survey of the most significant theories of community and to introduce him to methods of community research. Before this can be done, however, it is necessary to examine the word *community* itself. Unfortunately, it is no easy task to say just what sociologists mean by this term. Sometimes its meaning is extremely difficult to specify.

Hence, in Chapter 1 the concept of community is examined. It is argued that sociologists use the word *community* in essentially three ways. First, it is often used as a synonym: at one time or another prisons, religious organizations, minority groups, members of the same profession, and even military establishments have been referred to as communities. Secondly, the word *community* is often used to refer to a moral or spiritual phenomenon. Today men and women the world over are supposedly engaged in a "search for community," i.e., a quest for unity and involvement with other human beings. Finally, the word *community* is used to refer to those units of social and territorial organization which dot the face of the earth and which can also be called hamlets, villages, towns, cities, or metropolitan areas. It is an interest in these units of social and territorial organization which has prompted the writing of this book.

In Chapter 2 the reader's attention is focused on some of the forms which territorial communities can assume. More specifically, an attempt is made to spell out some of the characteristics of rural, urban, and metropolitan communities. Are there major and significant differences between these three communal types? If so, what are these differences? Once these questions are answered, we shall be in a good position to examine theories of community structure and process.

1

The Concept of Community

From its inception as a discipline, sociology has been plagued by inconsistency and ambiguity in some of its basic terminology. Indeed, some words which are used almost daily by the sociologist take on so many shades of meaning that it is difficult to endow them with scientific precision. The word *community* definitely falls into this category. As an element in the sociological vocabulary, this term has been used in so many ways that it has been described as an omnibus word.[1] In this book, however, we shall use the word *community* to refer to those units of social and territorial organization which, depending upon their size, may also be called hamlets, villages, towns, cities, or metropolitan areas. Before we examine this concept of community, perhaps we need to look at some of the other ways in which this illusive term has been used.

Community: A Word of Many Uses

One need not explore far into the literature of sociology before encountering the term *community*. For alert readers this can become a source of utmost confusion. David W. Minar and Scott Greer, for example, refer to factories, trade unions, cor-

[1] George A. Hillery, Jr., "Villages, Cities, and Total Institutions," *American Sociological Review*, **28** (October, 1963), p. 779.

porations, and professions as communities,[2] and at various times reference is made to prison communities, military communities, religious communities, academic communities, and so on, through a seemingly endless array of social phenomena. These multiple usages of the term *community* may be unavoidable but they nonetheless make things difficult for those who seek to study communities as a distinct form of social and territorial organization. Furthermore, the fact that a word can be used in several different ways diminishes its usefulness for purposes of scientific communication. For example, Herbert J. Gans has described the emergence of a small "community" of Jewish families in a predominantly Gentile suburb of Chicago.[3] The way in which Gans uses the term *community* seems to be perfectly appropriate. However, if this or any other small, closely knit minority group constitutes a community, then a great deal of mental gearshifting must occur before one refers to the great cities of the world or the thousands of smaller towns and villages scattered across the face of the earth as communities. Likewise, if the American military establishment represents a community,[4] then one can question whether a small group of Jewish families also constitutes a community. Are we not stretching the concept of community to that point at which it loses all meaning and becomes useless for scientific purposes? Do a minority group, a large city, and a complex military organization have enough in common that they can be referred to by the same term? They should only be called the same thing if they are *like* units of social organization.

These remarks rest on theoretical rather than practical grounds. Sociologists will undoubtedly continue to use *community* as a catch-all term for a long time to come. However,

[2] David W. Minar and Scott Greer, *The Concept of Community: Readings with Interpretations* (Chicago: Aldine Publishing Company, 1969), p. 140.

[3] See Herbert J. Gans, "Park Forest: The Birth of a Jewish Community," *Commentary*, 11 (April, 1951), pp. 330–39.

[4] For a discussion of "military communities" see Maurice R. Stein, *The Eclipse of Community: An Interpretation of American Community Studies* (New York: Harper & Row, 1964), pp. 175–98.

The Concept of Community

this practice can only cause confusion. Furthermore, in many cases the use of the term *community* denotes a lack of conceptual rigor. If the sociologist is talking about a social group, then he should refer to it as such and fit it into one of the many typologies of social groups. Similarly, if the object of investigation is a subculture (e.g., "the academic community"), then the vocabulary of subcultural analysis should be used. This is not to deny of course that there are some units of social organization which do not fit anywhere in the landscape of sociological terminology. Among the examples which can be cited are prisons, convents, mental hospitals, orphanages, and army barracks. We need more research which focuses upon these entities so that their basic properties can be determined. Erving Goffman, for example, has suggested that prisons, convents, mental hospitals, and kindred organizations share so many characteristics that they can be lumped into one category. He suggests that the term *total institution* be assigned to this category.[5]

Moral Communities and Mass Society

Whenever we encounter the term *community* we should ask ourselves whether the writer is guilty of using an illusive concept in a careless, imprecise way. At the same time we must also be aware of the fact that the writer may be using the word *community* in a philosophical sense. Indeed, *community* is sometimes used to refer to a moral or a spiritual phenomenon. This seems to be true in the case of Minar and Greer. In discussing their concept of community, they tell us that "it expresses our vague yearnings for a commonality of desire, a communion with those around us, an extension of the bonds of kin and friend to all those who share a common fate with us." [6]

Table 1-1 provides us with a preliminary overview of this concept of community and contrasts it with its opposite, mass

[5] See Erving Goffman, "Characteristics of Total Institutions," in Maurice R. Stein, Arthur J. Vidich, and David Manning White (eds.), *Identity and Anxiety: Survival of the Person in Mass Society* (New York: The Free Press, 1960), pp. 449–79.

[6] Minar and Greer, *The Concept of Community,* p. ix.

society. In the left-hand column of this table a few basic characteristics of "moral communities" are listed, the right-hand column gives the reader a clue to some of the characteristics of mass societies. Our listing of characteristics is by no means complete. Many other characteristics of "moral communities" and "mass societies" could be delineated.

Table 1-1. Selected Characteristics of Moral Communities and Mass Societies

Moral Communities	Mass Societies
Identification Members of the moral community have a deep sense of belonging to a significant, meaningful group.	*Alienation* Members of mass society have a deep sense of being "cut off" from meaningful group associations.
Moral Unity Members of the moral community have a sense of pursuing common goals and feel a oneness with other community members.	*Moral Fragmentation* Members of mass society pursue divergent goals and feel no sense of oneness with other members of the mass society.
Involvement Members of the moral community are submerged in various groups and have a compelling need to participate in these groups.	*Disengagement* Members of mass society have no meaningful group memberships and feel no compulsion to participate in the collective activities of various groups.
Wholeness Members of the moral community regard each other as whole persons who are of intrinsic significance and worth.	*Segmentation* Members of mass society regard each other as means to ends and assign no intrinsic worth or significance to the individual.

This table makes it immediately apparent that this concept of community is far from unidimensional. Rather, community as a moral phenomenon seems to involve a sense of identity and unity with one's group and a feeling of involvement and wholeness on the part of the individual. In short, the term *community* has been used to refer to a condition in which human beings find themselves enmeshed in a tight-knit web of meaningful relationships with their fellow human beings. In contrast to this "sense of community" are the conditions which supposedly prevail in modern society. During recent years scholars have become increasingly concerned with the place of the individual in mass society, and if one is to judge from the prodigious amount of literature on the subject, it can only be concluded that twentieth-century man is alienated, frustrated, and alone. Again, it is the opposite of this condition which several scholars choose to call community.

Among the sociologists who have championed this concept during recent years is Robert A. Nisbet. According to Nisbet, one of the fundamental themes of the twentieth century is that of a "quest for community." This quest arises from the fact that conditions in modern society do not give the individual a sense of security and fulfillment. In commenting on the modern political state, for example, Nisbet points out that

the state does not even serve the security need. No large scale organization can really meet the psychic demand of individuals because, by its very nature, it is too large, too complex, too bureaucratized, and altogether too aloof from the residual meanings which human beings live by. *The state can enlist popular enthusiasm, can conduct crusades, can mobilize on behalf of great "causes," such as wars, but as a regular and normal means of meeting human needs for recognition, fellowship, security, and membership, it is inadequate.*[7]

[7] Robert A. Nisbet, "Moral Values and Community," *International Review of Community Development*, No. 5 (1960), p. 82. Italics added. For a more complete statement of Nisbet's thesis see his *Community and Power: A Study in the Ethics of Order and Freedom* (New York: Oxford University Press, 1962).

In short, although modern society can offer man the miracles of mass democracy (or mass totalitarianism), mass education, mass production, and mass communications, it cannot offer him the security and belongingness which seem to accompany a sense of well-being. Hence, the only alternative to the continued spread of alienation in the twentieth century "are communities small in scale but solid in structure." [8] According to Nisbet, only "they and they alone can be the beginning of social reconstruction because they respond, at the grass roots, to fundamental human desires: living together, working together, experiencing together, being together." [9]

Baker Brownell adopts much the same perspective in his discussion of the human community.[10] Although the term *community* has several shades of meaning for Brownell, it is above all "the cooperative fullness of action, the sense of belonging, the face-to-face association with people well known." [11] Thus, Brownell limits the term *community* to "a potentially or practically face-to-face group in which a member may be easily in another's presence and where in the day-by-day comings and goings of life they may and do 'run across' each other with familiarity and without surprise." [12] On the other hand, the large bureaucratic organization, the modern state, and the sprawling metropolitan region constitute something other than community. Human relationships in entities of this type are, according to Brownell, of a secondary, noncommunal nature.

It is clear that Nisbet and Brownell are representatives of a great intellectual tradition which has viewed community from a humanistic perspective. Certainly it cannot be denied that their concept of community points to conditions in modern society that are of the utmost significance. Along with urbanization, rapid population growth, and the increasing complexity

[8] Nisbet, "Moral Values and Community," p. 82.
[9] Ibid., p. 82.
[10] See Baker Brownell, *The Human Community: Its Philosophy and Practice for a Time of Crisis* (New York: Harper & Row, 1950).
[11] Ibid., p. 209.
[12] Ibid., p. 199.

of modern society has apparently come a heightened sense of alienation and anxiety. Furthermore, the term *community* seems to be the only one which fully captures the sense of oneness for which Nisbet and Brownell so convincingly appeal. *Shared culture* is much too inclusive, whereas *primary group* is much too concrete. For some time to come those who study territorial communities will probably have to share their term with scholars who take note of man's continuous search for meaning and security in an increasingly complex world.

The Community in Sociological Perspective

Today most sociologists use the word *community* to refer to such units of social and territorial organization as hamlets, villages, towns, cities, and metropolitan areas. In brief, the term *community* refers to the places in which people maintain their homes, earn their livings, rear their children, and, in general, carry on most of their life activities. Thus, Hillery has found that at least three major elements enter into most sociological definitions of community, including (1) geographic area, (2) social interaction, and (3) common tie or ties.[13] Because of its basis in careful research we shall accept Hillery's contention that a "community consists of persons in social interaction within a geographic area and having one or more additional common ties." [14] It will be noted that this definition includes a territorial variable (geographic area), a sociological variable (social interaction), and a psychocultural variable (common ties). Each of these must now be elaborated upon.

The Community as a Territorial Unit

Hillery's definition reminds us that communities exist in a spatial milieu. Indeed the community has been referred to as

[13] George A. Hillery, Jr., "Definitions of Community: Areas of Agreement," *Rural Sociology,* **20** (June, 1955), p. 118.
[14] Ibid., p. 111.

a spatial unit, a cluster of people living within a specific geographic area, or as simply "a place." It is, however, somewhat difficult to analyze thoroughly all facets of the spatial dimension of communities. Perhaps some progress can be made in this direction by pointing out (1) that territorial factors help to account for the location, universality, and persistence of communities and (2) that community members constantly modify the territorial milieu in which they live. Both the influence of territorial variables on community life and the influence of the community on its spatial milieu must be considered.

Territory as an Independent Variable. It seems clear that territorial and geographical variables help to account for the location and growth potential of communities. Generally speaking, communities are most likely to appear at locations where rich natural resources exist or where transportation routes make permanent settlement germane. An especially favored site for new settlements is where resources and potentially adequate transportation routes converge, providing that there is a population base for the new community to draw upon. However, there are two qualifications which must be attached to this statement. First, whether something constitutes a "resource" depends upon social and cultural definitions. The "resource" may be physical (oil, water, and so on), recreational, climatic, or agricultural. Secondly, regardless of the resource potential of an area, a new community will not appear nor will an old community grow unless adequate transportation routes are present or can be developed. At the same time it should be obvious that the transportation and community growth relationship has many of the features of the chicken or the egg dilemma. Accessibility is a major variable affecting the emergence of communities, but as communities grow the transportation routes which link them to the outside world are constantly improved.

It is also clear that territorial and geographic factors help to explain the universality and persistence of communities. Although man has achieved many things, he must still meet most of his needs in a local area. Modern air transportation has indeed made it possible to eat breakfast in New York City and dinner in Los Angeles. Yet during a more extended period of time the individual must work, eat, sleep, and acquire goods and services in a severely delimited area. In short, communities appeared because man cannot transcend space. They also appeared because the satisfaction of man's social and psychological needs involves "nearness." According to Kingsley Davis, "it is no accident that people cluster together. Nearness facilitates contact, furnishes protection, and makes easier the organization and integration of the group." [15]

Territory as a Dependent Variable. Although territorial variables influence the location and growth dynamics of communities, the way in which people adjust and adapt to their territorial milieu still depends a great deal upon their cultural heritage and technical know-how. Terrain is malleable and may be modified by direct action or as a latent consequence of other activities. Thus, deserts have been made to bloom and brush-covered mountainsides have been converted into plush residential areas. In fact, the development of modern construction equipment has made it less necessary for man to choose his territorial milieu with care and more possible for him to shape diverse physical environments to meet his needs. This increased ability to modify and manipulate the physical environment may well number among the miracles of the twentieth century.

Of even more importance are the many ways in which local territories have been modified as a latent consequence of laws, values, and economic activities. It is clear, for example, that both laws and values have influenced patterns of land settlement in the United States. Generally speaking, the United States has been settled along "isolated farmstead" lines, with the accompanying village trade center. The dominance of this pattern of land settlement can be partly explained by the emphasis which American pioneers placed upon individualism and partly

[15] Kingsley Davis, *Human Society* (New York: The Macmillan Company, 1948), p. 311.

by the Quadrangular Survey and Homestead Acts.[16] However, a value system unique to the Latter-day Saints (Mormons) led to the emergence of the village pattern of land settlement in Utah and scattered parts of Arizona, New Mexico, Idaho, and Alberta, Canada.[17] Of equal significance are the many ways in which physical environments have been modified as a by-product of economic activities. Unfortunately, this has often involved the devastation of timberland, the gutting of mountain chains, and the pollution of air and water supplies. Because of man's apparent willingness and capacity to destroy his own physical environment, during recent years we have seen an upsurge of interest in improving the environment and in preserving natural resources.

Academic Approaches to the Territorial Variable. Our comments should make it clear that territorial variables cannot be ignored in the sociological study of communities. In fact, several approaches have been used to study the community as a territorial entity. Among other things, attention has been centered upon patterns of land settlement.[18] We have realized that man must live in proximity to his fellow man but that this need can be met in more than one way. Likewise, much research has focused upon the delineation of community boundaries.[19] To several sociologists it has seemed significant to establish meaningful community boundaries and to study the ties which exist

---

[16] Carl C. Taylor, Walter Goldschmidt, and Glen Taggart, *Patterns of Rural Settlement,* United States Department of the Interior, Bureau of Reclamation, Columbia Basin Joint Investigation Problem 10 (Washington, D.C.: Government Printing Office, 1947), p. 7.

[17] There are several good discussions of the "Mormon Village" pattern of land settlement. For example, see Lowry Nelson, *The Mormon Village: A Technique and Pattern of Land Settlement* (Salt Lake City: The University of Utah Press, 1952).

[18] See Taylor, Goldschmidt, and Taggart, *Patterns of Rural Settlement;* and Nelson, *The Mormon Village.* See also Lowry Nelson, Charles E. Ramsey, and Coolie Verner, *Community Structure and Change* (New York: The Macmillan Company, 1960), pp. 33–45.

[19] About the earliest such research was that of Charles J. Galpin. See his *The Social Anatomy of an Agricultural Community* (Madison: Wisconsin Agricultural Experiment Station Bulletin 34, 1915).

between the community and its hinterland. Finally, the ecological approach to the study of urban communities hardly needs to be mentioned. A rich body of theory and research has emerged which attempts to explain the "whys" and "hows" of city growth and the spatial relationships between man and his environment, his institutions, and his fellow man. This body of theory and research is reviewed in Chapter 3 of the present text.

The Community as a Unit of Social Organization

There is equally widespread agreement that the community is a basic unit of social organization. However, even a cursory survey of the literature suggests that there is little agreement upon how best to describe the community as a sociological entity. Broadly speaking, there have been two approaches to this problem. First, the community has been viewed as a social group or, more recently, as a social system. Second, the community has been analyzed as a network of interaction. In reality, these are not two distinctly different approaches to the study of communities. Our subsequent discussion will show that they have much in common.

The Community as a Social Group. To E. T. Hiller must go the credit for suggesting that the community is one among many social groups. According to Hiller, social groups have several basic properties, including a body of members, one or more tests of membership, a collection of assigned roles, and a set of norms.[20] Presumably all these properties are an integral part of community structure and hence it is legitimate to view the community as a social group.

That communities do possess these properties, at least to some degree, is obvious. All communities have a body of members (or a population) and demand certain things of those persons who want to enjoy full membership in the community. Likewise, each community assigns various roles to its members and has a set of norms to which these members are expected

[20] E. T. Hiller, "The Community as a Social Group," *American Sociological Review,* 6 (April, 1941), p. 189.

to conform. However, if the community is to be viewed as a social group, then it must be differentiated from other types of social groups. In discussing Hiller's work, Albert J. Reiss handles this problem quite simply by pointing out that "a community system differs from other systems in that locality is a datum in the integration of the system." [21] In short, the fact that communities have a territorial dimension distinguishes them from other social groups.

A more difficult question is whether it is scientifically profitable to view the community as a social group. Is the most to be learned about communities by treating them as a special form of social group or should they, for purposes of analysis, be treated as distinct forms of social organization? The answer to this question depends upon the learnings of the individual sociologist. On the one hand, much is to be gained by pinpointing the similarities between what may at first glance appear to be dissimilar units of social organization. The community does have something in common with other types of social groups, and these common elements should be identified. On the other hand, if we refer to the community as a social group, we may be stretching the term *social group* to a point at which it loses much of its conceptual power. If both an informal gathering of two or three persons and a large metropolitan area can be referred to as social groups, then the term itself loses much of its usefulness for purposes of scientific communication.

Today the social group approach to community analysis has few adherents. Instead it has become fashionable to analyze the community as a social system. Roland L. Warren, for example, defines the community as "that combination of social units and systems which perform the major social functions having locality relevance." [22] Although the approach to community analysis suggested by Warren is complex and multifaceted, his argument seems to be that the community is a total system con-

[21] Albert J. Reiss, "The Sociological Study of Communities," *Rural Sociology,* **24** (June, 1959), p. 127.

[22] Roland L. Warren, *The Community in America* (Chicago: Rand McNally & Company, 1963), p. 9.

sisting of smaller subsystems. These subsystems, in turn, perform the "locality relevant" functions of socialization, social control, social participation, mutual support, and production, distribution, and consumption.[23] A similar approach is taken by Irwin T. Sanders in his text *The Community: An Introduction to a Social System.*[24]

In reality, the social system approach is probably most accurately viewed as a refined version of the "community as a social group" approach. Social systems, like social groups, have a body of members, a normative structure, and one or more tests of membership. In social system theory the latter take the form of geographical, psychological, and social boundaries. All of this adds up to one thing: the application of social system theory to the community does not appear to be an entirely new innovation as it might first be thought. Rather, social system theory incorporates the social group approach into a more comprehensive frame of reference.

Regardless of whether the social system approach to community analysis represents a major breakthrough or not, it does make clear the importance of the community as a unit of social organization. As we examine the hierarchy which begins with the two-person group and ends with national societies, the community emerges as the first subsystem which can potentially meet the full range of man's physiological, psychological, and social needs.[25] The small group cannot do this nor can the nuclear family, the church, the government, or a voluntary association. This may well be what Robert H. McIver had in mind when he said that,

> Any circle of people who live together, who belong together so that they share not this or that particular interest, but a

[23] Ibid., p. 9.

[24] Irwin T. Sanders, *The Community: An Introduction to a Social System,* 2nd ed. (New York: The Ronald Press, 1966).

[25] This perspective on the community was first brought to the author's attention in an article by Conrad M. Arensberg. See Conrad M. Arensberg, "The Community as Object and as Sample," *American Anthropologist,* **63** (April, 1961), pp. 241–61.

whole set of interests wide enough and complete enough to include their lives, is a community. . . . The mark of a community is that one's life may be lived wholly within it, that all one's relationships may be found within it.[26]

Although this fullness of scope is seldom found in modern American communities, it is the rule in many primitive communities. Furthermore, although it might prove stifling, many Americans potentially can meet all of their basic life needs in their home community. This is not true of any social unit of less complexity than the community.[27]

The Community as a Network of Interaction. As an alternative to the social system approach, some writers prefer to view the community as a network of interaction. Before examining the interactional approach, two things should be noted. First, the social system and interactional approaches are not discrete, distinct ways of analyzing the community. Rather, they have much in common. As a matter of fact, the chief point of articulation between the two approaches lies in the postulate that interaction occurs not only between individuals but also between groups and institutions. Secondly, a distinction must be made between the approach which views the community as a network of interaction and what is known as community action theory. Interaction is, of course, a rather standard conceptual tool in sociology and it is quite understandable that sociologists use this tool in their efforts to analyze the community. On the other hand, community action theory seeks to distinguish activities which are communal in nature from those which are not.[28] Quite often community action theorists have the explicit goal of shedding light on the dynamics of planned community change and

[26] Robert M. MacIver, *Society: Its Structure and Changes* (New York: Ray Long & Richard R. Smith, Inc., 1931), p. 9.

[27] Some persons, of course, may spend their entire lives in "total institutions." This is only possible, however, because others, in this case the staff, play roles which link the institution to the larger community.

[28] See Willis A. Sutton, Jr., "Toward a Universe of Community Actions," *Sociological Inquiry,* **34** (Winter, 1964), pp. 48–59.

development. Thus, a leading writer on community action concludes one of his discussions by stating that his concern has been "with the development of theory which would support research that would contribute effectively to the growing community organization and development movement." [29]

With these comments in mind, we can examine the community as a network of interaction. One of the chief problems inherent in the interactional approach to community analysis is that conditions in the modern community do not completely square with those definitions of interaction which are accepted by most sociologists. In brief, interaction is usually defined as a face-to-face encounter between two or more people in which each person takes the other into account. Obviously the involvement of every member of the community in a network of interaction of this type never occurs, except perhaps in the smallest rural hamlet. In most communities the number of actors (i.e., large size of population) and a lack of common interests prevents such contact from occurring.

Those who view the community as a network of interaction attempt to overcome this conceptual problem in one of two ways. As we noted before, one solution is to maintain that not only do individuals interact, but that interaction also occurs between the various groups and institutions of which the community is composed. Those who take this position usually view the community as a chain of input, output relationships in which each subsystem receives needed inputs from other subsystems and, in turn, contributes to the other subsystems and to the total community system. These inputs and outputs may take the form of financial contributions, physical resources, social pressures, a labor force, and so forth.[30] Likewise, those who view the community as a network of interacting subsystems often refer to the community's horizontal and vertical axes. The horizontal axis "involves the relationship of individual to individual or of

[29] Harold F. Kaufman, "Toward an Interactional Conception of Community," *Social Forces,* **38** (October, 1959), p. 17.

[30] Warren, *The Community in America,* p. 294.

group to group within the locality" while the vertical axis "involves the relationship of the individual to a local interest group and of that interest group to a regional, state, or national organization." [31] This is simply a shorthand way of indicating that interaction can occur between two social units which occupy a similar level in the total community system or between two social units, one of which is more inclusive than the other.

There is at least one major advantage in viewing the community as a network of interacting subsystems: it serves well as a tool by which to describe systematically the interrelationships between various units of which the community is composed. At the same time, the proponents of this approach need to specify more clearly the nature of interaction between groups and to explore the mechanisms by which this interaction occurs. Perhaps the key question which must be raised concerns the mechanisms by which groups actually interact. In brief, do members of the interacting groups merge and form a larger group, or are members of the involved groups represented by group leaders in the process of interaction?

The second major approach that is taken by those who view the community as a network of interaction is to point out that interaction at the community level often displays characteristic themes and patterns. When these themes and patterns become generalized to the point that they are characteristic of interaction between both individuals and groups, they are referred to as the basic social processes. The basic social processes are cooperation, competition, and conflict. The subprocesses by which cooperation is furthered and competition and conflict mitigated are accommodation, amalgamation, and assimilation. Those who used these concepts to analyze the American community are heavily in debt to the pioneering work by Park and Burgess, in which the significance of the social processes was made clear.[32]

[31] Roland L. Warren, "Toward a Reformulation of Community Theory," *Human Organization,* 15 (Summer, 1956), p. 8.

[32] Robert E. Park and Ernest W. Burgess, *Introduction to the Science of Sociology* (Chicago: University of Chicago Press, 1921).

To be more specific, it has been suggested many times that the American community is an arena of competition and that competition is the key to progress at both the local and national level. Similarly, it has become rather stylish to view the American community as an arena of conflict, and the number of studies which focus upon specific instances of community conflict increases yearly. However, those who study communities in terms of the social processes often overlook the central role of cooperation in community life. In actuality, it is only because men cooperate with each other that viable communities are maintained. This follows from the fact that conflict can become costly and dysfunctional for the community system and that competition does not always lead to the solution of basic community problems. Hence, whenever competition or conflict are encountered, further exploration usually reveals an underlying dimension of cooperation. In even the most conflict-ridden communities most people still cooperate with the police, still support their churches and schools, and still subscribe to basic social norms. Similarly, competition rarely occurs in raw, cutthroat form. In the final analysis, competition is an essentially cooperative process in which the parties to the interaction agree upon which goals to compete for and upon the ways by which these goals may be legitimately achieved.

The study of villages, cities, and metropolitan areas in terms of cooperation, competition, and conflict can yield significant insight into the sociological dimensions of community life. Among other things, it forces one to explore the very basis upon which communal organization rests: cooperation is seemingly the fundamental theme underlying all other social processes at the community level. Furthermore, the "social processes" approach provides a useful tool for analyzing the dynamics of any given community. Social relationships in some communities may be of a cooperative nature, whereas in other communities competition or even conflict may reign supreme. There is no question, for example, that the black subcommunity in some of our large cities is more likely to be conflict-ridden than a middle-class suburb. In many cases, however, these three processes are so interwoven that it is meaningless to characterize the community as being an arena of cooperation, competition, or conflict. All three processes are present in varying degrees.

Miscellaneous Approaches. In addition to these general approaches there are more specialized approaches which have been used to analyze communities. Two of these require brief mention. First, a number of books and articles have focused upon social class at the community level and, indeed, among the most widely hailed community studies are those concerned chiefly with local stratification systems.[33] For the most part these studies have not led to a comprehensive theory of community structure and process. Rather, their authors have sought insight into a phenomenon which has national as well as local dimensions. Secondly, during recent years students of community life have developed a keen interest in community power and in the processes by which decisions are made at the local level.[34] Although some of these studies are both insightful and interesting, a theory of community which has power as its key variable has yet to be developed. For the most part the frequently heated debates concerning community power have centered around methodological rather than theoretical questions.[35]

[33] Among the best-known studies are Allison Davis and Burleigh Gardner, *Deep South* (Chicago: University of Chicago Press, 1941); John Dollard, *Class and Caste in a Southern Town* (New Haven: Yale University Press, 1937); A. B. Hollingshead, *Elmtown's Youth* (New York: John Wiley & Sons, Inc., 1949); W. Lloyd Warner et al., *Democracy in Jonesville* (New York: Harper & Row, 1949); and W. Lloyd Warner and Paul S. Lunt, *The Social Life of a Modern Community* (New Haven: Yale University Press, 1946).

[34] One of the best-known accounts of a community power structure was made by Robert S. and Helen M. Lynd in their *Middletown in Transition: A Study in Cultural Conflicts* (New York: Harcourt Brace Jovanovich, Inc., 1937), Chapter 3. Another well-known study is Floyd Hunter's *Community Power Structure: A Study of Decision Makers* (Chapel Hill: University of North Carolina Press, 1953).

[35] For a sampling of this literature see William V. D'Antonio and Eugene C. Ericksen, "The Reputational Technique as a Measure of Community Power: An Evaluation Based on Comparative and Longitudinal Studies," *American Sociological Review,* **27** (June, 1962), pp. 362–76; M. Herbert Danzgar, "Community Power Structure: Problems and Continuities," *American Sociological Review,* **29** (October, 1964),

The Community as a Psychocultural Unit

A third element in many sociological definitions of community stresses the idea that there are common ties or bonds between community members. As a matter of fact, sociologists have not been totally insensitive to the dimension of community which has been explored in depth by Nisbet, Brownell, and others working in the humanistic tradition. However, sociologists of an empirical bent do differ from the humanists in that the former insist that common ties and bonds are but one aspect of the complex reality subsumed under the term *community*. The term should only be used to refer to those units of social organization which have a territorial dimension.

There is little agreement as to whether these common ties are psychological or cultural in nature. Thus, Roland L. Warren suggests that the degree to which persons psychologically identify with local social systems varies from community to community,[36] whereas Irwin T. Sanders devotes a chapter of his text to a discussion of community traditions and values.[37] The psychological perspective hypothesizes that people gain a sense of security because they identify with their community, whereas advocates of the cultural perspective maintain that this identification exists because community members share common values, norms, and goals. Both of these ideas are encompassed in the concept of community sentiment as it has been used by MacIver and Page, that is, "An awareness of sharing a way of life as well as the common earth." [38]

---

pp. 707–17; Nelson W. Polsby, "Three Problems in the Analysis of Community Power," *American Sociological Review,* **24** (December, 1959), pp. 796–802; John Walton, "Substance and Artifact: The Current Status of Research on Community Power Structure," *American Journal of Sociology,* **71** (January, 1966), pp. 430–38; and Raymond E. Wolfinger, "Reputation and Reality in the Study of Community Power," *American Sociological Review,* **25** (October, 1960), pp. 636–44.

[36] Warren, *The Community in America,* p. 13.

[37] Sanders, *The Community,* pp. 99–112.

[38] Robert M. MacIver and Charles H. Page, *Society: An Introductory Analysis* (New York: Holt, Rinehart and Winston, Inc., 1949), p. 10.

The Psychocultural Dimension. Before we examine the functional consequences of community sentiment it might be well to indicate some of the elements of which it is composed. As a cultural variable, community sentiment involves, first, a sharing of common values, beliefs, and goals. These may arise from many sources, and especially from the historical milieu out of which the community grew. These values, beliefs, and goals of course may be focused upon many things. Florence Kluckhohn and Fred Strodtbeck, for example, suggest that most cultural systems have value orientations pertaining to man's relationship to nature, to the supernatural, to time, to the modality of human activity, and to other men.[39] Similarly, as a cultural variable, community sentiment also involves norms, that is, community members have a set of shared behavioral expectations to which they supposedly conform. As a psychological concept, community sentiment encompasses many things, including a feeling of "we-ness." Presumably, many community members think of each other as "we" and of other persons as "they." It has also been argued that whatever psychological security and stability the individual enjoys comes to him by virtue of his community membership. Perhaps in an era in which family names mean little and in which society is extremely complex the only way that an individual can place himself in the larger scheme of things is by claiming his identity from his home community.

Most of the statements in the preceding paragraph are, in the present writer's thinking, quite debatable. For one thing, few modern communities have a cultural system that is completely distinct from that of the larger society. Rather, modern man is confronted both with cultural phenomena which originate at the local level and with those which have their origin in the larger society. Similarly, it is doubtful that common values and psychological identification really typify the modern com-

[39] Florence R. Kluckhohn and Fred L. Strodtbeck, *Variations in Value Orientation,* (New York: Harper & Row, 1961), pp. 11–20.

munity. Theoretically, the existence of common values and psychological identification should effectively stifle deviancy and disorganization, yet crime, mental illness, and social unrest are among the basic problems confronting modern man. For that matter, community sentiment would appear to be the opposite of alienation, but again one of the fundamental themes of the twentieth century is that most people are alienated and alone. This suggests that the inclusion of common ties and/or psychological identification in sociological definitions of community needs careful examination, qualification, and documentation. Do most persons actually identify with their community? Is the modern community characterized by a set of common values and norms which originate at the local level? Unfortunately, not enough research has been carried out to answer these questions fully, but it seems clear that one cannot glibly answer them in the affirmative.

Consequences and Implications. Even though psychocultural variables have a questionable place in definitions of community, it might be well to indicate some of the potential consequences and implications of community sentiment for individuals and for the community as a social system.

The consequences of community sentiment for individuals are obvious and require only brief mention. Community sentiment potentially gives the individual something to draw upon for pattern and stability in a complex world and is, theoretically, the opposite of alienation and insecurity. Yet it is entirely possible that strong community sentiment can hamper individual creativity and adjustment. In fact, in modern society a high degree of commitment to local values and goals may well be dysfunctional for a person, for he must survive in a social milieu which places a premium upon individualism and unfettered mobility. Hence, in the final analysis psychocultural variables underlie one of the fundamental dilemmas facing modern man. Presumably, most individuals need the security and acceptance which comes from being wholly committed to an identifiable social system. At the same time, this commitment may retard personal development, hamper careers, and frustrate the achievement of other hopes and desires that the individual may possess.

The possible breakdown of community sentiment also has tremendous implications for the community itself. Obviously, all communities have a crucial interest in the development of healthy, stable personalities. Crime, mental illness, divorce, and social unrest not only are personal tragedies but also entail multiple costs for the community. It might be argued that one way to avert tragedies of this type is to give the individual a sense of identification with his community. However, the achievement of widespread community sentiment involves a seemingly hopeless paradox. The key to psychological identification is *involvement,* that is, a willingness on the part of the individual to participate in local community affairs. At the same time, meaningful community involvement, if it develops at all, occurs only among those who readily identify with their communities. We have already questioned whether many people fall into this category.

Community sentiment also has a number of implications for social control. Indeed community sentiment can be a powerful force which leads the individual to conform to community values, beliefs, and norms. Alan Wheelis makes this clear when he says,

> One who lives out his life in the town of his birth derives much superego support from proximity to family and relatives, and from their continuing expectations of him. They know what kind of person he is, and they expect him to continue being that kind of person. If the culture of the community is relatively homogeneous, conscience is strengthened also by the continuing pattern of known traditions, customs, and values. Unopposed mores are not subject to critical scrutiny, but they are taken for granted. . . . Life under such conditions is orderly and predictable.[40]

[40] Alan Wheelis, *The Quest for Identity* (New York: W. W. Norton & Company, Inc., 1958), p. 100.

Wheelis continues by pointing out that,

> Probably there is no one who is not more liable to steal, to
> lie, or commit adultery in a foreign land than at home. Some
> persons, indeed, travel for just this purpose—to lose an un-
> wanted reinforcement of conscience. For them wanderlust is
> not a lust for wandering, but a wandering for lust—an effort
> to achieve abroad a license for which one could not forgive
> himself at home. Many persons do not need to go far: the
> annual business convention in America is notorious in this
> respect. Things happen in motels that do not happen in homes,
> and towels are swiped in distant hotels by persons who would
> not steal a pin in their home towns. In these ways our in-
> creased mobility diminishes the external support for con-
> science.[41]

Wheelis makes the interrelationship between common values,
psychological identification, and social control so clear that
further comment is unnecessary.

Summary

In this chapter we have indicated some of the different ways
in which the term *community* has been used. At times it is used
as a synonym for such units of social organization as minority
groups, subcultures, social institutions, political states, and so
forth. Secondly, the term *community* has also been adopted by
humanists to refer to the condition in which people enjoy meaningful fellowship with other people. The humanists of course
are concerned with matters of the highest significance and *community* seems to be the only term which fully encompasses the
condition for which Nisbet, Brownell, and others so forcefully
appeal. Finally, *community* has been used as a generic term
which encompasses those units of social and territorial organization which, depending upon their size, may also be called
hamlets, villages, towns, cities, or metropolitan areas. It should

[41] Ibid., p. 101.

be clear that the present writer's interest is in the analysis of these units.

We have also attempted to present the reader with an analysis of the term *community* as it is used in this book. That many sociologists agree upon the inclusion of geographic area, social interaction, and common ties in definitions of the term need not be demonstrated. This has already been done by Hillery. However, the validity of including these elements in definitions of community does require exploration, especially in light of the fact that sociologists have experienced difficulty in differentiating the community from other units of social organization. Although some of the statements made in this chapter are tentative, the following observations seem to be warranted:

1. The community differs from other units of social organization in that it has a firm territorial base. Above all, communities represent an organizational pattern through which persons meet their daily needs in a local area. This is perhaps the major criterion by which the community can be delineated from other units of social organization. Although it is true that families, churches, schools, and so forth exist in a territorial milieu, we do not usually think of them as units of territorial organization. Rather, they are a part of a larger territorial unit, the community, which is potentially able to meet the full range of man's physiological, psychological, and social needs.

2. Although there is some disagreement concerning the best way to describe the community as a unit of social organization, there is no question but that the community must be analyzed in terms of interaction, as a social group or as a social system. Communities consist of people in interaction with other people. This implies that communities do have definite patterns of social organization. Furthermore, the community is a rather unique form of social organization, again because it is potentially able to meet the full range of man's needs. Families meet some needs, as do churches, governments, and schools, but none of these institutions can simultaneously provide men with food, clothing, and shelter, with a marriage partner, with a

sense of belonging, with intellectual stimulation, and so on, through the seemingly endless list of human wants. In the hierarchy of social organization, communities emerge as the first social unit which can claim such all-inclusiveness as a needs-meeting facility.

3. For the sake of agreement with other sociologists it would be desirable if we could argue that the community is a basic unit with which people identify and from which they gain a sense of security and belonging. However, the preceding analysis suggests that this may not be the case. The contention that members of the modern community share common ties and bonds needs to be seriously examined. If these ties and bonds did exist, then it seems unlikely that contemporary scholars would constantly remind us that twentieth-century man is alienated, frustrated, and alone. As a matter of fact, it might be more realistic to suggest that viable common ties have broken down at the community level and that the answer to many of our deepest problems is to restore the common bonds which seem no longer to typify the social life of modern communities.

Bibliography

Baltzell, E. Digby. *The Search for Community in Modern America.* New York: Harper & Row, 1968.

Brownell, Baker. *The Human Community: Its Philosophy and Practice for a Time of Crisis.* New York: Harper & Row, 1950.

Freilich, Norris. "Toward an Operational Definition of Community," *Rural Sociology,* **28** (June, 1963), pp. 117–27.

Hiller, E. T. "The Community as a Social Group," *American Sociological Review,* **6** (April, 1941), pp. 189–202.

Hillery, George A., Jr. "Definitions of Community: Areas of Agreement," *Rural Sociology,* **20** (June, 1955), pp. 111–23.

————. "Villages, Cities, and Total Institutions," *American Sociological Review,* **28** (October, 1963), pp. 779–91.

Miner, David W., and Scott Greer (eds.). *The Concept of Community.* Chicago: Aldine Publishing Company, 1969.

Nelson, Lowry, Charles E. Ramsey, and Coolie Verner. *Community*

Structure and Change. New York: The Macmillan Company, 1960.

Nelson, Lowry. *The Mormon Village: A Technique and Pattern of Land Settlement*. Salt Lake City: The University of Utah Press, 1952.

Nisbet, Robert A. *Community and Power: A Study in the Ethics of Order and Freedom*. New York: Oxford University Press, 1962.

————. "Moral Values and Community," *International Review of Community Development*, **5** (1960), pp. 77–85.

Reiss, Albert J. "The Sociological Study of Communities," *Rural Sociology*, **24** (June, 1959), pp. 118–30.

Sanders, Irwin T. *The Community: An Introduction to a Social System,* 2nd ed. New York: The Ronald Press, 1966.

Schnore, Leo F. "The Community," in Neil J. Smelser (ed.). *Sociology: An Introduction*. New York: John Wiley & Sons, 1967.

Warren, Roland L. *The Community in America*. Chicago: Rand McNally & Company, 1963.

————. "Toward a Reformulation of Community Theory," *Human Organization,* **15** (Summer, 1956), pp. 8–11.

2

Major Community Types

We have faced the laborious task of indicating what we shall mean by the term *community*. In essence we have said that a community is a unit of social and territorial organization in which people live, work, attend church and school, and carry on a host of other activities which are a part of daily living. Indeed, communities are unique in that all of a person's needs can potentially be met within them. At the same time, it is immediately apparent that communities differ greatly from one another. Thus, both Houston and New Deal have at least one thing in common: they are both communities in the state of Texas. Yet the differences between Houston and New Deal appear to be much more significant than their similarities. The same is true of Los Angeles and Pumpkin Center, California, of Louisville and Gooserock, Kentucky, and of Salt Lake City and Dutch John, Utah. Hence, in this chapter we must take a close look at major community types.

Rural and Urban Communities: A Survey of Differences

It is rather easy to specify the goals which should be pursued in this chapter. We should be able to derive a scheme for classifying communities by type which is simple, theoretically relevant, and unambiguous. Unfortunately this is probably an impossible task. For one thing there are literally hundreds of variables which could be used to differentiate between types of communities. We could, for example, classify communities according to the size and density of their population, their ecological characteristics, their legal status, their sociocultural characteristics, or their predominant economic activity. Furthermore, there is no foolproof way to decide whether the variables which we might choose to distinguish between types of communities are meaningful and important ones. Other variables might do the job better. To make matters even worse, if a combination of two or more variables was used to distinguish between types of communities there would be no guarantee that they would correlate with one another: on one variable community A might be urban whereas on another variable it might be rural. Therefore, in this chapter we shall not attempt to derive a highly sophisticated classification of types of communities. Rather, we shall examine some of the chief differences between rural and urban communities and look rather closely at the metropolitan area and the communities that are drawn into its orbit. A good place to begin is by examining some of the demographic differences between rural and urban communities.

Demographic Differences

Population size is often cited as one of the most important differences between rural and urban communities. There are several advantages to differentiating between types of communities on the basis of this variable, including the fact that accurate data on population size are readily available in many countries. Moreover, population size obviously has a profound effect on other facets of community life. Within a given culture we can often make some crude hypotheses about the nature of a community by simply knowing the number of people who live in that community. It is, however, extremely risky to do this when one is conducting cross-cultural research. A community with 20,000 population that is located in an underdeveloped country may be much more rural than a community of 10,000 that is located within the United States.[1] This suggests of course that there are difficulties associated with the use of population size in classifying communities as rural or urban. For one thing, it cannot be assumed that population size always correlates with the more complex cluster of traits implied by the terms *rural* and *urban*.[2] In the final analysis it is these broad rural–urban differentials which must be built into an adequate classification of communities. Similarly, on the surface it might appear that the use of population size in differentiating between types of communities would involve no methodological problems. This is partially true in the United States, where the Bureau of the Census to some extent has devised standardized techniques for enumerating community populations. On the other hand, the dangers of making international comparisons of communities on the basis of population size are great. Gibbs and Davis, for example, point out that "there is no assurance that persons included as city residents in one country are not excluded in other countries, and vice-versa."[3] Furthermore, they suggest that "even within the same country there may be little uni-

[1] Because of this, Gideon Sjoberg tells us that "in practice it is difficult, if not impossible, in cross-cultural research to take size as the sole criterion of what is urban. It is evident, for instance, that communities of, say, 5,000 differ considerably in India, Mexico, and the United States, and any analysis predicated on size alone is a poor one. . . . In other words, it is often essential to specify the social conditions under which size is taken as the criterion for urban centers." Gideon Sjoberg, "Theory and Research in Urban Sociology," in Philip M. Hauser and Leo F. Schnore (eds.), *The Study of Urbanization* (New York: John Wiley & Sons, Inc., 1965), p. 164.

[2] See Otis Dudley Duncan, "Community Size and the Rural-Urban Continuum," in Paul K. Hatt and Albert J. Reiss, Jr. (eds.), *Cities and Society* (New York: The Free Press, 1957), pp. 35–45; Richard Dewey, "The Rural–Urban Continuum: Real but Relatively Unimportant," *American Journal of Sociology,* 66 (July, 1960), pp. 60–66; and Philip M. Hauser and Leo F. Schnore, *The Study of Urbanization,* especially p. 511.

[3] Jack P. Gibbs and Kingsley Davis, "Conventional Versus Metropolitan Data in the International Study of Urbanization," *American Sociological Review,* 23 (October, 1958), p. 505.

formity from one province or state to another or from one city to another in drawing the urban boundaries."[4] Even in the United States this can become a problem because of the fact that some communities are underbounded, others overbounded, and yet others bounded in a realistic manner.

Another major difficulty inherent in differentiating between types of communities on the basis of population size is that communities fall along a continuum in terms of this variable. Hence, the choice of cutting points between rural and urban communities is arbitrary. For research personnel in the United States 2,500 and 50,000 constitute the most familiar cutting points. The United States Bureau of the Census uses a population of 2,500 as the basic figure for differentiating between rural and urban territories and the concept of Standard Metropolitan Statistical Area as defined by the same agency hinges upon the requirement that the community in question have a central city of at least 50,000 inhabitants. However, it has been argued that both the rural–urban and the metropolitan cutting points are unrealistically low. At a later point in this chapter we shall examine these arguments.

Another index of rurality or urbanity that is frequently used is the ratio of population to land area (i.e., population density). Some years ago Louis Wirth argued that density of population has a profound impact on community structure,[5] and more recently Smith and Zopf have argued that "differences in the density of population color many important features of rural and urban life."[6] Again, however, it cannot be assumed that population density always correlates with degrees of "rurality" or "urbanity" or for that matter with size of population. A high population density, like a high population size, does not necessarily mean that the members of the community are "urbane"

[4] Ibid., p. 505.

[5] See Louis Wirth, "Urbanism as a Way of Life," *American Journal of Sociology,* 44 (July, 1938), pp. 14–16.

[6] T. Lynn Smith and Paul E. Zopf, Jr., *Principles of Inductive Rural Sociology* (Philadelphia: J. A. Davis Company, 1970), p. 26.

in their attitudes and behavior. Likewise, Kingsley Davis is undoubtedly correct when he points out that,

> A hundred people may happen to live very close together, separated by open country from other dense settlements, but the place would ordinarily be called a "hamlet" or "village" rather than a town or city. To qualify as an urban place in the eyes of most observers, a settlement would have to embrace a more substantial population and a larger area. In other words, we implicitly recognize not only the factor of density but also the absolute population and the absolute area.[7]

Because of these considerations the researcher who uses population density to differentiate between rural and urban communities should bear two things in mind. First, even though population density may be a satisfactory measure of urbanity in the developed countries, it is not in the underdeveloped world. In many of the emerging nations population densities are extremely high in essentially rural, agricultural areas.[8] Secondly, if population density is used as a measure of urbanity, this must always be in conjunction with population size or some other variable. Otherwise, data on population density tell us nothing about the community. There are also methodological problems entailed in the use of population density as a device for differentiating between types of communities. Obviously, the population density of an underbounded community should not be compared with that of another community whose boundaries extend far into the adjacent rural territory.

Ecological Differences: The Community and Its Hinterland

Several writers have suggested that cities and metropolitan areas could not emerge until working relationships were estab-

[7] In Jack P. Gibbs, *Urban Research Methods* (Princeton, N.J.: D. Van Nostrand Company, Inc., 1961), p. xvii.

[8] For one example see Joel M. Halpern, *The Changing Village Community* (Englewood Cliffs, N.J.: Prentice-Hall, Inc., 1967), pp. 83–86.

lished between the community and its hinterland.[9] Among other things, the urbanite has always had to obtain food, fuel, and fiber from the hinterland population. More recently the urbanite has had to look to the hinterland for choice residential sites, and commercial and business ventures on the scale which we find them in the modern urban community can only thrive if they get the trade of persons who live far out in the hinterland. This suggests that a second major difference between rural and urban communities lies in the nature of their hinterlands. Generally speaking, rural communities have hinterlands which are small and underdeveloped, whereas urban communities tend to have large, well-developed hinterlands. In fact, this may be one of the most accurate ways of distinguishing between types of communities.

Hinterlands may be conceptualized in several ways. One possibility is to conceive of hinterlands in demographic and ecological terms. This involves an inquiry into the number of inhabitants in the territory surrounding a community and into the size and shape of this territory. However, it is nonsensical to delineate a hinterland of this type unless the inhabitants of the territory have viable relationships with the community in question. These relationships may be of various kinds. First, they may entail exchange between the community and the surrounding territory. This exchange may be manifested in periodic shopping trips to the community center, visiting friends who live in the community center, and the utilization of community-based facilities by the hinterland population. Secondly, the community–hinterland relationship may involve economic ties. Indeed, the traditional concept of *hinterland* implies economic interdependence between a city with its commerce and industry and the agricultural hinterland. Finally, the hinterland can be delineated in terms of patterns of influence. With the emergence of mass media of communication the urban community can, and often does, influence a vast geographic area, at least in terms of shaping values, opinions, attitudes, and knowledge.

[9] See, for example, Philip M. Hauser and Leo F. Schnore, *The Study of Urbanization*, p. 2.

It is no easy task to measure the size and degree of development of a community's hinterland and one must keep his definition of *hinterland* constant from community to community. One way to meet the latter requirement is through the use of Hawley's concepts of primary, secondary, and tertiary community areas.[10] The primary community area is that relatively small area which surrounds the central community. Its residents work, purchase groceries, and meet other recurrent needs in the central community. It seems safe to assume that all communities have primary areas, although their nature depends partly upon the size of the community: the primary area associated with a rural community is often sparsely settled and accessible only by poor roads, whereas the primary area of a large city may be densely settled and criss-crossed by freeways running in all directions. On the other hand, small rural communities simply do not have secondary and tertiary areas. Basically, a secondary community area is one in which the exchange between the community center and the hinterland occurs on a sporadic, irregular basis and pertains to "the retail purchase of durable goods, wholesale distribution, specialized medical, legal, and financial services, rare forms of entertainment, etc." [11] More often than not, the rural community lacks a highly developed secondary area and is instead located within the secondary area of a more urban community. Finally, a tertiary community area is found only in conjunction with the most metropolitan of communities. Quite often these communities perform specialized services for an extremely large hinterland, or tertiary, area. Hawley points out, for instance, that "Chicago is the transportation hub and the livestock market for the whole of the United States; New York and London are the world's financial centers; and Hollywood, New York, and Paris are fashion centers for the world." [12]

[10] Amos H. Hawley, *Human Ecology: A Theory of Community Structure* (New York: The Ronald Press Company, 1950), pp. 255–58. Hawley's concept of *community area* and our concept of *hinterland* appear to be identical.
[11] Ibid., p. 256.
[12] Ibid., p. 257.

It would seem that the presence or absence of a highly developed secondary area surrounding the community center would constitute an excellent basis for distinguishing between rural and urban communities, especially in cultural areas where emphasis is placed upon trade and commerce. If a particular community serves as a retail, financial, wholesale, medical, and legal center for a large area, we would undoubtedly think of it as urban regardless of its size or density of population. During recent years urban geographers, under the leadership of Walter Cristaller, have apparently arrived at essentially the same conclusion. In reference to the work of these urban geographers in classifying communities by type, Raymond Murphy points out that "most of these studies, like Cristaller's theoretical one, are based on the idea that the services a city performs for the surrounding area—its central services—rather than its size or governmental status should determine its position in the [rural–urban] hierarchy." [13] This is simply another way of saying that an urban community is one which has a highly developed secondary area.

Sociocultural Differences

One of the fundamental tasks which sociologists have set for themselves has been to specify the social and cultural differences between rural and urban communities. It is regrettable that little agreement has been reached concerning these differences, because they are of basic importance. Variables such as population size, population density, and community–hinterland relationships are perhaps no more than convenient indexes of the more important social and cultural differentials which exist between communities.

One of the best-known attempts to specify the characteristics of urban areas was made by Louis Wirth.[14] Before examining

[13] Raymond E. Murphy, *The American City: An Urban Geography* (New York: McGraw-Hill Book Company, 1966), pp. 83–84.
[14] See Louis Wirth, "Urbanism as a Way of Life," pp. 1–24.

the specific traits which Wirth attributed to urbanism, we should note that this University of Chicago sociologist said nothing about the rural community. Although it may be safe to make inferences about the rural community from Wirth's analysis of urbanism, it must be stressed that these are no more than inferences. Furthermore, Wirth maintained that the characteristics that he attributed to the city were the function of large population size, high density of population, and the heterogeneous character of urban populations. On the latter variable, heterogeneity, Wirth's thinking appears to have been somewhat confused. On the one hand, he clearly viewed the heterogeneity of urban populations as an independent variable which influences the sociocultural characteristics of cities. After examining Wirth's article, however, one must conclude that heterogeneity itself is partly attributable to high population size and density.

In any event, Wirth's description of urbanism is detailed and multifaceted. In his critique of Wirth's work Richard Dewey, for example, lists nearly fifty traits which Wirth ascribed to urbanism or to the urban personality.[15] It appears, however, that this multitude of specific traits can be summarized as follows:

1. Urbanism is characterized by the segmentalization of human relationships. This entails the predominance of secondary over primary contacts and a means–end-oriented form of role playing.

2. Urbanism fosters sophistication, rationality, and a utilitarian accent in interpersonal relationships. This cluster of traits, in turn, leads to reserve, indifference, and a blasé outlook, and to the anonymity and depersonalization of the individual.

3. Urbanism is characterized by a high division of labor and a high degree of role specialization.

4. Urbanism depends upon communication via the mass media and the expression of individual interests by a process of delegation. Wirth maintains that "the individual counts for

[15] Dewey, "The Rural–Urban Continuum," pp. 61–62.

little, but the voice of the representative is heard with a deference roughly proportional to the numbers for whom he speaks." [16]

5. Urbanism is characterized by formal mechanisms of social control.

6. Urbanism encourages the individual to develop a relativistic perspective and a tolerant stance toward individual differences.

7. Urbanism implies a complicated and multidimensional class structure. High rates of vertical mobility are typical of the city.

8. Finally, we have noted that Wirth associated heterogeneity with urbanism. According to him the large population found in urban areas leads to a heightened range of individual variation and the urban milieu, for various reasons, encourages and rewards individuality.

The fact that Wirth associated so many traits with urbanism makes it extremely difficult to summarize his argument and to indicate briefly the traits which would, by inference, be associated with rurality. Presumably, a rural community would display such features as homogeneity of population, a predominance of primary relationships, and social control on an informal basis.

Wirth's and similar analyses have been subject to rather heavy criticism. Among others, Harold L. Wilensky and Charles N. Lebeaux question the "traditional view" and argue that the form of urbanism described by Wirth was a passing, transitional phenomenon resulting from high rates of industrialization and immigration.[17] Today, they maintain, a mature industrial order is emerging which does not have secondary contacts, superficiality, and the subjugation of the individual as its hallmarks. Indicative of the type of evidence with which Wilensky and

[16] Wirth, "Urbanism as a Way of Life," p. 14.

[17] Harold L. Wilensky and Charles N. Lebeaux, *Industrial Society and Social Welfare* (New York: The Free Press, 1965), pp. 121–33. Paperbound.

Lebeaux support their thesis is the following comment about the modern family:

> With striking consistency the recent studies of urban life underscore the nuclear family as the basic area of involvement for all type of urban populations. *We find not a madly mobile, restless mass, disintegrating for want of intimate ties,* but an almost bucolic contentment with the narrow circle of kin and close friends, with the typical urbanite spending most of his leisure with the family at home, caring for the children, watching television, maintaining the home, reading.[18]

This image of urbanism clearly contradicts the traditional view of urbanism as it was articulated by Wirth.

Perhaps the most penetrating criticism of the traditional view of urbanism is that offered by Richard Dewey.[19] Dewey maintains that many of the traits which Wirth assumed to be associated with urbanism are not a product of high population size and density at all. Rather, they are part of the general cultural setting within which cities appear. Urbanism, so Dewey's argument runs, is a trait associated with entire societies rather than with communities of a specific size. This is why one finds "small rural communities which are secular, civilized, dynamic, and highly literate as well as large, sacred, essentially primitive, illiterate, and relatively static urban communities." [20] At the same time, however, Dewey does not argue that the size and density of their populations is the only major difference between "rural" and "urban" communities. Rather, he sees five major sociocultural differences between rural and urban communities. The first of these differences centers around ano-

[18] Ibid., p. 129. Italics added.

[19] Dewey, "The Rural–Urban Continuum," pp. 60–66.

[20] Ibid., p. 65. Today most sociologists accept the idea that "urbanism" is a trait associated with entire societies rather than with communities of a specific population size. However, Smith and Zopf maintain that the differences between the "country and the city" are still strong and important. See Smith and Zopf, *Principles of Inductive Rural Sociology,* Chapter 2.

nymity. Although Wilensky and Lebeaux are probably correct when they suggest that the urbanite is not as anonymous and alienated as advocates of the traditional view maintain, it is nonetheless true that the urbanite can find anonymity if he so desires. On the other hand, in order to escape the scrutiny of family and neighbors the rural dweller may have to leave his home community. A second major characteristic which Dewey attributes to cities is a high division of labor. Indeed, he points out that "whereas a small rural community can present an un-differentiated occupational pattern, a city of a million most certainly cannot. Great complexity in the division of labor *can* exist in an industrial culture's city, but a certain minimum *must* exist." [21] Thirdly, he argues that heterogeneity is characteristic of large cities and that it increases as the city increases in size. Although Dewey does not make it clear, presumably this heterogeneity involves people of all types and from all walks of life as well as a multitude of organizations and associations. Fourthly, impersonal and formally prescribed relationships are likely to flourish in the urban milieu. Dewey echoes the widely accepted principle that it is impossible for the urbanite to develop primary relationships with all the people with whom he comes into contact. Finally, Dewey argues that in an urban milieu people are ranked on the basis of overt symbols of status. This observation has been documented by several investigators, including T. E. Lasswell.[22]

Because his argument is sound, the variables identified by Dewey will be used in our discussion of rural and urban communities. Other writers, the most notable of which are Ferdinand Tonnies and Robert Redfield, have also contributed much to our understanding of the sociocultural differences between rural and urban communities. However, a detailed discussion of the contributions made by these two men must wait until Chapter 4.

[21] Ibid., p. 65.
[22] T. E. Lasswell, "Social Class and Size of Community," *American Journal of Sociology,* **64** (March, 1959), pp. 505–508.

Major Community Types

We have now enumerated some of the variables which can be used to distinguish between different types of communities. These variables can now be utilized in a discussion of some of the forms which territorial communities actually take. Specifically, we shall explore rural and urban communities in more detail. Within the latter category we must look at both the city and the metropolitan area. It could easily be argued that this classification of types of communities is grossly oversimplified. However, one could also question whether much is to be gained by drawing fine distinctions between hamlets, villages, towns, cities, and metropolitan areas. Certainly it is not necessary to do so in order to understand the concept of community itself.

Rural Communities

Demographic Characteristics. To Americans the most obvious feature of the rural community is its small population. However, the point at which a community ceases to be rural and becomes urban instead is open to debate. In the United States some students of community life follow the practice employed by the U.S. Bureau of the Census and designate a population of 2,500 as the cut-off point between rural and urban. Thus all communities of under 2,500 population, whether incorporated or not, might be classified as rural, whereas those with a population of 2,500 or more might be classified as urban. There is fairly widespread agreement, however, that the figure of 2,500 is unrealistically low. It is indeed difficult to think of communities with 2,500 inhabitants as being urban, especially when they are compared to great cities with their millions of people. Because of this Gibbs and Davis suggest that for purposes of international comparison a population of 10,000 represents a more satisfactory cut-off point between rural and urban,[23]

[23] Gibbs and Davis, "Conventional Versus Metropolitan Data," p. 511.

whereas Fenton Keyes presents data which indicate that 25,000 might represent a good cut-off point between rural and urban communities, at least in the United States.[24] Similarly, Philip M. Hauser maintains that "in practice, many comparative international studies use populations in places of 20,000 or more as urban because the data are generally available on that basis and because an agglomeration of this size is not likely to retain rural characteristics." [25] The latter portion of Hauser's statement is of course debatable.

It is not the intention of the present writer to resolve this question. However, the present discussion does raise again the possibility that population size is not of intrinsic significance in distinguishing between types of communities. At the risk of being repetitious, it must be reiterated that a large population by itself does not guarantee that a community will be "urbanlike" in its social and cultural characteristics. About the best that can be said is that as a community gains in population the likelihood that its members will be urban in their values, attitudes, and behavior is increased. In any event, if we must select a cut-off point between rural and urban communities on the basis of population size, it should be at that population size at which the social and cultural characteristics of the community change from rural-like to urbanlike.

It is even more difficult to offer a definitive proposition concerning the population densities of rural communities. In the United States rural communities generally tend to be characterized by relatively low population densities. This is the result of many things, including the fact that in rural America one simply does not find many plots of land that are crowded with multiple-family dwelling units. In countries in which land is in extremely short supply, however, one can find communities that have an extremely high density of population but that are basically rural. Halpern, for instance, describes one Indian village

[24] Fenton Keyes, "The Correlation of Social Phenomena with Community Size," *Social Forces,* **36** (May, 1958), pp. 311–15.
[25] Hauser and Schnore, *The Study of Urbanization,* p. 10.

which had, as of 1951, a population density of approximately 4,700 per square mile.[26] This is as high as or higher than the average population density of many large American cities. Again, population density, taken alone, may be almost worthless as a measure of degrees of urbanization. It is debatable whether one can even hypothesize that there is a direct correlation between population density and the probability that a community will be urban in its social and cultural characteristics.

The Rural Community and Its Hinterland. A second characteristic of the rural community is its small and sometimes undeveloped hinterland.[27] Indeed, we have already discussed the possibility that most rural communities have only a primary community area. The evidence at hand seems to bear this out. Normally the rural community serves as a shopping and service center for its own residents and for the surrounding farm population, and both of these groups sometimes trade in larger communities.[28] Furthermore, the ties between the village and its hinterland may be weak. Aside from serving as a center where they purchase their daily commodities, worship, and send their children to school, the village may perform no other functions for families which live in its hinterland. Their thoughts, attitudes, and opinions are shaped and formed by messages diffused from larger communities. Similarly, today most people "buy" durable goods, expert medical attention, legal advice, and financial services from "sellers" in a nearby, but nonetheless large, city.

Sociocultural Characteristics. Much credit must be given to Richard Dewey for suggesting that urbanism is a trait that is associated with entire societies. It is because of this fact that

[26] Joel M. Halpern, *The Changing Village Community,* p. 68.

[27] For a description of several rural villages and their hinterlands see Irwin T. Sanders and Douglas Ensminger, *Alabama Rural Communities: A Study of Chilton County* (Montevallo: Alabama College Bulletin No. 1A, July, 1940).

[28] See Arthur J. Vidich and Joseph Bensman, *Small Town in Mass Society: Class, Power and Religion in a Rural Community* (Princeton, N.J.: Princeton University Press, 1958).

Major Community Types   43

a particular community may clearly be rural in terms of population size but still display many of the characteristics that are associated with urbanism. It must be remembered that in large measure the entire population of the United States is urbanized and that the differences that we shall now discuss are a matter of degree.

The first thing that might be pointed out about the resident of a rural community is that he is supposedly enmeshed in a tight-knit web of social relationships. This makes it impossible for him to remain anonymous for very long. The newcomer to a rural community often finds that his neighbors know a great deal about him even before he takes up residence in the community, and rural youth often lament the fact that they cannot escape the ever-watchful eyes of kin and neighbors. In short, the rural dweller is both visible and known. This means that he normally does not experience that type of anonymity which leaves one feeling isolated and alone, but that he may not enjoy the freedom and privacy that is enjoyed by the urban dweller. Furthermore, the rural dweller is also likely to become one strand in a web of informal primary relationships. Not only is he on a friendly, first-name basis with his next-door neighbor, but he has that relationship with most of the people with whom he comes into contact.

Because primary relationships predominate, rural dwellers are frequently ranked on the basis of personal characteristics rather than on the basis of overt symbols of status. The questions that residents of the rural community ask of each other supposedly have little to do with one's income, education, and occupation. The values which people hold and the practices that they engage in are the things which determine social rank in the rural community.[29] The end product of social ranking in the rural community is a simple stratification system as compared to that of the city, although the class system of small towns is apparently more complex than might be thought.

In most cases the rural community is characterized by homo-

[29] For evidence bearing on this point see ibid., especially Chapter 3.

geneity in both people and institutions. In many rural communities the surnames of most residents reveal their common ethnicity and, by national standards, the vast majority of residents may belong to the same social class. Homogeneity of this type is almost never found in the urban area. Similarly, the range of organizations and services available in the rural community is limited.[30] Some rural communities have only a few churches and a few small business concerns. They may lack even a local school and a viable unit of government. This restricted range of organizations and services is simply not encountered in the city. Indeed, if a community's facilities are this limited, it might properly be classified as rural, even though it has a large population.

Another dimension of this homogeneity is the low division of labor which typifies most rural communities. In fact, the entire occupational structure of the rural community is often built around agriculture and meeting the needs of the farm population.[31] In a few rural communities the dominant economic activity shifts from agriculture to manufacturing or to operating resort and recreational facilities. This low division of labor of course must be measured in terms of the occupational structure of the rural community itself. Today it is relatively common for individuals who are employed in the city to live in small hinterland communities. Thus, a complete enumeration of the residents of an essentially rural community may uncover podiatrists, key-punch operators, and nuclear physicists as well as persons engaged in farming. The former are obviously a part of the urban labor force even though they live in a rural setting.

Rural Communities: The Delineation of Subtypes. We have already hinted that rural communities can be classified on the basis of their dominant economic activity. Is the community

[30] See Fenton Keyes, "The Correlation of Social Phenomena with Community Size," pp. 311–15.

[31] Because of this Smith and Zopf maintain that "among all the differences which have been noted between the rural and urban portions of society, the occupational difference seems to have the most fundamental importance." Smith and Zopf, *Principles of Inductive Rural Sociology,* p. 24.

primarily an agricultural center? A mining center? A manufacturing center? A resort and recreational center? When distinctions of this type contribute to one's study of community structure and process, it is perfectly legitimate to make them. Likewise, a leading student of rural community life, Lowry Nelson, has drawn a distinction between three types of rural communities: the hamlet, the small village, and the large village.[32] Nelson's classificatory scheme is based on population size alone. Thus, he applies the term *hamlet* to all communities which have a population of 250 or less, the term *small village* to all communities which have a population of 250 to 1,000, and the term *large village* to all communities which have a population of 1,000 to 2,500. He also distinguishes between towns and small cities. Towns, according to Nelson, have a population greater than 2,500 but less than 5,000, whereas small cities have a population of between 5,000 and 10,000. Some of our earlier comments, however, should make it clear that this classificatory scheme, based as it is on population size alone, may not tell us much about rural communities as units of social and cultural organization. Only field research can reveal whether there are major social and cultural differences between hamlets and small villages, or between small villages and large villages.

Urban Communities: Cities and Metropolitan Areas

After discussing Wirth's concept of urbanism, anything further said about the urban community may be redundant. However, something might be gained by examining the more salient characteristics of the modern city and metropolitan area.
Demographic Characteristics. Little needs to be said about the size of urban communities. In terms of numbers the urban community begins where the rural community leaves off. Population size might also be used to draw a distinction between minor urban communities and metropolitan communities. The U.S. Bureau of the Census, for example, classifies as urban all places,

[32] See Lowry Nelson, *Rural Sociology,* 2nd ed. (New York: American Book Company, 1955), p. 87.

whether incorporated or not, which have a population of 2,500 or more.[33] However, if an urban place has 50,000 or more inhabitants, it is designated as a Standard Metropolitan Statistical Area. In addition to including the central city, a Standard Metropolitan Statistical Area also includes the county in which the city is located, plus contiguous counties "if according to certain criteria they are essentially metropolitan in character and socially and economically integrated with the central city." [34]

In the United States, then, the student of community life might be on fairly safe ground if he applied the term *metropolis* to communities which have a total population of 50,000 or more. Of course he might want to use additional criteria which would assure that the community in question actually possesses metropolitan characteristics. At the same time there is fairly widespread agreement that a population of 50,000 is really not large enough to distinguish between metropolitan communities and smaller urban places. William A. Robson, for instance, maintains that a community should have a central city with at least 300,000 population and a total population of at least 400,000 if it is to qualify for metropolitan status.[35] Similarly, Hans Blumenfeld defines a metropolis as "a concentration of at least 500,000 people living within an area in which the traveling time from the outskirts to the center is no more than about 40 minutes." [36]

Cities also tend to have high population densities. This can be attributed to tightly circumscribed city boundaries, a preponderance of small lots, and a large number of multifamily dwelling units. Thus, on occasion large cities have within their boundaries areas in which population densities exceed 100,000 per square mile: the over-all population densities of cities may run into the thousands. It is a bit more difficult to generalize

[33] For further discussion see Raymond E. Murphy, *The American City: An Urban Geography,* pp. 9–10.

[34] Ibid., p. 17.

[35] William A. Robson, *Great Cities of the World,* 2nd ed. (New York: The Macmillan Company, 1957), p. 31.

[36] Hans Blumenfeld, "The Modern Metropolis," *Scientific American,* 213 (September, 1965), p. 64.

about the population densities of metropolitan communities. They tend to be high near the center of the community and to decrease as one moves outward.

Ecological Characteristics. If we follow Hawley's analysis, relatively little needs to be said about the urban community and its hinterlands (i.e., community areas). One can presume that all cities and metropolitan communities have primary community areas. It also seems safe to assume that all except perhaps the smallest urban communities (assuming that the cut-off point between rural and urban communities is set at 2,500) have secondary areas. People constantly journey to the city and the metropolitan area to purchase durable goods and to obtain specialized medical, financial, and legal services. In addition, it is in the city and the metropolitan area, rather than in the rural community, that we find the wholesale distributor, the international airport, and regional newspapers and television stations. Finally, most large metropolitan communities have tertiary community areas. The worldwide influence of such great metropolitan centers as New York, London, Paris, Tokyo, and Moscow is obvious.

Sociocultural Characteristics. The social characteristics of urban communities can be easily summarized. Among other things, the urban dweller can supposedly remain anonymous if he so desires. This does not mean that the urbanite necessarily feels cut off from group ties, but only that there are places where he can go and not be known by anyone. This, in turn, makes it necessary to rely upon the police, courts, and other regulatory bodies to provide for social control. These agencies cannot deal with the minutia of human behavior. Therefore, minor patterns of deviance are sometimes ignored by urban dwellers. However, the fact that urban dwellers must rely upon secondary mechanisms of social control does not mean that social control on a primary basis has disappeared completely. Most urbanites are still responsive to pressures exerted upon them by family, friends, and even passing acquaintances. In fact, a person who does not experience these pressures or respond to them is to be pitied. He is a truly anomic, alienated human being.

That the urban community is characterized by heterogeneity in people and organizations scarcely needs to be pointed out. It is in the urban community that one finds people of all races, religious, and creeds, people who hold a wide variety of value orientations and who have a variety of life styles. One way in which this heterogeneity is manifested is in a very high division of labor. In the urban community a range of occupational specialties is found that is unknown in the rural community. In addition, a wide range of organizations and services is found. If one desires a wide choice of churches or schools, if one wishes to patronize a podiatrist or a burlesque show, he would be best advised to look to the city rather than the country.

Finally, the class structure of the modern urban community is exceedingly complex and the social rank of the individual is often determined on the basis of impersonal criteria. Such variables as education, income, and occupation often serve to determine who one associates with and how one is evaluated by passing acquaintances. In daily encounters with strangers even less personal criteria are used to evaluate the individual. This is made clear by Richard Dewey when he says,

> When people interact socially, they must, except on rare occasions, know the status of their associates, and the pervasive anonymity of the large city demands some means of identifying the functionaries essential to daily living there. The waitress, the clerk, the policeman, the priest, and others must be identified. Even the less uniform symbols of "good standing" are important in the city. A salesman whose clothes were soiled and ill pressed and whose face and hair were unkempt could stand little chance of gaining an audience with a perspective customer in the city.[37]

This is in marked contrast to the rural community. In the latter, a person's status may not become fully crystallized until his neighbors have the opportunity to study his behavior and beliefs.

[37] Dewey, "The Rural–Urban Continuum," pp. 65–66.

A Further Look at the Metropolitan Community

The movement of the world's population from rural to urban areas has been going on for a long, long time. The gigantic metropolitan community is, however, a product of the twentieth century. Amos H. Hawley, for example, points out that "few phenomena are more representative of the trend of modern society with its increasing emphasis on large-scale organization than is the emergence and rapid development of the metropolitan community during the past fifty odd years." [38] Similarly, Philip M. Hauser presents data which indicate that "by the end of the century 42 percent of the world's people may be resident in places of 100,000 or more as contrasted with 20 percent in 1960, 5.5 percent in 1900, and 1.7 percent in 1800." [39] Within the United States trends in metropolitan growth are even more dramatic and the metropolitan community has indeed become the "city" of the twentieth century. It therefore behooves us to examine the metropolitan community in more detail. A good place to begin is with an analysis of some of the factors which have contributed to metropolitan growth.

The Logic of Metropolitan Growth: Edward C. Banfield

Edward C. Banfield has shed a good deal of light on some of the factors which have made the emergence of metropolitan communities in the United States inevitable. [40] One of these factors is demographic in nature, i.e., there has been a steady and continuous stream of migrants (both from within the country and from overseas) into American cities during the twentieth

[38] Amos H. Hawley, *The Changing Shape of Metropolitan America: Deconcentration Since 1920* (New York: The Free Press, 1956), p. 1.
[39] Philip M. Hauser, "The Chaotic Society: Product of the Social Morphological Revolution," *American Sociological Review,* **34** (February, 1969), p. 4.
[40] See Edward C. Banfield, *The Unheavenly City: The Nature and Future of Our Urban Crisis* (Boston: Little, Brown and Company, 1970), Chapter 2.

century. Because of their sheer numbers, the urban community has expanded outward and become the sprawling entity that it is today. Banfield devotes considerable effort to explaining why it has been the "well-off" rather than the "not well-off" that have moved to the periphery of the metropolitan community, but this need not concern us here. At the same time, population pressure alone does not totally explain the outward expansion of the city. Rather, population pressure operated in combination with two other factors to make the emergence of the metropolitan community inevitable. The first of these factors was technological in nature. Banfield tells us that "if it is feasible to transport large numbers of people outward (by train, bus, and automobile) but not upward or downward (by elevator), the city must expand outward." [41] Finally, a third set of factors which made metropolitan growth possible, and indeed inevitable, were those of an economic nature, i.e., "if the distribution of wealth and income is such that some can afford new housing and the time and money to commute considerable distances to work while others cannot, the expanding periphery of the city must be occupied by the first group (the 'well-off') while the older, inner parts of the city, where most of the jobs are, must be occupied by the second group (the 'not well-off')." [42]

The Structure of the Metropolitan Community

At first, it might appear that the metropolitan community is simply an extremely large city. However, students of the urban community do not necessarily take this point of view. Rather, they see the "metropolis" as a series of interdependent communities, one of which exercises dominance over the rest. Indeed, one of the most famous students of the metropolitan community in America, Roderick D. McKenzie, has noted that the metropolitan community "absorbs varying numbers of

[41] Ibid., p. 23.
[42] Ibid., p. 23.

separate local communities into its economic and cultural organization"[43] and further states that "the city of former days is really being replaced by a new entity, the metropolitan community, with a distribution of people shading off from extreme congestion to relative sparseness, yet with some uniformity of character."[44] Similar ideas lie behind the concept of Standard Metropolitan Statistical Area as it has been developed by the U.S. Bureau of the Census.[45]

When these threads of thought are drawn together, the image of the metropolitan area which emerges is that of a very large central city which is surrounded by a number of smaller communities and residential areas. The boundaries between the central city, its satellites, and its suburbs may merge to such an extent that they have only legal significance. Nonetheless, students of the metropolitan community have found it helpful to analyze the "metropolis" in terms of three components: the central city, the suburban ring with its suburban and satellite comunities, and the rural–urban fringe. These three components of the metropolitan community are shown in Figure 2-1.

The Central City. The heart of any metropolitan community is its central city. In fact, it would be hard to visualize a metropolitan community without a densely settled urban core.

To be more specific, the central city is utilized by two distinct occupants. The most prominent of these occupants are various business and commercial organizations. Even today the huge skyscraper buildings that are found in the central city are the headquarters for large department stores, financial institutions, specialty shops, legal firms, giant corporations, medical

43 Roderick D. McKenzie, *The Metropolitan Community* (New York: McGraw-Hill Book Company, 1933), p. 7.

44 R. D. McKenzie, "The Rise of Metropolitan Communities," in President's Research Committee on Social Trends, *Recent Social Trends in the United States,* one-volume ed. (New York: McGraw-Hill Book Company, 1933), p. 444.

45 For a discussion of "Standard Metropolitan Statistical Areas" see U.S. Bureau of the Census, *U.S. Census of Population 1960, Part A, Number of Inhabitants* (Washington, D.C.: U.S. Government Printing Office, 1961), pp. xxiii–xxviii.

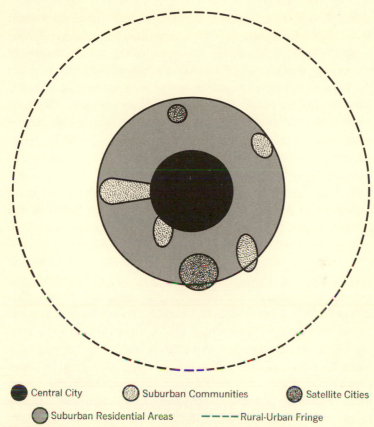

● Central City   ◉ Suburban Communities   ◉ Satellite Cities

◉ Suburban Residential Areas   – – – – Rural-Urban Fringe

Figure 2-1. Structure of the metropolitan community.

specialists, and advertising agencies. At the same time, we must remember that millions of people still live within the central city. In the United States these inner-city residents are often the most disadvantaged members of the society. Scott Greer puts it well when he states that the central city "has exclusive possession of most nonassimilating ethnics (the darker-skinned migrants) and most of the very poor (the dwellers in congested, aged residential areas inherited from an earlier epoch)." [46]

[46] Scott Greer, *The Emerging City: Myth and Reality* (New York: The Free Press, 1962), p. 84.

Major Community Types   53

Needless to say, the central city has, at least in the United States, been in a state of continuous flux and change. In the residential sector, this change has manifested itself in the steady movement of white persons out of the central city. As a result, the modern central city has become a community that is populated mainly by black Americans,[47] Puerto Ricans, Mexican-Americans, and other minority groups. Change in the central city, however, has not been confined to the residential sector. At one time the central city, among other things, provided a locus for factories, warehouses, railroad yards, and truck terminals. Like the more affluent white population, however, these organizations have long since moved to the periphery of the metropolitan area, where open land is available for expansion, storage, and parking.[48]

The Suburban Ring. The typical metropolitan community is characterized by a suburban ring or fringe which surrounds the central city. Like the central city, the suburban ring consists of two components. First, the suburban ring usually encompasses vast tracts of land which are devoted to residential uses. Indeed, Dobriner describes portions of the suburban ring well when he comments that "moving out into the inner (or suburban) ring the quality of the housing improves. The apartment houses all but disappear, and the modern single-family house on the 60 by 100 plot, the universal symbol of suburban America, stands triumphant everywhere." [49] Secondly, the suburban ring is also dotted with suburban and satellite communities. These two communal types must be explored in more detail.

The distinction between "suburbs" (or suburban communities) and satellite cities is well established in the literature. In fact, as early as 1925 Harlan Paul Douglas recognized that a dis-

[47] For documentation see Philip M. Hauser and Leo F. Schnore, *The Study of Urbanization,* Chapters 14 and 15.

[48] For an analysis of changes in the central city see Hans Blumenfeld, "The Modern Metropolis," p. 71.

[49] William M. Dobriner, *Class in Suburbia* (Englewood Cliffs, N.J.: Prentice-Hall, 1963), p. 162.

tinction can be made between "suburbs of production" and "suburbs of consumption." [50] The first of these terms reminds us that within the suburban ring of many metropolitan communities one can find subcenters in which manufacturing and related types of activity are dominant. These centers of production which may dot the suburban ring are referred to as satellite cities. As such they not only provide jobs for their own residents but for workers who commute from other subcommunities within the metropolitan complex. Because jobs are available in the satellite community, its residents may not be particularly dependent on the central city.

The residents of a suburb, on the other hand, are quite dependent on the central city. Thus, Alvin Boskoff tells us that the "suburbs" consist of "those urbanized nuclei located outside (but within accessible range) of central cities that are politically independent but economically and psychologically linked with services and facilities provided by the metropolis," [51] whereas Walter T. Martin defines a "suburb" as "the relatively small but formally structured community adjacent to and dependent upon a larger central city." [52] Furthermore, he suggests that two features distinguish the suburb from other community types: the physical and political separation of suburbs from the central city and the economic dependence of the suburb on the central city.[53] The latter characteristic manifests itself in the fact that residents of suburbs frequently work in the central city and make most of their major purchases there. It is because of this that Janowitz refers to the suburb as a "community of limited liability." [54]

[50] Harlan Paul Douglas, *The Suburban Trend* (New York: The Century Co., 1925), pp. 74–92. See also Leo F. Schnore, "Satellites and Suburbs," *Social Forces,* **36** (December, 1957), pp. 121–29.

[51] Alvin Boskoff, *The Sociology of Urban Regions,* 2nd ed. (New York: Appleton-Century-Crofts, 1970), p. 109.

[52] Walter T. Martin, "The Structure of Social Relationships Engendered by Suburban Residence," *American Sociological Review,* **21** (August, 1956), p. 447.

[53] Ibid., p. 447.

[54] Morris Janowitz, *The Community Press in an Urban Setting* (New York: The Free Press, 1951), pp. 222–25.

In addition to encompassing satellite cities and suburban communities, the suburban ring also contains residential subdivisions which do not seem to be directly affiliated with any particular community. Indeed, the term *suburbia* conjures up the image of a housing development which is homogeneous both in architecture and in the characteristics of its inhabitants. In the first edition of his book, however, Alvin Boskoff suggested that there are basically three types of residential suburbs.[55] The first, the traditional upper-class suburb, is inhabited by long-established, high-status families, and little turnover of population occurs. For obvious reasons upper-class suburbs are concentrated in older sections of the country, such as near Boston, New York, and Philadelphia. The second type of residential development is what Boskoff calls the stable middle-class suburb. Suburban residential areas of this type are populated by middle-class families and are usually located in the newest sections of the suburban ring. The final type of suburban residential area that Boskoff identifies is the "packaged" suburb. These are mass-produced suburban housing developments intended for those families who wish to enjoy the amenities of suburban living but who cannot afford residences in the middle-class suburbs.[56]

Rural–Urban Fringe. There is some confusion in the literature concerning whether there are one or two rings surrounding the central city. Some writers are content with drawing a distinction between the central city and the metropolitan ring. Most urban sociologists, however, argue that the metropolitan ring can and should be divided into the suburban ring and the rural–urban fringe.

[55] Alvin Boskoff, *The Sociology of Urban Regions* (New York: Appleton-Century-Crofts, 1962), pp. 134–35. Boskoff takes a somewhat different approach to the classification of types of suburbs in the second edition of his book. See pp. 113–19. Yet another classification of types of suburbs is offered by S. D. Clark. See his *The Suburban Society* (Toronto: University of Toronto Press, 1966), especially pp. 15–18.

[56] For a thorough description of a "packaged" suburb see Bennett M. Berger, *Working Class Suburb: A Study of Auto Workers in Suburbia* (Berkeley: University of California Press, 1960).

The Concept of Community

There are some serious problems entailed in delineating both the inner and the outer boundaries of the rural–urban fringe.[57] Nonetheless, the nature of the rural–urban fringe itself is easily specified. The rural–urban fringe consists of that belt of land which lies between the rather densely populated suburban fringe and that part of the city's rural hinterland which is devoted almost entirely to farming.[58] As such the rural–urban fringe is characterized by mixed land use. Within the rural–urban fringe one can find scattered residential developments, small communities, industries which cannot operate in heavily populated areas, and of course farms and unused lands. Indeed, the rural–urban fringe is exactly what its name implies: it represents the fusion of rural and urban ways of life on the outskirts of large metropolitan communities.

Murphy suggests that at one time the rural–urban fringe had more than its fair share of problems.[59] In many cases people were drawn to the rural–urban fringe by the promise of inexpensive lots and low taxes. At the same time, the rural–urban fringe frequently lacked building codes and zoning ordinances and thus its development occurred in a random, haphazard fashion. Furthermore, the two units of government most typically found in the rural–urban fringe, the county and the school district, were often unable to provide a growing population with adequate schools, police and fire protection, roads, and other public facilities. The fringe resident, as a result, often found that he was paying rather high taxes for services which were inferior to those received by the urban resident. During recent years, however, this picture may have improved considerably. Fringe residents have undoubtedly benefited from the increased standard of living which most members of our society enjoy and from the fact that the federal government has become

[57] See Raymond E. Murphy, *The American City,* pp. 43–45.

[58] For a much more extensive and sophisticated definition and delineation of the rural–urban fringe see Robin J. Pryor, "Defining the Rural–Urban Fringe," *Social Forces,* **47** (December, 1968), pp. 202–210.

[59] See Raymond E. Murphy, *The American City,* pp. 45–48. See also Walter Firey, "Ecological Considerations in Planning for Urban Fringes," *American Sociological Review,* **11** (August, 1946), pp. 411–21.

more and more willing to pay part of the bill for improvements that are made at the local level.

Summary

The goal of this chapter has not been to offer an elaborate scheme by which communities can be classified by type. Of course it would be highly desirable if one could spell out an accurate, simple way to differentiate between rural and urban communities. The value of this classificatory scheme would be enhanced even further if it allowed us to distinguish between types of rural communities (hamlets, villages, and so on) and types of urban communities (cities and metropolitan communities). However, in previous drafts of this manuscript, the writer has simply found it impossible to derive a scheme for classifying communities by type which is logical and upon which any two sociologists can agree!

Hence, we have attempted to do two things in this chapter. First, some of the differences between rural and urban communities have been indicated and discussed. That the rural community differs from the urban community in its demographic characteristics, the nature of its hinterlands, and its sociocultural features should be obvious. Whether these differences are of great importance is a matter that can be debated. Secondly, in the latter half of this chapter we have tried, in effect, to give the reader a profile of rural and urban communities. Special emphasis has been placed upon the metropolitan community, because it is the community of the twentieth century and of the future. Most of the readers of this book will live and work in huge metropolitan areas.

Anyone who writes a chapter of this type faces several risks. Among other things, there is a danger that an ethnocentric bias will intrude itself into his work. For example, the present writer is entirely aware that there are communities in every corner of the world and that a sociologically acceptable discussion of community types should apply to all communities, regardless of whether they are located in Asia, Africa, Europe, or the Americas. The fact of the matter is, however, that our comments probably apply with most accuracy to communities within the United States. This is inevitable given the fact that much of the literature which we have been forced to draw upon is written for the American student of American community life. Likewise, our discussion may convey the impression that there is a great gulf between the rural and the urban community and that these are two totally distinct forms of communal and social organization. This simply is not the case. We must always remember that all Americans, regardless of whether they live in small villages or large cities, are a part of a larger society in which urbanism is the order of the day. There is every reason to think that in virtually every country of the world the differences between rural and urban become less significant with each passing decade.

Bibliography

Banfield, Edward C. *The Unheavenly City: The Nature and Future of Our Urban Crisis.* Boston: Little, Brown and Company, 1970.

Bell, Wendell, and Marion T. Boat. "Urban Neighborhoods and Informal Social Relations," *American Journal of Sociology,* **62** (January, 1967), pp. 391–98.

Berger, Bennett M. *Working Class Suburb: A Study of Auto Workers in Suburbia.* Berkeley: University of California Press, 1960.

Blumenfeld, Hans. "The Modern Metropolis," *Scientific American,* **213** (September, 1965), pp. 64–74.

Bogue, Donald J. *The Structure of the Metropolitan Community.* Ann Arbor: University of Michigan Press, 1950.

Bollens, John C., and Henry J. Schmandt. *The Metropolis.* New York: Harper & Row, 1965.

Boskoff, Alvin. *The Sociology of Urban Regions,* 2nd ed. New York: Appleton-Century-Crofts, 1970.

Clark, S. D. *The Suburban Society.* Toronto: University of Toronto Press, 1966.

Dewey, Richard. "The Rural–Urban Continuum: Real but Relatively Unimportant," *American Journal of Sociology,* **66** (July, 1960), pp. 60–66.

Dobriner, William M. *Class in Suburbia.* Englewood Cliffs, N.J.: Prentice-Hall, Inc., 1963.

———— (ed.). *The Suburban Community.* New York: G. P. Putnam's Sons, 1958.

Duncan, Otis Dudley. "Community Size and the Rural–Urban Continuum," in Paul K. Hatt and Albert J. Reiss, Jr. (eds.), *Cities and Society: The Revised Reader in Urban Sociology.* New York: The Free Press, 1957.

———— et al. *Metropolis and Region.* Baltimore: The Johns Hopkins Press, 1960.

Firey, Walter. "Ecological Considerations in Planning for Urban Fringes," *American Sociological Review,* **11** (August, 1946), pp. 411–21.

Gans, Herbert J. *The Levittowners: How People Live and Politic in Suburbia.* New York: Pantheon Books, 1966.

Gibbs, Jack P., and Kingsley Davis. "Conventional Versus Metropolitan Data in the International Study of Urbanization," *American Sociological Review,* **23** (October, 1958), pp. 504–14.

Gottman, Jean. *Megalopolis: The Urbanized Northeastern Seaboard of the United States.* New York: The Twentieth Century Fund, 1961.

Green, Constance McLaughlin. *The Rise of Urban America.* New York: Harper & Row, 1965.

Greer, Scott. *The Emerging City: Myth and Reality.* New York: The Free Press, 1962.

Halpern, Joel M. *The Changing Village Community.* Englewood Cliffs, N.J.: Prentice-Hall, Inc., 1967.

Hauser, Philip M., and Leo F. Schnore (eds.). *The Study of Urbanization.* New York: John Wiley & Sons, 1965.

Keller, Suzanne. *The Urban Neighborhood: A Sociological Perspective.* New York: Random House, 1968.

Keyes, Fenton. "The Correlation of Social Phenomena with Community Size," *Social Forces,* **36** (May, 1958), pp. 311–15.

Lasswell, T. E. "Social Class and Size of Community," *American Journal of Sociology,* **64** (March, 1959), pp. 505–508.

McKelvey, Blake. *The Emergence of Metropolitan America 1915–1966.* New Brunswick, N.J.: Rutgers University Press, 1968.

McKenzie, Roderick D. *The Metropolitan Community*. New York: McGraw-Hill Book Company, 1933.

————. "The Rise of Metropolitan Communities," in President's Research Committee on Social Trends, *Recent Social Trends in the United States,* one-volume ed. New York: McGraw-Hill Book Company, 1933.

Mann, Peter H. "The Concept of Neighborliness," *American Journal of Sociology,* **60** (September, 1954), pp. 163–68.

Martin, Walter T. "The Structure of Social Relationships Engendered by Suburban Residence," *American Sociological Review,* **21** (August, 1956), pp. 446–53.

Murphy, Raymond E. *The American City: An Urban Geography*. New York: McGraw-Hill Book Company, 1966.

Pryor, Robin J. "Defining the Rural–Urban Fringe," *Social Forces,* **47** (December, 1968), pp. 205–15.

Schnore, Leo F. "Satellites and Suburbs," *Social Forces,* **36** (December, 1957), pp. 121–29.

Smith, Joel, William H. Form, and Gregory P. Stone. "Local Intimacy in a Middle-Sized City," *American Journal of Sociology,* **60** (November, 1954), pp. 276–84.

Wilensky, Harold L., and Charles N. Lebeaux. *Industrial Society and Social Welfare*. New York: The Free Press, 1965. See especially Chapter V.

Wirth, Louis. "Urbanism as a Way of Life," *American Journal of Sociology,* **44** (July, 1938), pp. 8–20.

Wood, Robert C. *Suburbia: Its People and Their Politics*. Boston: Houghton Mifflin Company, 1958.

two

Theories of Community

A vast body of literature has emerged which pertains to communities. This literature is so widely scattered throughout textbooks, monographs, scientific journals, and even popular magazines that it is, for all practical purposes, inaccessible to all but the most serious student of community life. To search it out requires months, if not years, of effort.

Hence, in the next five chapters of this text an attempt is made to explore some of the most significant literature on community structure and process. To be more specific, in Chapter 3 the reader's attention is drawn to theories of human ecology. There are several different schools of human ecology but they all have one thing in common: they seek to explain the physical layout and growth dynamics of cities. Indeed, theories of human ecology shed light on the spatial organization of cities and are based on the assumption that the distribution of demographic, economic, and social phenomena within the city follows regular, recurrent, and predictable patterns. In Chapter 4 we turn our attention to constructed type theories of community. In actuality, constructed types are rather complex entities and their characteristics cannot be specified at the present time. It should be noted, however, that many theorists have made use of constructed types in their efforts to analyze community structure and change. Perhaps the most famous of these theorists was Ferdinand Tonnies, whose *Gemeinschaft und Gesellschaft* laid the foundation for the further development of the constructed-type approach to community analysis. Among the other theorists who have worked within the constructed-type tradition and whom we shall consider in Chapter 4 are Robert Redfield, Robert MacIver, Carle Zimmerman, Gideon Sjoberg, Roland L. Warren, and George A. Hillery, Jr. Chapter 5 of this text differs from its companion chapters in that it borrows theoretical systems from general sociology and explores their relevance for community analysis. Specifically, this chapter deals with functionalism and social system theory. In the present writer's thinking, the chief contribution which social system theory makes to community analysis is that it gives meaning to the term *community structure* and clarifies the way in which various components of the community, such as its groups and institutions, are interrelated. Functionalism supplements this by reminding us that any social system is a complex, multifaceted whole and that there are human and social needs which must be met if a community is to persist through time. Another approach to community analysis is explored in Chapter 6. In this chapter we use community action theory to examine patterns of action at the local level and as a tool which helps us to understand the role of power and leadership in community affairs. Finally, in Chapter 7 we consider theories of community change and development. Today many communities are changing at an extremely rapid rate and unless these change processes are understood, we cannot claim to have a full understanding of the modern community.

To the best of the writer's knowledge this fivefold classification of types of community theory encompasses the dominant sociological approaches to community analysis. It is true of course that a great deal of literature on the community can be found which does not fit into this scheme. It should be noted, however, that the focus of this text is on the *community as a whole* rather than upon the groups and institutions which are typically found *within* the community. It is in this respect that the present text differs from many of the other textbooks on community life.

3

Human Ecology

The city has always provided man with a source of fascination and wonder. To some it has been a place to fear and detest, a seat of corruption and decay, whereas others have regarded it as the center of all progress. One of the most penetrating analyses of the city, however, has not come from the many philosophers, poets, and reformers who have loudly praised or condemned it, but from a small group of social scientists called human ecologists. It is from human ecology that some of the most elaborate and most controversial theories of community have been derived.

There is of course more than one approach to human ecology. Certainly the blueprint for human ecology set forth by Robert E. Park is significantly different than that developed by Walter Firey some years later. However, all those working within the ecological tradition seem to agree that the foremost goal of human ecology is to explain the spatial organization and growth dynamics of urban communities. Furthermore, it is almost essential that human ecologists work on the assumption that the growth and resulting layout of the city, its population, and its institutions follow regular, recurrent patterns. Hence, it becomes the task of the human ecologist to discover basic patterns of city growth and to explain why cities tend to take on characteristic spatial configurations.

Historical Development

Even though the term *human ecology* dates back only to 1921, writings which might be classified as ecological in nature go back as far as the early years of the nineteenth century.[1] Indeed, although the term was coined by Robert Park it is impossible, chronologically speaking, to identify the first human ecologist. Some possibilities, however, are M. de Guarry de Champnouf, who as early as 1825 investigated the spatial distribution of criminal acts in France,[2] and Charles Booth, whose classic studies of London and its people contain many of the insights that were later rediscovered and explored by the Chicago ecologists.[3] Nor can the social morphological approach as developed by Emile Durkheim and Maurice Halbwachs be ignored.[4] In fact, one of the shortcomings of the Chicago ecologists was that they did not indicate that they were working within an already established tradition.

This is not a major criticism of the human ecologists who were based at the University of Chicago during the 1920's and the 1930's. It was they who gave human ecology its theory and many of its methods, and history seems to dictate that Robert Park be declared the father of modern human ecology. It was Park who coined the term, provided the basic assumptions for a theory of human ecology, and most importantly, stimulated other outstanding scholars to seek a thorough understanding of the city. Furthermore, the truly significant contribu-

[1] For a review of some of these studies see Yale Levin and Alfred Lindesmith, "English Ecology and Criminology of the Past Century," *Journal of Criminal Law and Criminology,* **27** (March, 1937), pp. 801–16.

[2] See M. C. Elmer, "Century-Old Ecological Studies in France," *The American Journal of Sociology,* **39** (July, 1933), pp. 63–70.

[3] Charles Booth, *Life and Labour of the People in London* (London: Macmillan Company, Limited, 1902), Vols. 1–8.

[4] For a brief review of the social morphological approach see Maurice Halbwachs, *Population and Society: Introduction to Social Morphology,* translated by Otis Dudley Duncan and Harold W. Pfautz (New York: The Free Press, 1960), pp. 7–29.

tions of Park and his associates were not erased when classical ecology was brought under severe criticism during the late 1930's. Perhaps the greatest tribute paid to Robert Park and his University of Chicago colleagues was that many of those who questioned the validity of classical ecology later developed their own theories of urban spatial organization.

Classical Ecology

Some of the major theories of human ecology may now be examined. Specifically, we need to look at the classical, neo-orthodox, sociocultural, and social area approaches to ecological analysis.[5] The obvious launching point is with the classical school of human ecology as it developed at the University of Chicago during the second and third decades of the twentieth century.

Basic Assumptions

One of the fundamental assumptions made by Robert E. Park and his associates was that human society consists of two levels of organization, the biotic and the social.[6] The biotic level is not unique to man but is found wherever living things share a common habitat. Perhaps the most important feature of the biotic level is that it is characterized by close-knit patterns of interdependence between its cohabitants and is therefore essentially communal in character. Because this level of organization is common to all forms of life one of Robert Park's basic aims was to determine the applicability of principles of plant and animal ecology to the study of human communities. In contrast, the social level exists only among human beings and

[5] This classification of types of human ecology is taken from George A. Theodorson (ed.), *Studies in Human Ecology* (New York: Harper & Row, 1961).

[6] For example, see Robert E. Park, "Human Ecology," *The American Journal of Sociology,* **42** (July, 1936), pp. 1–15.

involves relationships which only man is capable of creating and sustaining. Because the dichotomy between the biotic (communal) and social levels of organization is of central importance to classical ecology, it must be examined in more detail.

The first thing which should be pointed out about the biotic or communal level is that it is not a product of deliberate and rational activities. Rather, its organizational pattern is automatically determined as numerous individuals congregate in a limited territory, such as within the boundaries of a city. Hence, the forces giving the community its shape and structure are impersonal and subsocial, a product of natural distributive processes of which man is normally not aware. Furthermore, the classical ecologists assume that the relationships which exist at the biotic level are symbiotic, that is, they consist of impersonal patterns of coexistence and interdependence. Although the inhabitants of a human community are not always aware of it, they are dependent upon each other in much the same way that the plants or animals found in any given area are dependent upon each other for their survival. Finally, and most importantly, the classical ecologists maintain that the patterns of organization which typify the biotic level result from certain impersonal processes of competition. Thus, James A. Quinn points out that,

> Park, Burgess, and McKenzie . . . emphasize the importance of impersonal, continuous, universal "competition" among living organisms, which in the long run selects and distributes the populations and institutions of an area. This impersonal interaction "without social contact" results, so they say, in a basic underlying areal structure that serves as a foundation on which the consensus aspects of social structure arise.[7]

Because the concept of competition is of central importance in classical ecological theory, it will be considered in more detail below.

[7] James A. Quinn, *Human Ecology* (Englewood Cliffs, N.J.: Prentice-Hall, Inc., 1950), p. 297.

In contrast to the biotic level of organization, the social level consists of a network of interpersonal relationships. Its hallmarks are consensus and communication. Thus, Park frequently pointed out that community life always has its impersonal, competitive (i.e., biotic) aspects, but that "men and women are bound together by affections and common purposes; they do cherish traditions, ambitions, and ideals that are not all their own. . . ." [8] The fact that men do have these ties of sentiment and common purpose gives rise to social organization.

There are several things which we must note. First, Park has occasionally been criticized on the grounds that he overlooked the fact that human relationships do involve consensus and communication. Although this criticism may apply to some of his followers, it is obviously not applicable to Park himself. As a matter of fact, some of his most penetrating insights dealt with the role of communication and consensus in social organization.[9] Nonetheless, Park did regard the fundamental task of human ecology to be that of exploring and explaining the biotic or communal level of organization. He, along with his followers, maintained that consensus and communication grew out of man's struggle for existence on an impersonal level. It is this struggle for existence which determines patterns of urban spatial organization.

The Central Role of Competition

We have already suggested that the classical ecologists saw competition as the central factor which determines the spatial organization of the city. This competition arises because the amount of land that it is feasible for a city to occupy is limited

[8] Robert Ezra Park, *Human Communities* (New York: The Free Press, 1952), p. 180. This citation originally appeared in an article entitled "Sociology, Community, and Society," in Wilson Gee (ed.), *Research Methods in the Social Sciences* (New York: The Macmillan Company, 1929).

[9] For example, see Robert E. Park, "Reflections on Communication and Culture," *American Journal of Sociology,* **44** (September, 1938), pp. 187–205.

and must be allocated to many different groups and institutions. At the same time, all these groups and institutions must be accommodated simply because they are dependent upon one another: both business and industry may desire the same land, but neither wishes to see the other destroyed. This is what the term *symbiosis* implies, and is why the classical ecologists speak of competitive cooperation rather than of a type of competition which borders on conflict. In short, urban spatial organization does not result from the attempt of one group or institution to eliminate other groups or institutions. Rather, it results from the fact that each group or institution tries to find a niche in the community which it can profitably occupy. The community could not persist through time if the majority of its groups and institutions was not eventually accommodated.

To be more specific, competition centering around the use of land and competition for residential sites are the two main forces which determine the spatial organization of cities. The first, competition centering around the use of land, arises out of the fact that various groups and institutions have preferred locations in terms of the city as a whole. Sometimes these overlap and conflict. As a result, the question continually arises as to whether a given piece of land shall be used for commercial, industrial, institutional, or residential purposes. Presumably, this problem is resolved through the process of competition, with the economically most powerful groups and institutions being the winners. Because commercial and industrial interests usually have the most power in the competitive struggle, they control the vital land near the center of the city and/or at the intersection of main transportation routes. Other groups and institutions must then find convenient locations on the land which remains available. This is known as the *principle of dominance* in classical ecological theory.

In addition to the allocation of land to various commercial, industrial, and institutional interests, land must also be distributed to various residential groups. Because of this the classical ecologists maintain that urban spatial organization is also influenced by competition between various socioeconomic, racial, and ethnic groups for residential sites. Presumably, the wealthiest people get the choicest land and other residential groups get that which remains. Because the most preferred residential locations are often near the outskirts of the city, a gradient is established with the wealthiest persons living some distance away from the center of the city and the poorest and most disadvantaged living on what little land is available for residential purposes within the already crowded centers of business and industry. Other groups compete for the land between these two extremes.

The Ecological Processes

The classical ecologists therefore view competition as a master process affecting the spatial organization of the city. However, there are other processes which come into play, partly as a concomitant of competition and partly as independent forces impinging upon city growth and organization. These ecological processes are centralization, concentration, segregation, invasion, and succession and were first delineated by Roderick D. McKenzie.[10]

The first of these, centralization, refers to the tendency for selected institutions and services to cluster near the city's focal points of transportation and communication. As the city gains in population and evolves a high division of labor, relatively specialized commercial interests seek locations in the central business district. The chief reason for this lies in the fact that these specialized shops and services must be accessible to large numbers of persons. A department store which handles only expensive, high-quality merchandise or an exclusive health food store must be exposed to a large market if it is to realize a profit, because the percentage of the population which uses these services is small. In brief, the central business district

[10] See R. D. McKenzie, "The Scope of Human Ecology," *Publications of the American Sociological Society,* **20** (1926), pp. 141–54.

represents that one point of greatest average convenience for all persons who might utilize the facility or service in question. Similarly, McKenzie argued that with the passage of time the central business district comes to dominate not only the city, but also the surrounding hinterland with its villages and small towns.[11] The small-town grocery is gradually absorbed by the huge chain store, with its centralized offices and distribution facilities, and the small-town bank disappears as its functions are absorbed by its more powerful urban competitors. Thus centralization is a twofold process which involves both the expansion and proliferation of services offered in the central city and the increasing dominance of the central city over its hinterland.

Competition has a key role to play in this process. Arnold Rose, for example, points out that "merchants specializing in a certain product—such as wholesale clothing or used cars— may find it expedient and profitable to settle near one another so that customers can 'shop around.'"[12] Hence, although two department stores are in competition for the consumer's dollar, they may nonetheless benefit by being located in proximity to one another. Being so located means that a large number of potential customers are attracted to the area and that these customers can compare and choose among the goods offered by the department stores. This is a prime example of what the classical ecologists mean by competitive cooperation. Likewise, the tendency for businesses located in the hinterland to lose their independence reflects, in a real sense, the operation of competition. The small-town grocery or bank simply lack the capital and population base to meet the challenge posed by commercial interests located within the city.

The classical ecologists recognized that there are limits to the amount of centralization which can occur. Competition for land within the central city causes an increase in land values to

[11] Ibid., p. 150.
[12] Arnold M. Rose, *Sociology: The Study of Human Relations,* 2nd rev. ed. (New York: Alfred A. Knopf, 1965), p. 521.

a point at which further expansion is economically unfeasible. Furthermore, the central city can become so congested that businessmen and shoppers alike find it extremely costly, both in time and patience, to visit it regularly. Thus, a considerable amount of decentralization may eventually occur. Indeed, one of the fundamental facts of urban life today is the increasing tendency for stores, professional offices, industries, and entertainment facilities to seek suburban locations. The result is that suburban areas often assume many of the same characteristics and go through many of the same processes that were originally manifested in the central city. They become little cities in themselves.

The second subprocess, concentration, has been conceptualized in two distinctly different ways by the ecologists. First, it has occasionally been used to refer to the tendency for some parts of the city to become extremely congested and overcrowded while other parts remain sparsely populated. As a concept developed by McKenzie, however, concentration refers to the tendency for the population of urban areas to increase as a result of migration from outlying regions. During recent years, for example, metropolitan areas have grown at the expense of small towns and villages. Concentration has been the core process underlying urbanization in the United States and in many other countries.

This tendency toward population concentration in urban centers can also be attributed to competition. As McKenzie explains it, "the degree of concentration attained by any locality is . . . a measure of its resources and location advantages as compared to those of its competitors." [13] To be more specific, the relative size of markets, availability of raw materials, and number of jobs available determines the extent to which competing urban centers can draw persons into their orbit. At the same time, heavy migration into an urban area obviously increases the amount of competition which occurs within its

[13] McKenzie, "The Scope of Human Ecology," p. 147.

boundaries, and especially that for residential sites. Drastic overcrowding such as in New York's Harlem is to a great extent the result of continuous and heavy in-migration from rural areas and from the Southern states. Competition among these newcomers for housing has forced rental prices up to a level equal to, or greater than, those found in the more desirable sections of the city.

The third major ecological subprocess identified by McKenzie is segregation. This refers to the tendency for various groups and institutions to locate in separate and distinct parts of the city. Segregation helps to account for the fact that some parts of the city are characterized by upper-class housing, a minority group population, certain types of industry, or whatever. Presumably, the process of segregation manifests itself in about the same way in all large, rapidly growing cities; thus certain patterns of segregation become almost universal.

There are several things that must be noted about the concept of segregation as it is employed in classical ecological theory. First, it refers only to the tendency for similar ecological units to cluster in proximity to one another. The classical ecologists say little about that type of segregation which arises from racial prejudice and discrimination. Second, like the other ecological processes, segregation refers both to an ongoing process of change and to the end product of this change.[14] To be more specific, the classical ecologists concerned themselves not only with the fact that various parts of the city are characterized by different patterns of land use but with the reasons why this is the case. Why do cities have black belts, better residential areas, wholesale districts, and areas in which vice runs rampant? Finally, the classical ecologists maintained that segregation is the primary factor leading to the emergence of natural areas. Because segregation brings together people who are racially, economically, or socially homogeneous, they tend also to share common interests, bonds, and needs. Because the concept of

[14] See Quinn, *Human Ecology*, p. 353.

"natural area" is an important one in classical ecological theory, more will be said about it in later parts of this chapter.

That competition is the chief sorting and selecting mechanism in this process of segregation is entirely clear. The wealthy become isolated from the poor because of their greater ability to command and control choice residential sites. On the other hand, certain minority groups are unable to compete at all and must therefore take up residence in the least desirable sections of the city. Likewise, it has already been indicated that centralization leads to a certain amount of ecological segregation as specialized shops and service facilities outbid all other interests for locations in the central city. One ecologist has suggested that the processes of centralization and segregation can proceed so far that even within retail shopping districts one finds "shoe stores in one or two adjacent blocks; men's and women's clothing stores in another sector; and florists and other units combined in still other locations." [15]

The fourth and fifth ecological subprocesses that were identified by McKenzie are invasion and succession. These two concepts draw one's attention to the fact that the spatial organization of the city is constantly in a state of flux and change. Various pieces of land are constantly changing hands and areas once devoted to one type of activity are given over to new ones.

To be more specific, invasion refers to a situation in which one group or institution encroaches upon the territory held by another group or institution. More often than not the involved territories are adjacent to one another, but this does not have to be the case. For example, invasion occurs when the central business district begins expanding into immediately adjacent areas, but it also occurs when commercial establishments begin appearing in suburban residential areas. Similarly, a particular population group (e.g., the city's nonwhites) may move into an adjacent residential area or it may begin filtering into a far removed suburb. In short, invasion can be traced to either (1)

[15] Amos H. Hawley, *Human Ecology* (New York: The Ronald Press, 1950), pp. 279–80.

outward growth and expansion from the original territory or (2) permanent movement from one territory to another.

The classical ecologists have used the term *succession* in more than one way. As defined by McKenzie, however, succession refers to a completed process of invasion, i.e., the complete conversion of an area from one use to another. Succession would therefore occur when an area that was formerly residential becomes totally commercial, or when a residential area that was formerly restricted to whites becomes inhabited by nonwhites alone. This means that succession is a temporal as well as a territorial phenomenon. It entails the replacement of old population groups by new ones and the appearance of new and different institutional types in a given area. This may require years of continuous and steady change.

The Concentric Zone Hypothesis

The ecologists were firmly convinced that these processes, and especially competition, operate in every large city. Because of this they hypothesized that as the city grows it tends to assume certain clearly delineated patterns of spatial organization. Specifically, it was the classical ecologists who developed the concentric zone hypothesis. According to Ernest Burgess, who originally suggested this hypothesis, the city tends to become divided up into five distinct zones. (See Figure 3-1.) These zones, and the forces which supposedly lead to their emergence, are as follows:

1. Zone I consists of the central business district and is found in every city of moderate to large size. According to Burgess it is where "we expect to find the department stores, the skyscraper office buildings, the railroad stations, the great hotels, the theaters, the art museum, and the city hall." [16] This

---

[16] Ernest W. Burgess, "The Growth of the City: An Introduction to a Research Project," in Robert E. Park, Ernest W. Burgess, and R. D. McKenzie (eds.), *The City* (Chicago: University of Chicago Press, 1925), p. 52.

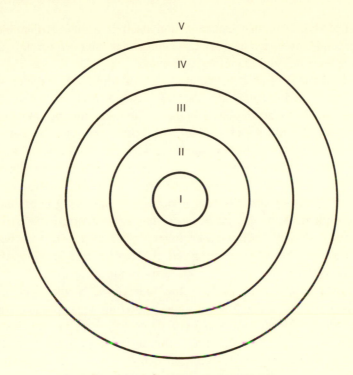

Zone I	Central Business District. Large department stores, skyscrapers, large hotels, theaters, and so on.
Zone II	Zone of Transition. Slum housing, skid-row hotels and drinking establishments, industry, and so on.
Zone III	Zone of Independent Workingmen's Homes. Modest homes interspersed with an occasional school, park, corner grocery, and so on.
Zone IV	Zone of Better Residences. Single-family dwellings, apartment houses, and bright-light areas.
Zone V	Commuters' Zone. Suburban residential areas, satellite cities, and so on.

Figure 3-1. The concentric zone pattern. [Adapted from R. E. Park, E. W. Burgess, and Roderick D. McKenzie, *The City* (Chicago: University of Chicago Press, 1925), p. 55.]

area inevitably becomes the hub of economic, political, and cultural activities for the city and its hinterland. Needless to say, the central business district is a product of centralization and on occasion becomes the victim of decentralization. It will be recalled, however, that centralization itself is partly attributable to competition among various commercial interests for favorable locations and numerous customers.

2. Zone II is aptly called the zone of transition. As such it forms a circle around the central business district. Within it are usually found the city's slum districts, immigrant colonies, part of the black belt, centers of crime and vice, rooming house districts, and some light industry. The individuals who live in this zone often have only one thing in common. They are the losers in the competitive struggle through which different parts of the city are allocated to various groups and institutions. This may be because they have rejected the competitive struggle itself (the criminal, hobo, or derelict) or because they have not been given the opportunity to compete (black Americans and other minority group members).

Two basic forces lead to the emergence of the zone of transition. First, this zone is allocated to those people and institutions who are not permitted to occupy land in any other part of the city. They are frequently unable to bear the costs of living further distances from the central city, or if they are, land may not be made available to them. For example, the American Negro, because of both prejudice against him and his disadvantaged economic condition, is given no choice but to occupy the dilapidated, rundown sections of the city. Similarly, houses of prostitution, cheap hotels, and skid-row drinking establishments would never draw a sufficient number of customers in a middle-class suburban shopping center and obviously would not be permitted in such areas.

The dilapidation which characterizes the zone of transition, however, is not directly attributable to the types of people and institutions which occupy it. Rather, it can be traced to the fact that this zone is the chief target of invasion by the central business district. Indeed, the term *zone of transition* implies that this part of the city is constantly in a state of flux and change, invasion and succession. The process involved is made clear by Walter C. Reckless when he says,

The improved property in these mobile, decaying neighborhoods that are in the direct line of business expansion is allowed to run down, to deteriorate, for upkeep generally results in a total loss to the owner, since business only ordinarily demands the site. These deteriorated dwellings of the slum, because of their undesirability, can command but very low rents. It is unavoidable that the poor and vicious classes share the same locality in the city's junk heap.[17]

Reckless' last sentence once more underscores the fact that the classical ecologists consider urban spatial organization to be the result of uncontrolled, impersonal processes.

3. The third zone delineated by Burgess, that of independent workingmen's homes, is chiefly residential in character. As such this zone is "inhabited predominately by factory and shop workers," [18] whose homes are smaller, older, and of frame construction. Burgess also suggested that quite often the inhabitants of Zone III moved there from the Zone of Transition. They are, in effect, people who have escaped from the slum. At the same time, these persons, or their sons and daughters, frequently aspire to residence in Zone IV, with its restricted residential areas, its apartment house regions, and its "bright-light" districts.

Burgess does not discuss the forces which lead to the emergence of the Zone of Independent Workingmen's Homes. However, it once more seems obvious that competition has a key role to play. The inhabitants of this zone have acquired the means to escape from the slum, but they still lack the ability to compete for residential sites in the "best" sections of the city.

4. The fourth ring is called the Zone of Better Residences. The standard housing type found in this area is the single-family dwelling unit, but Burgess indicated that in Chicago Zone IV was becoming increasingly characterized by apartment

[17] Walter C. Reckless, "The Distribution of Commercialized Vice in the City: A Sociological Analysis," *Publications of the American Sociological Society,* **20** (1926), p. 175.
[18] Burgess, "The Growth of the City," p. 56.

houses and residential hotels.[19] In any event, it is in this section of the city that one finds the homes of small businessmen, professional people, clerks and salesmen, and other members of the native-born middle class.[20] However, Zone IV is not devoted exclusively to residential uses. It is also an area in which local shopping centers or "satellite loops" appear. It is not a bit uncommon to find commercialized areas within this zone which contain banks, supermarkets, drugstores, and restaurants. In addition, Burgess also suggested that Zone IV may have its clusters of motion pictures theaters, cabarets, and smart hotels. Burgess referred to these entertainment centers located within the Zone of Better Residences as "bright-light" areas.

5. The Commuter's Zone was the final one delineated by Burgess. The inner side of this zone is bounded by the Zone of Better Residences, but its outer periphery may be quite amorphous. Within the Commuter's Zone are found a variety of small hamlets, towns, and suburban areas that are not legally integrated with the central city, but that are nonetheless dependent upon it for goods, services, and jobs. These satellite communities are "in the main, dormitory suburbs, because the majority of men residing there spend the day at work in the Loop (central business district), returning only for the night." [21] At the same time, the characteristics of these satellite communities are varied: they range all the way from quiet, upper-class "bungalow" districts to gaudy entertainment centers. With the appearance of these satellite communities, the city has indeed become metropolitan in character.

Many of the same processes which account for the emergence of Zones I, II, and III help to account for Zones IV and V. The latter zones are also a product of competition, for in them dwell the winners in the competitive struggle for land. The fact that the desirable land near the outskirts of the city is controlled by

[19] See E. W. Burgess, "Urban Areas," in T. V. Smith and L. D. White (eds.), *Chicago: An Experiment in Social Science Research* (Chicago: University of Chicago Press, 1929), p. 116.
[20] Ibid.
[21] Ibid., p. 117.

Theories of Community

middle- and upper-class groups explains why less advantaged members of the urban population are frequently crowded into slums and ghettos. No other locations are made available to them. Furthermore, the recent suburbanization of American cities can be traced to the combined effects of decentralization, segregation, invasion, and succession. Suburbs are obviously a product of continuous and rapid decentralization and are among the most homogeneous, "segregated" areas found in the modern city.

Before we leave the concentric zone hypothesis, a few concluding observations are in order. First, the present writer has followed Burgess' own description of the city and its spatial organization as closely as possible. This is because the focus of this book is on *theories of community* rather than on *the community itself*. If Ernest Burgess were alive today, he might well revise his hypothesis in order to take into account recent developments in urban spatial organization. Secondly, it must be stressed that Burgess saw the formation of concentric zones as an ongoing process. He points out, for example, that under conditions of rapid population growth the city constantly expands outward in such a way that, for example, what was once a part of Zone II becomes a part of Zone I. Finally, the concentric zone hypothesis has been criticized because there are many factors which can interfere with the emergence of perfect concentric circles. Burgess apparently anticipated these criticisms when he said that

> neither Chicago nor any other city fits perfectly into this ideal scheme. Complications are introduced by the lake front, the Chicago River, railroad lines, historical factors in the location of industry, the relative degree of the resistance of communities to invasion, etc.[22]

Whether the concentric-zone hypothesis itself has any validity is a different question. It will be considered in later parts of this chapter.

Although the concentric zone hypothesis has consistently

[22] Burgess, "The Growth of the City," pp. 51–52.

received the most attention, there have been other theories of urban spatial organization. One of these is Homer Hoyt's sector theory.[23] Basically, Hoyt maintains that cities tend to become divided into a number of sectors which radiate out from the central business district. (See Figure 3-2.) Some of these sectors

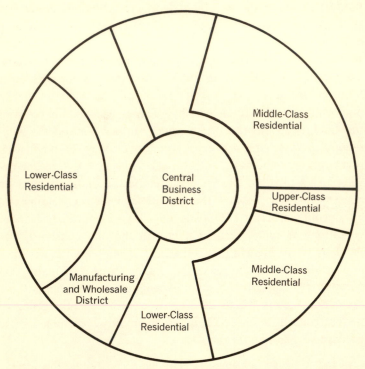

Figure 3-2. The sector theory of urban spatial organization. [Adapted from Chauncey D. Harris and Edward L. Ullman, "The Nature of Cities," *Annals of the American Academy of Political and Social Science,* **242** (November, 1945), p. 12.]

are devoted to residential use whereas others are devoted to industrial and related uses. Those sectors that are residential in nature may, in turn, display a pattern wherein the poorest

[23] See Homer Hoyt, *The Structure and Growth of Residential Neighborhoods in American Cities* (Washington, D.C.: U.S. Government Printing Office, 1939), Chapter 6.

Theories of Community

districts are located near the central business district whereas the best residential areas are found near the periphery of the city. Hoyt argues that this pattern results from the tendency for different groups and institutions to expand along the major transportation routes leading from the central city to the periphery: residential areas expand along one route, industrial establishments along another, and so forth. Another well-known theory of urban spatial organization is Harris and Ullman's multiple-nuclei theory.[24] Put most simply, Harris and Ullman argue that the city has not one but several nuclei or centers. (See Figure 3-3.) Each of these centers is devoted to different

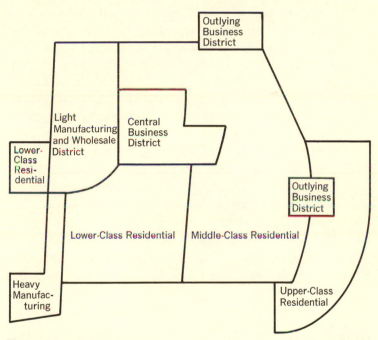

Figure 3-3. The multiple-nuclei pattern of urban spatial organization. [Adapted from Chauncey D. Harris and Edward L. Ullman, "The Nature of Cities," *Annals of the American Academy of Political and Social Science,* **242** (November, 1945), p. 12.]

[24] See Chauncey D. Harris and Edward L. Ullman, "The Nature of Cities," *The Annals of the American Academy of Political and Social Science,* **242** (November, 1945), pp. 7–17.

activities. Thus, one nuclei may be devoted exclusively to wholesaling, another to governmental functions, and yet a third to financial activities. Harris and Ullman have developed four principles which supposedly account for the emergence of these separate nuclei. These principles may be summarized as follows:

1. Certain groups and institutions demand specialized facilities if they are to flourish. Heavy industry, for example, requires large acreages whereas the retail business district must be located so as to be conveniently accessible to the majority of the city's population.
2. Certain groups and institutions benefit from being located in proximity to one another. Large retail establishments, for example, benefit from being located in the same general part of the city. This brings a large number of potential customers to the area. These customers can compare and evaluate the price and quality of the goods offered by the different establishments.
3. Certain unlike groups and institutions find it disagreeable and disadvantageous to be located in proximity to one another. It is, for example, more pleasant to have as one's next-door neighbor a person of similar background and values than it is to have a large, noisy industrial plant as one's next-door neighbor.
4. Finally, the inability to pay high rents forces some groups and institutions to cluster together. In most cities there is a limited amount of land which can be obtained at relatively low cost. This land is often taken up by lower-quality housing developments, bulk wholesaling or storage facilities, and other groups and institutions which need large amounts of land at a low price.

Natural Areas

If the classical ecologists had concluded their analysis of the city with the concentric zone hypothesis, they would have been guilty of gross oversimplification. Even though it is reasonable to hypothesize that the city is divided into a series of concentric zones and that each zone is homogeneous in comparison to the others, it is also reasonable to suggest that the various zones themselves display a considerable diversity of people and institutions. The Zone of Transition, for example, supposedly contains a black belt, immigrant colonies, centers of crime and vice, a skid row, a rooming house district, and areas of light industry. Because of this the classical ecologists developed their final major concept, that of natural areas.

The concept of natural area has several different dimensions. From a geographic point of view it refers to the smallest meaningful territorial unit found within the city. Because of features of the landscape (rivers, hills, and so on) and such man-made barriers as railroads, highways, and parks, the city becomes divided into a number of small, semi-isolated areas. Sometimes this isolation is rather complete, as is the case when a modern freeway splits one formerly well-integrated neighborhood into two completely distinct ones. This simple illustration also suggests why the resulting areas are said to be natural, that is, "they are the unplanned, natural product of the city's growth."[25]

Of more importance is the fact that each natural area tends to become segregated in terms of the type of people and institutions found within its boundaries. In short, natural areas are homogeneous units found within the heterogeneous urban milieu. There are several ways by which this segregation might be explained, but once again the classical ecologists relied upon the competitive struggle for land as their key explanatory variable: wealthy, powerful groups gain control of the most desirable natural areas, whereas weak, disadvantaged groups and institutions find their niche in less desirable areas. Furthermore, because of the homogeneous character of each natural area, these small units of urban spatial organization tend to become culturally distinct from one another. Robert Park, for example, tells us that "every natural area has, or tends to have, its own peculiar traditions, customs, conventions, standards of decency

[25] Harvey W. Zorbaugh, "The Natural Areas of the City," *Publications of the American Sociological Society,* **20** (1926), p. 191.

and propriety, and, if not a language of its own, at least a universe of discourse, which is appreciably different for each local community." [26] Thus when someone refers to Chinatown or Skid Row we not only think of a district that can be plotted on a map, but of a section of the city which has its own unique social and cultural patterns.

During recent years the concept of natural area has been somewhat ignored by those who continue to work within the ecological tradition. Nonetheless, this concept was central to classical ecological theory. For one thing, the assumption that the city is divided into a number of natural areas rounds out the picture which the classical ecologists painted of urban spatial organization. In essence, they suggested that the city is a complex mosaic of zones and subareas, each of which represents a "pocket" into which the heterogeneous urban population is sorted and segregated. Furthermore, the classical ecologists made brilliant use of natural areas in their research. Among other things, they were able to show that different natural areas become characterized by high or low crime rates, by varying degrees of family disorganization, and by different types of mental illness.[27] Indeed, the research conducted by the Chicago ecologists was fully as important as their contributions to ecological theory. Finally, one of the Chicago ecologists, Harvey W. Zorbaugh, made it clear that the existence of natural areas has numerous implications in terms of the efficient administration of city government. Put most simply, Zorbaugh suggested that far too often the city's political units cut across and ignore the boundaries of natural areas and that, because of this, our desire to make political units meaningful to their inhabitants is frustrated. This problem is well illustrated by a community council which "set out to make a community of a section of the city including a colony of 6,000 Persians, a

[26] Park, *Human Communities,* p. 201.

[27] An excellent summary of some of these studies is contained in Maurice R. Stein, *The Eclipse of Community: An Interpretation of American Community Studies* (Princeton, N.J.: Princeton University Press, 1960), pp. 34–46.

belt of some 4,000 Negroes, a colony of 1,000 Greeks, a rooming house population of 25,000, Towertown—Chicago's Greenwich Village—and Chicago's much vaunted Gold Coast." [28] The utter futility of attempting to bring such a diversity of people together into one "community" of interest and association is obvious.

The Growing Tide of Criticism

During the 1920's and the early 1930's the Chicago ecologists worked feverishly to develop their conceptual scheme. By 1935 their work was essentially complete, at least in its main outlines. Human ecology had reached the stage in its development at which it included the dichotomy between biotic and social levels of organization, the concentric-zone hypothesis, and the concept of natural area. Furthermore, the assumption that competition is the key variable influencing urban spatial organization had been taken for granted. However, classical ecology barely reached this stage when it came in for a period of rather severe and devastating criticism. The critics of classical ecology not only questioned its validity as a theoretical system but also raised questions about some of the empirical findings that were reported by the Chicago ecologists.

As a system of theory, classical ecology was attacked on several grounds. About the most serious of these attacks centered around the dichotomy that was drawn between the biotic and social levels of organization. A particularly vocal critic in this regard was Milla A. Alihan, who argued that the classical ecologists were themselves unable to make the distinction between biotic and social levels a meaningful one: although they focused upon spatially distributed phenomena, they were eventually forced to rely upon social and cultural variables to explain their observations.[29] Similarly, Warner E. Gettys argued

[28] Zorbaugh, "The Natural Areas of the City," p. 194.
[29] See Milla A. Alihan, *Social Ecology: A Critical Analysis* (New York: Cooper Square Publishers, 1964), pp. 81–84. This volume was originally published in 1938 by Columbia University Press.

that the concept of "biotic level" in classical ecological theory was symbolic of a form of biological and geographic determinism. Thus,

> In spite of statements in the literature to the contrary, there is considerable evidence that the ecologists held to a theory of biological and/or geographic determinism in human affairs. In other words, men and their institutions are represented as being spatially, temporally and occupationally distributed by the operation of forces either inherent in the biological nature of man or existing external to man in the so-called "natural world." [30]

Finally, August B. Hollingshead strongly and convincingly argued that sociocultural systems influence every facet of human affairs, including those of an ecological nature. Among other things, cultural norms and values dictate that personal, cooperative relationships will also have a role to play in determining the spatial organization of communities.[31]

In addition to these basic criticisms, the emphasis that the classical ecologists put on competition as the key variable determining urban spatial organization was also attacked. Alihan, for example, seriously questioned the validity of designating competition as "the primary, the universal, and the fundamental process" determining the physical layout of the city.[32] Could not some other process, such as cooperation, conflict, or assimilation, be arbitrarily chosen as an explanatory variable and a theory of human ecology built upon this base? This of course would be a meaningless question if we could demonstrate that competition is the key process influencing the spatial organization of the city. The problem in doing this, however, is indicated by Amos Hawley when he states that,

[30] Warner E. Gettys, "Human Ecology and Social Theory," *Social Forces,* **18** (May, 1940), p. 470.

[31] A. B. Hollingshead, "A Re-examination of Ecological Theory," *Sociology and Social Research,* **31** (January–February, 1947), pp. 194–204.

[32] Alihan, *Social Ecology,* p. 91.

A related problem exists with regard to the observability of the operation of competition. The specific sequence of changes by which a homogeneous aggregate is converted into a differentiated and interdependent population has not been described in detail. Consequently it is almost impossible to indicate what to look for in order to see competition in action. This situation is not improved by pointing out that the process is a type of interaction, that is, a process of mutual internal modification. Ecologists, unfortunately, lack the technique for the observation of internal phenomena. Defined in terms of competitive interaction, ecology amounts to little more than the contemplation of a concept.[33]

Thus, the entire theoretical system developed by the classical ecologists represented but one approach to the explanation of ecological phenomena. Furthermore, their key explanatory variable, competition, had the disadvantage that it did not lend itself to direct observation and empirical verification. Classical ecological theory was at best an untested, *post hoc* interpretation of urban growth dynamics.

Many of the hypotheses put forth by the classical ecologists were also questioned on empirical grounds. The classical ecologists did use Chicago as their research arena but they maintained that the same ecological processes were operative in all large and growing cities. Presumably, all such cities would be characterized by five concentric zones and would be divided into natural areas. As might be expected, this hypothesis was soon put to empirical test.

One of the earliest of these tests was conducted in 1938 by Maurice R. Davie. After carefully identifying twenty-two "natural or distinctive areas" within New Haven, Connecticut, and collecting a considerable amount of data on each of these, Davie arbitrarily divided a map of the city into a series of concentric zones. The resulting analysis revealed that distance from the center of the city apparently had no influence upon the distri-

[33] Amos H. Hawley, "Ecology and Human Ecology," *Social Forces,* 22 (May, 1944), p. 401.

bution of social, economic, and ecological phenomena. As a result, Davie had to conclude that "the hypothesis of the concentric zone pattern . . . clearly does not apply to New Haven." [34] Among other things Davie found that the wealthiest and poorest sections of the city were practically equidistant from the central business district and therefore within the same zone. However, Davie did uncover one ecological pattern, this being that low-grade housing is found near centers of transportation and industry. A few years later another scholar, Paul K. Hatt, seriously questioned whether natural areas are basic units of urban organization. In research conducted in Seattle, Hatt found (1) that not all parts of the city are divided into natural areas and (2) that the number and type of natural areas found within a city depend exclusively upon the methods used in delineating them. Because of this Hatt concluded that natural areas are not real entities but that the concept itself might be useful for research purposes.[35] Finally, since as early as 1934 ecological studies have been conducted in countries other than the United States.[36] These studies reveal that in some parts of the world the ecological organization of cities is quite similar to that described by the Chicago ecologists but that in other places, such as Latin America, urban spatial organization differs radically from the pattern found in the United States.

[34] Maurice R. Davie, "The Pattern of Urban Growth," in George P. Murdock (ed.), *Studies in the Science of Society* (New Haven: Yale University Press, 1937), p. 159.

[35] Paul K. Hatt, "The Concept of Natural Area," *American Sociological Review,* **11** (August, 1946), pp. 423–27.

[36] For a sampling of these studies see Asael T. Hansen, "The Ecology of a Latin American City," in E. B. Reuter (ed.), *Race and Culture Contacts* (New York: McGraw-Hill Book Company, 1934), pp. 124–42; Theodore Caplow, "The Social Ecology of Guatemala City," *Social Forces,* **28** (December, 1949), pp. 113–35; Theodore Caplow, "Urban Structure in France," *American Sociological Review,* **17** (October, 1952), pp. 544–49; Erdmann Deane Beynon, "The Morphology of the Cities of the Alfold," *Geographical Review,* **27** (April, 1937), pp. 328–29; and Fernando Peñalosa, "Ecological Organization of the Transitional City: Some Mexican Evidence," *Social Forces,* **46** (December, 1967), pp. 221–29.

Neo-orthodox Ecology

By the mid-1940's classical ecology had been subjected to rather severe criticism. However, even though one particular brand of human ecology had been almost utterly destroyed, interest in the study of ecological phenomena persisted.

The first major innovation in ecological theory was pioneered by two men, James A. Quinn and Amos H. Hawley, and is often referred to as neo-orthodox ecology. As the name suggests, the neo-orthodox ecologists were basically in sympathy with the goals and purposes of the classical ecologists. They sought to correct the deficiencies in classical ecological theory rather than to replace it with some other theoretical scheme. Nonetheless, both Quinn and Hawley disagreed with the classical ecologists on several important issues. First, they thought that human ecologists should study more than the spatial distribution of social phenomena. This was certainly one of their tasks but there were also other things that the ecologists should investigate. Secondly, both men were suspicious of elevating competition to the status of a key explanatory variable. Both men recognized that the forces which influence the spatial organization of cities are extremely complex and involve many elements *in addition to* competition. Finally, both Quinn and Hawley objected to the rigid distinction that the classical ecologists made between the biotic and social levels of organization and maintained instead that all human relationships, including those of an ecological nature, are influenced by culture. At the same time, neither man treats culture as a basic concept in ecological theory. They still thought that the ecological structure of cities was the result of impersonal and largely subsocial forces.

James A. Quinn

Although Quinn and Hawley agree on the preceding points, there are some fundamental differences between the theories which they put forth. To be more specific, Quinn views human ecology as a branch of sociology. As such, it is a field which investigates one facet of human interaction. However, the type of interaction which ecologists study is considerably different than the type studied by the general sociologist. Quinn summarizes the differences between social and ecological interaction when he says,

> Ecological interaction occurs upon different levels from those of truly social interaction. Human social interaction involves consensus, exchange of meaning through symbolic communication, and imaginative playing of the roles of others. Ecological interaction, in contrast, involves only an indirect, impersonal form of mutual modification by which each living man influences others by increasing or decreasing the supplies of environmental factors upon which the others depend.[37]

It is this process of ecological interaction which gives the modern community its basic spatial and functional structure. Specifically, Quinn assumes that the way in which scarce environmental factors, such as land and jobs, are allocated to various ecological units is the chief force determining urban spatial organization. It should be noted, however, that ecological interaction is not always synonymous with competition. The allocation of land, resources, and jobs can also involve cooperation and mutual aid.

Even though the study of ecological interaction is very important to Quinn, in the final analysis it is only a means by which we can gain understanding of ecological structure. Basically, the concept of ecological structure refers to two different but interrelated phenomena. First, it encompasses the division of labor found at the community level. The division of labor is properly a part of ecological study simply because it involves impersonal, subsocial relationships and represents one facet of man's adjustment to the environment. Secondly, ecological struc-

[37] James A. Quinn, "Human Ecology and Interactional Ecology," *American Sociological Review,* **5** (October, 1940), p. 722.

ture also includes the spatial organization of the community. Unlike the classical ecologists, Quinn apparently subscribes to no one theory of urban spatial organization. Instead he argues that the spatial organization of cities depends upon patterns of ecological interaction which are to some extent unique to each community. This does not mean, however, that there are no principles which govern urban growth dynamics. Rather, Quinn hypothesizes that four basic factors determine the location of ecological units within a community. The four factors are as follows.

1. *Minimum cost.* Quinn's first hypothesis is that ecological units tend to distribute themselves throughout a given area so as to minimize the cost of adjusting to other ecological units and to the environment. One can assume, for example, that when other conditions are equal, heavy industries will locate where the costs of transporting labor, raw materials, and the finished product are kept to a minimum. It should be noted, however, that Quinn includes within the concept of "cost" not only expenditures of time, money, and energy but also various noneconomic factors. Thus, he points out that the prestige value of an area must be taken into account in calculating the costs or rewards attached to any given location. In any event, it is Quinn's opinion that "the hypothesis of maximum satisfaction at minimum cost affords a general guiding principle to the interpretation of the spatial patterning of areas." [38]

2. *Minimum ecological distance.* The hypothesis of minimum ecological distance is simply an extension of the hypothesis of minimum costs. According to this hypothesis ecological units distribute themselves throughout an area so as to minimize the total ecological distance between them and the other ecological and social units upon which they depend. This helps to explain why industries tend to locate in proximity to one another: they utilize each other's products. Likewise, schools and churches normally locate near the residential areas that they serve.

[38] Quinn, *Human Ecology,* p. 285.

3. *Median location.* The hypothesis of median location states that "the most efficient location for any ecological unit is at the median (weighted) of all units which are to be transported to and from it." [39] Included among these latter units are "the environmental resources which it (the original unit) utilizes, the other units on which it depends, and the other units that it serves." [40] The reader will note of course that this hypothesis is simply a restatement, in different terms, of the hypotheses of minimum ecological distance and minimum ecological cost.

4. *Intensiveness of utilization.* The hypothesis of intensiveness of utilization takes into account the fact that two or more ecological units may have a common median and therefore desire the same site. In situations of this type Quinn argues that "that ecological unit tends to occupy the common median which can utilize it most intensively." [41] If two ecological units are in competition for the same location, presumably that unit which serves the most persons and realizes the most profit from occupying the sought-after location will gain control of it.

In summary, Quinn maintains that considerations of cost and distance determine patterns of spatial organization at the community level. His is therefore an economic interpretation of ecological structure: the spatial organization of communities results from the tendency for ecological units to minimize their costs and maximize their satisfactions by occupying that one point in space which represents the most efficacious location vis-à-vis other ecological units.[42] This of course is the chief point upon which Quinn's theory may be criticized. It is assumed that the typical community is organized in a highly

[39] James A. Quinn, "Discussion of Hollingshead's 'Community Research: Development and Present Condition,'" *American Sociological Review,* **13** (April, 1948), p. 148.

[40] Quinn, *Human Ecology,* p. 286.

[41] Ibid., p. 288.

[42] According to Quinn, there are three different kinds of ecological units, i.e., (1) single living organisms, (2) a group that produces or consumes as a unit, and (3) any specialized function, such as a store or factory, that occupies a spatial position of its own. See ibid., p. 280.

rational and efficient manner with respect to the movement of both goods and people. This rationality and efficiency is supposedly the product of impersonal and subsocial forces.

Amos H. Hawley

Of the human ecologists Amos H. Hawley takes the broadest view of the field, its scope and its purposes. Evidence of this comes when, in defining human ecology, Hawley states,

> ecology is concerned with the elemental problem of how growing, multiplying beings maintain themselves in a constantly changing but ever restricted environment. . . . The subject of ecological inquiry then is the community, the form and development of which are studied with particular reference to the limiting and supporting factors in the environment. . . . It attempts to determine the nature of community structure in general, the types of communities that appear in different habitats, and the specific sequence of change in community development.[43]

Because human ecology has as its primary task the analysis of community structure, it is important that we understand the meaning that Hawley assigns to this term. Basically, Hawley considers community structure to consist of those mechanisms by which a population organizes itself for survival in a particular habitat. Among the most important of these mechanisms is a division of labor appropriate to the needs and characteristics of the community in question. Because of this Hawley considers his analysis of urban service institutions to be within the scope of human ecology.[44] In this study he examines the correlation between the size and composition of different urban populations and the number of commercial institutions found within the area they inhabit.

[43] Hawley, "Ecology and Human Ecology," p. 403.
[44] See Amos H. Hawley, "An Ecological Study of Urban Service Institutions," *American Sociological Review,* **6** (October, 1941), pp. 629–39.

Like Quinn, Hawley does not consider the fundamental task of human ecology to be that of analyzing the spatial distribution of social phenomena. However, he does argue that there is a general tendency for all communities to display a series of zones that are roughly concentric but never perfectly homogeneous. Furthermore, he maintains that instead of having a single center, the modern community has its central business district plus a series of subcenters. The ecological units which occupy these centers are those which are least able to withstand the friction of space, that is, the cost and time involved in locating at more distant points. Those units with a maximum need for accessibility are the ones which become most centralized.

Sociocultural Ecology

Neo-orthodox ecology has its merits as an explanation of the spatial organization of American cities. In a society which places great emphasis upon economic gain, considerations of cost and profit do influence the location of many ecological units. Nonetheless, the neo-orthodox ecologists make two assumptions which can be questioned. The first is that space—more particularly, distance—is simply a given to which people must adjust. No recognition is accorded the fact that regardless of how it is measured, the distance between two points is itself a matter of cultural definition. In some cultures five miles may appear to be a great distance, whereas in other cultures something located five miles away may be defined as nearby. Secondly, the neo-orthodox ecologists also assume that ecological units always seek that location where their costs, largely defined in economic terms, are kept to a minimum. However, there is much reason to think that economic rationality is not the only factor which influences urban spatial organization.

Because of the difficulties inherent in these two assumptions, yet another approach to ecological theory has been developed. This approach, known as sociocultural ecology, views social and cultural variables as the chief factors influencing the spatial organization of cities. The leading proponent of this approach is Walter Firey, whose study *Land Use in Central Boston* has become a classic.[45] According to Firey, there are two basic forces which determine urban spatial organization. First, he does not deny that "rational adaption," or the minimization of costs and the maximization of satisfactions, influences the location of ecological units. However, he does argue that rational adaption is itself a culturally defined and culturally relative concept. To illustrate, Firey suggests that the retail business district as found in the modern American city is the outgrowth of a particular value configuration which emphasizes the constant acquisition of material goods. Purchasing entails a considerable expenditure of time and "what is more important, it involves a rational comparison of price and quality at different markets." [46] Hence, it is "rational" for selected retail outlets to cluster near the center of the city. This makes them readily accessible to the individual shopper and allows him to compare the quality and price of goods offered by the different stores. Presumably, "rational adaption" would entail something quite different in a culture which does not place a premium upon the acquisition of material goods.

Secondly, Firey also argues that sentiment and symbolism have an impact upon urban spatial organization. That this may be the case seems to be amply documented by Firey's extensive analysis of the ecological structure of Boston.[47] For example, one of Boston's most fashionable residential areas, Beacon Hill, has preserved its identity and character despite its proximity to the central business district and despite the fact that the land could be used in much more profitable ways. The reason for this is that Beacon Hill has been consistently viewed by its

[45] Walter Firey, *Land Use in Central Boston* (Cambridge, Mass.: Harvard University Press, 1947).

[46] Ibid., p. 256.

[47] For a brief summary of Firey's findings see his "Sentiment and Symbolism as Ecological Variables," *American Sociological Review,* **10** (April, 1945), pp. 140–48.

residents as a center of profound cultural and historical significance. Thus, numerous attempts to convert it to more "rational" uses have been effectively thwarted. The Boston Commons, a large plot of land located in the center of the city, provides another illustration of the role of sentiment and symbolism in determining the ecological structure of the city. There are many different ways in which the retention of the Commons is uneconomical in terms of commercial values, but again all attempts to convert it to more "rational" uses have been frustrated. The Commons symbolizes many individual and collective traditions to the residents of Boston and has, in effect, become a sacred object to them. Intangible forces such as these are the ones which, according to Firey, determine the spatial organization of the city.

Another interesting example of the role of sociocultural variables in influencing urban spatial organization can be observed in Salt Lake City and some of Utah's other urban communities. The visitor to these cities, if he is the least observant, will immediately notice that the streets run due north and south and east and west, that most of these streets are exceptionally wide, and that barns and farm equipment sheds are frequently found on residential sites well within the city limits. In fact, it becomes immediately apparent that the larger cities of Utah are not the product of the same forces which gave shape and form to our large Eastern cities. Rather, they are the result of careful, consistent planning.

In order to explain the somewhat unique pattern of spatial organization found in Utah cities, it is necessary to examine both the environmental conditions under which these communities were settled and the value configurations of the people who settled them. When these communities were founded (circa 1848 to 1860), the environment was an untamed one which virtually dictated that all settlers, including farmers, locate their homes in proximity to one another, that is, within what later became the city limits. Among other things, this was the only feasible method of gaining protection against the hostile tribes of Indians which roamed the area, and more importantly, it fostered the close, intimate cooperation that was required to make the arid, undeveloped land productive.

An even more significant influence upon the spatial organization of Utah cities was the belief in millennialism that is characteristic of Mormonism. According to the doctrines of the Church of Jesus Christ of Latter-day Saints (Mormonism), North America has been chosen to be the scene of gathering in the last days and, furthermore, the specific site of this gathering is to be the Salt Lake Basin. As a result, it has always been a dominant passion of the Mormons to build a perfect city as a "dwelling place of the Savior and those human beings freed from selfishness, greed, and vanity and thus perfected after the order of their tradition." [48] Among the specifications for this utopian city were that all streets should be eight rods wide and oriented toward the four points of the compass, that the city should be exactly one mile square, and that each block within the city should contain ten acres and be divided into twenty one-half-acre residential sites. The important thing to note is that this was not only a master plan of utopian dimensions. It also became a plan of action that was at least partially carried out.

Our examples from Boston and Salt Lake City are sufficient to illustrate the sociocultural approach to the analysis of ecological phenomena. In effect, the sociocultural ecologists argue that the spatial organization of cities is almost wholly determined by various social and cultural forces, including value configurations, spatially referred sentiments, and traditions that are held in high esteem. Obviously this approach has a tremendous appeal among social scientists who regard culture as a concept which possesses extremely high explanatory power. However, one crucial implication of the sociocultural approach must be pointed out. If the social and cultural forces which influence urban spatial organization are at least partly unique to each

[48] Albert L. Seeman, "Communities in the Salt Lake Basin," *Economic Geography,* **14** (July, 1938), p. 306.

city, then each community should have its unique patterns of spatial organization. Whether students of human ecology are willing to abandon the search for uniformities in urban spatial organization is open to question.

Social Area Analysis

Social area analysis represents yet another approach to the study of ecological phenomena.[49] However, social area analysis differs from the other approaches to human ecology in that it does not advance a full-blown theory of urban spatial organization. Rather, the proponents of social area analysis are concerned only with patterns of differentiation and stratification as they are manifested in urban areas. In brief, social area analysis is essentially a research technique by which we can study the spatial distribution of different population groupings that are typically found in urban settings.

To be more specific, social area analysis is used to identify urban census tracts whose population is similar in terms of three key variables. The three variables, which were originally delineated by Eshref Shevky and Marilyn Williams, are social rank, urbanization, and segregation.[50] The first, social rank, is essentially a measure of the socioeconomic status of the population which inhabits the census tract in question and utilizes census data relating to occupation and education. The second, urbanization, is reflective of the degree of "familialism" present in the census tract. This variable is measured by the use of census data relating to fertility differentials, differentials in the number of females in the labor force, and differentials in the

[49] Social area analysis was first discussed in Eshref Shevky and Marilyn Williams, *The Social Areas of Los Angeles: Analysis and Typology* (Berkeley: University of California Press, 1949). The basic theory and computational procedures used in social area analysis were elaborated upon in Eshref Shevky and Wendell Bell, *Social Area Analysis: Theory, Illustrative Application and Computational Procedures* (Stanford, Calif., Stanford University Press, 1955).

[50] Ibid., especially pp. 33–57.

number of single-family detached dwelling units. Finally, the third variable, segregation, is indicative of significant differentials in the composition of census tract populations and requires the use of census data relating to racial and ethnic composition and to nativity.[51] Some time ago Wendell Bell suggested that much could be gained by way of clarification if the term *economic status* was substituted for *social rank, family status* for *urbanization,* and *ethnic status* for *segregation.*[52]

These three variables obviously reflect fundamental and meaningful distinctions between the different population groupings found in American society.[53] Certainly in the large American city distinctions are made between white- and blue-collar groups, family- and nonfamily-oriented groups, and native-born whites and the members of various minority groups. Furthermore, there is often a strong correlation between these factors and the values which people hold, their life chances, and their modes of living. Hence, a social area simply consists of one or more census tracts which display a unique configuration of these traits as measured by the indexes of social rank, urbanization, and segregation.

From the standpoint of human ecology, several valuable things may be achieved through the use of social area analysis. First, social area analysis constitutes a potentially powerful tool

[51] These variables are described in greater detail in Eshref Shevky and Wendell Bell, *Social Area Analysis,* pp. 17–18.

[52] Wendell Bell, "The Utility of the Shevky Typology for the Design of Urban Sub-area Field Studies," *Journal of Social Psychology,* **47** (February, 1958), p. 72.

[53] It is important to note that the proponents of social area analysis see the city as a reflection of the society in which it is found. Thus, Shevky and Williams tell us that "every city is a product of its time and can only be understood in terms of the society in which it comes into being." (Shevky and Williams, *The Social Areas of Los Angeles,* p. 2.) It should also be noted that the differentials measured by the indexes of social rank, urbanization, and segregation are of relatively recent origin: they have come in the wake of rapid industrialization and the continuing trend toward heterogeneity in the racial and ethnic composition of American society.

by which to ascertain whether there are predictable, recurrent patterns in urban spatial organization. By identifying social areas within several different cities and then comparing them, any generalizations which can be made about the spatial distribution of social phenomena within urban settings should become immediately apparent. This can be done without incurring the expense of conducting field surveys or personally observing the cities in question. Second, social area analysis also represents an excellent method for studying ecological change as it occurs between two or more consecutive census dates. This simply requires that the social areas within a city be identified and that data taken from the different censuses be compared. Has the population of some census tracts changed enough to qualify them for inclusion in different social areas? Have new social areas emerged? What seems to be the over-all pattern of change? Third, social area analysis can be utilized in a similar way to compare the spatial organization of different cities at one point in time. Among other things, this may reveal regional differences in urban ecological structure and lead to the identification of certain types of cities about which it is safe to make ecological generalizations. Finally, social area analysis represents an excellent way of selecting urban subareas for more intensive study.[54] Indeed, Shevky and Bell tell us that,

> The concepts of "natural area" and "subculture" are not unrelated to our concept "social area" for we view a social area as containing persons with similar social positions in the larger society. The social area, however, is not bounded by the geographical frame of reference as is the natural area, nor by implications concerning the degree of interaction between persons in the local community as is the subculture. We do claim, however, that the social area generally contains persons having the same level of living, the same way of life, and the same ethnic background; and we hypothesize that persons living in a particular type of social area would systematically differ with

[54] For example, see Wendell Bell, "The Utility of the Shevky Typology for the Design of Urban Sub-area Field Studies," pp. 71–83.

respect to characteristic attitudes and behaviors from persons living in another type of social area.[55]

If this is the case, social area analysis represents an excellent tool by which the urban sociologist can identify those parts of the city that he wishes to study in greater detail.

The proponents of social area analysis have a great deal of faith in their methodological approach. This is made clear by Shevky and Bell's statement that "we feel that the application of this typology to census and comparable data available for American cities will allow the beginning of the systematic accumulation of knowledge about the social organization, especially the stratification and differentiation, of American urban populations." [56] The faith which Shevky and Bell have in social area analysis seems to be at least partially justified. Thus, it appears that the three variables of social rank, urbanization, and segregation (or some modification thereof) do help to account for much of the variation between census tracts in terms of other variables upon which census data are collected.[57]

Summary

It has been several decades since human ecology had its inception at the University of Chicago. Since that time the human ecologists have not developed a single coherent theoretical system. Rather, human ecology has developed in a variety of different directions and several different explanations of ecological phenomena have been advanced. However, the human

[55] Shevky and Bell, *Social Area Analysis,* p. 20.

[56] Ibid., p. 2.

[57] A number of studies have been completed which use factor analysis to investigate the intercorrelations between social rank, urbanization, and segregation and a variety of other social phenomena which vary from tract to tract. Because of the highly technical nature of this material, it will not be considered in this text. The reader who wishes to pursue "factorial ecology" further should consult the excellent bibliography provided by Janet L. Abu-Lughod in her "Testing the Theory of Social Area Analysis: The Ecology of Cairo, Egypt," *American Sociological Review,* **34** (April, 1969), pp. 210–12.

ecologists have agreed that their fundamental task is to explain the spatial organization and growth dynamics of urban communities. This is a goal which Park, Burgess, Quinn, Hawley, Firey, and most other ecologists have held in common.

Needless to say, the success of this undertaking depends entirely upon whether there are basic similarities in the spatial organization of different cities. If this is the case then the common patterns should be identified and adequate explanations for them put forth. However, the literature reviewed in this chapter suggests that the search for predictable, recurrent patterns in urban spatial organization has not been as successful as one might hope. Although there are undoubtedly a few broad similarities in the spatial organization of cities, every city is apparently somewhat unique in this regard. If this is the case, then the very basis upon which human ecology rests is brought into question.

Even if we eventually find predictable, recurrent patterns of urban spatial organization, the significance of such findings can be questioned. There are many important facets of community life which exist quite independently of its spatial dimension. Indeed, the most significant thing about the community would seem to be that this is where man meets man. As a result, we are able to satisfy our biological, social, and emotional needs. Thus, the greatest need in community study today is for a continued probing of the sociological dimensions of community life and of the strictly human problems which have arisen as a concomitant of urbanization. This is not to suggest that ecological analysis has no role to play in efforts to solve these problems. In fact it can be vigorously argued that the physical environment in which the individual finds himself does have an influence upon his attitudes, behavior, and outlook on life. Squalor, dilapidation, and filth apparently are associated with crime, delinquency, mental illness, and many other social problems. Nonetheless, it must be remembered that the reasons for this are social, economic, and psychological. The physical environment is no more than the setting in which these problems occur.

Obviously, this is not a direct criticism of the human ecologists. These men have been among the most productive, thought-provoking social scientists the United States has produced. However, the ultimate value of human ecology itself must still be determined. Ample opportunity for doing this will exist as the city increasingly becomes the focus of intensive research. In any event, the human ecologists must be given credit for suggesting an approach to the study of urban communities which remains challenging and of high potential significance. There is nothing faulty or picayune about the problems the human ecologists have outlined for themselves.

There is no way to know whether interest in human ecology will persist, and if so, in what directions the field might develop. However, there are a few things which seem fairly obvious. First, it is still worthwhile to search for generalizations concerning the spatial organization of cities, but apparently these must be carefully qualified and of rather limited scope. Even though broad, all-inclusive formulations such as the concentric-zone hypothesis are apparently not feasible, there may still be some recurrent features in the spatial organization of American cities. Secondly, it seems apparent that the successful ecological theory of the future will be one which makes use of the insights contributed by sociologists, anthropologists, historians, and other social scientists. One must agree with Firey that urban spatial organization is the product of human relationships and social values rather than of subsocial and impersonal forces. Finally, a successful theory of human ecology will be one that is both change oriented and future oriented. Today most large communities are in a continuous state of flux and change. The value of any theory which fails to take this fact into account can be seriously questioned.

Bibliography

Abu-Lughod, Janet L. "Testing the Theory of Social Area Analysis," *American Sociological Review*, **34** (April, 1969), pp. 198–212.
Alihan, Milla A. *Social Ecology: A Critical Analysis*. New York: Columbia University Press, 1938.

Anderson, Theodore R., and Janice A. Egeland. "Spatial Aspects of Social Area Analysis," *American Sociological Review,* **26** (June, 1961), pp. 392–98.

Bell, Wendell. "The Utility of the Shevky Typology for the Design of Urban Sub-area Field Studies," *Journal of Social Psychology,* **47** (February, 1958), pp. 71–83.

Berry, Brian J., and Philip H. Rees. "The Factorial Ecology of Calcutta," *American Journal of Sociology,* **74** (March, 1969), pp. 445–91.

Burgess, Ernest W. "The Growth of the City: An Introduction to a Research Project," in Robert E. Park, Ernest W. Burgess, and R. D. McKenzie (eds.), *The City.* Chicago: University of Chicago Press, 1925.

————. "Urban Areas," in T. V. Smith and L. D. White (eds.), *Chicago: An Experiment in Social Science Research.* Chicago: University of Chicago Press, 1929.

Caplow, Theodore. "The Social Ecology of Guatamala City," *Social Forces,* **28** (December, 1949), pp. 113–35.

Davie, Maurice R. "The Pattern of Urban Growth," in George P. Murdock (ed.), *Studies in the Science of Society.* New Haven: Yale University Press, 1937.

DeFlour, Lois B. "Ecological Variables in the Cross-Cultural Study of Delinquency," *Social Forces,* **45** (June, 1967), pp. 556–70.

Elmer, M. C. "Century-Old Ecological Studies in France," *American Journal of Sociology,* **39** (July, 1933), pp. 63–70.

Firey, Walter. *Land Use in Central Boston.* Cambridge, Mass.: Harvard University Press, 1947.

————. "Sentiment and Symbolism as Ecological Variables," *American Sociological Review,* **10** (April, 1945), pp. 140–48.

Gettys, Warner E. "Human Ecology and Social Theory," *Social Forces,* **18** (May, 1940), pp. 469–76.

Hansen, Asael T. "The Ecology of a Latin American City," in E. B. Reuter (ed.), *Race and Culture Contacts.* New York: McGraw-Hill Book Company, 1934.

Harris, Chauncey D., and Edward L. Ullman. "The Nature of Cities," *The Annals of the American Academy of Political and Social Science,* **242** (November, 1945), pp. 7–17.

Hatt, Paul. "The Concept of Natural Area," *American Sociological Review,* **11** (August, 1946), pp. 423–27.

Hawley, Amos H. "Ecology and Human Ecology," *Social Forces,* **22** (May, 1944), pp. 398–405.

——. *Human Ecology.* New York: The Ronald Press, 1950.

Hollingshead, A. B. "A Re-examination of Ecological Theory," *Sociology and Social Research,* **31** (January–February, 1947), pp. 194–204.

Hoyt, Homer. *The Structure and Growth of Residential Neighborhoods in American Cities.* Washington, D.C.: U.S. Government Printing Office, 1939.

Levin, Yale, and Alfred Lindesmith. "English Ecology and Criminology of the Past Century," *Journal of Criminal Law and Criminology,* **27** (March, 1937), pp. 801–16.

McKenzie, R. D. "The Scope of Human Ecology," *Publications of the American Sociological Society,* **20** (1926), pp. 141–54.

Park, Robert E. "Human Ecology," *American Journal of Sociology,* **42** (July, 1936), pp. 1–15.

Peñalosa, Fernando. "Ecological Organization of the Transitional City: Some Mexican Evidence," *Social Forces,* **46** (December, 1967), pp. 221–29.

Quinn, James A. *Human Ecology.* Englewood Cliffs, N.J.: Prentice-Hall, Inc., 1960.

——. "Human Ecology and Interactional Ecology," *American Sociological Review,* **5** (October, 1940), pp. 713–22.

Reckless, Walter C. "The Distribution of Commercialized Vice in the City: A Sociological Analysis," *Publications of the American Sociological Society,* **20** (1926), pp. 164–76.

Seeman, Albert L. "Communities in the Salt Lake Basin," *Economic Geography,* **14** (July, 1938), pp. 300–308.

Shevky, Eshref, and Wendell Bell. *Social Area Analysis.* Stanford, Calif.: Stanford University Press, 1955.

Shevky, Eshref, and Marilyn Williams. *The Social Areas of Los Angeles: Analysis and Typology.* Berkeley and Los Angeles: University of California Press, 1955.

Sweetser, Frank L. "Factorial Ecology: Helsinki, 1960," *Demography,* **2** (1965), pp. 372–85.

Theodorson, George A. (ed.). *Studies in Human Ecology.* New York: Harper & Row, 1961.

Zorbaugh, Harvey W. "The Natural Areas of the City," *Publications of the American Sociological Society,* **20** (1926), pp. 188–97.

4

Constructed Types and Community Theory

Sociologists have made extensive use of constructed types. Among the most famous of these have been Emile Durkheim's analysis of organic and mechanical solidarity, Max Weber's modes of action orientation, Charles Horton Cooley's concept of the primary group, Becker's models of sacred and secular societies, and the pattern variables as delineated by Talcott Parsons.[1] Likewise, the process of type construction has been very popular in the study of human communities. It is to some of the constructed-type theories of community that we now must turn.

Constructed Types

The Nature of Constructed Types

Before we consider the major typological theories of community, the nature of constructed types and the processes involved in type construction must be examined. Although the process of type construction is used with regularity by the sociologist, there are few statements in the literature concerning the nature and purposes of constructed types. As a matter of

[1] John C. McKinney and Charles P. Loomis, "The Typological Tradition," in Joseph S. Roucek (ed.), *Contemporary Sociology* (New York: The Philosophical Library, Inc., 1958), pp. 557–71.

fact most texts on social research make no reference to constructed types, and many sociologists routinely engage in type construction without realizing it. Nonetheless, it is easy to specify the nature of a constructed type. A constructed type is basically a simplified and sometimes purposely exaggerated model of the personality, social, or cultural system that is being examined by the investigator. In type construction the investigator ignores the welter of details which characterize the phenomena he is examining and focuses upon those variables that are most significant or central in describing the system in question. For example, even a small rural community is obviously a very complex form of organization. However, the sociologist who uses type construction as his basic methodological tool might conclude that in its purest form the rural community is characterized by a completely homogeneous population, the dominance of the family over all other institutions, and social relationships of a primary nature.

It is important to note that constructed types are not a product of the investigator's imagination. Rather, a good constructed type is always based upon an intimate familiarity with empirical cases and can only be derived after careful, prolonged research on the phenomenon under consideration. To put the case differently, an adequate but simplified model of a personality, social, or cultural system cannot be advanced until the investigator is thoroughly acquainted with the many variables which characterize the system. At the same time, a constructed type is never a verbatim description of the system being studied. The reasons for this are twofold. First, by its very nature a constructed type is a simplified model of reality and only the *key* variables which typify the system are included in the model. The fact that a constructed type represents a simplification of reality is the very thing which makes it an extremely valuable tool in sociological analysis. Secondly, almost all constructed types are based upon an examination of more than one case. To be more specific, in type construction the peculiarities of individual cases are ignored and the focus is upon the variables that are common to all manifestations of the thing being studied. Howard Becker makes this point clear when, in discussing "typical" revolutions, he says that "the constructed type is merely a tool. Hence when the methodologically sophisticated sociologist talks about a type of revolution, his hearers can be very sure that it will never correspond exactly to any empirical instance, to any 'real' situation." [2]

Finally, the typologist often concerns himself not only with the system being studied but also with its polar opposite. In short, constructed types frequently are used to delineate the outermost limits of a rural–urban, sacred–secular, or some other important continuum. As will be seen, this practice can enhance immeasurably both the theoretical relevance and the pragmatic utility of the original constructed type. However, the delineation of the polar opposite is not an essential step in type construction. Contrary to what some students may conclude, Cooley did not offer a model of the secondary group as a polar opposite for his primary group, and some things that sociologists study simply do not have meaningful opposites. What, for example, is the polar opposite, the other extreme, of revolution?

The Utility of Constructed Types

In his discussion of type construction John McKinney makes it clear that typological procedures have an important role to play in theory construction and in the conduct of empirical research.[3] In the analysis of communities, for example, it appears that there are four ways in which constructed types are especially helpful. First, a good constructed type should shed light on the nature of various communities if they were ever encountered in pure form. Thus, although all modern communities are probably a complex mixture of rural and urban pat-

[2] Howard Becker, *Through Values to Social Interpretation: Essays on Social Context, Actions, Types, and Prospects* (Durham, N.C.: Duke University Press, 1950), p. 107.

[3] John C. McKinney, *Constructive Typology and Social Theory* (New York: Appleton-Century-Crofts, 1966).

Theories of Community

terns, by the use of type construction it is possible to identify and single out those variables that are unique and peculiar to rural communities. In effect, the sociological connotation of rurality can be sharpened and refined. The same would be true if a model of the urban community, the secular society, the inner-directed personality, the capitalist system, or whatever, were constructed. Secondly, type construction can be a powerful tool in the derivation of much-needed generalizations about communities. It hardly needs to be pointed out, for example, that each community is unique and has its own distinctive constellation of traits and patterns. Nonetheless, in type construction the theorist ignores the idiosyncratic features of the communities being studied and focuses only upon their shared traits. By doing so he is able to offer generalizations which apply to all communities falling within a particular class (e.g., rural communities). Thirdly, constructed types, especially when they represent the outer limits of a continuum, can be extremely useful in drawing comparisons between two or more communities. Quite frequently the question arises as to whether one community is more rural or more urban than another. This question and others like it can easily be answered by assessing the degree to which the communities in question deviate from the pure types which represent the polar ends of a rural–urban continuum. Finally, constructed types are frequently helpful in the study of social change and in making predictions about the path of development that a changing community may follow. A good polar typology of rural and urban communities, for example, should yield insight into the process of urbanization and indicate the traits that a community takes on as it becomes increasingly urban.

An Illustrative Polar Type

The significance and utility of constructed types can best be conveyed by a highly simplified example. For this purpose Figure 4-1 has been prepared. In this figure a crude polar

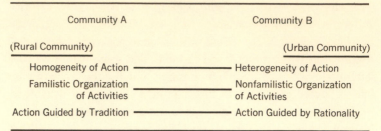

Figure 4-1. Patterns of action in rural and urban communities: an illustrative polar typology.

typology has been developed which indicates differences in patterns of human action between rural and urban communities. This typology is based on the assumption that patterns of human action in rural communities differ in very basic ways from those found in urban communities. Similarly, the degree of deviation of two fictitious communities from the "pure" type has been indicated. Although this typology is a product of armchair analysis, it does illustrate the uses to which constructed types may be put.

1. The typology helps us to understand how human activity might be patterned in both rural and urban communities if either were found in their purest form. For example, if a small, completely isolated community could be found, all its members might well be engaged in highly similar activities. Virtually *all* able-bodied adult males might spend winter, spring, summer, and fall in caring for the fields and livestock, whereas *all* adult females might devote their entire efforts to rearing children and running the household. Likewise, in the same community virtually all activities may be carried on in conjunction with other family members. In short, all work, recreation, worship, and education would involve interaction with kin rather than with nonrelated individuals. Finally, in our fictitious rural community, all human activity might well be guided by tradition. On the other hand, if the concept of *urban* is pushed to its logical limits, it would denote a communal form in which no

two people engage in the same activities or play identical roles, in which most human activity occurs in nonfamilial groups, and in which human action is guided by norms of rationality and expediency. It should be obvious that there are probably few communities which fit either of these models exactly. Nonetheless, it is the prerogative of the typologist to exaggerate in order to give meaning and utility to his concepts.

2. If the polar types suggested in Figure 4-1 were based on empirical research, they would constitute a set of generalizations relating to patterns of human action in rural as opposed to urban communities. If the peculiar and idiosyncratic features of individual rural communities are ignored and the common features of many rural communities focused upon, it might well be concluded that the activities of rural dwellers are homogeneous, that rural people do engage in a disproportionate amount of action involving other members of their family, and that the activities of rural people are to some extent dictated by tradition.

3. Assuming that the profiles for communities A and B actually represent their relative positions on a rural–urban continuum, then there is no question but that community A is more rural than community B. In short, a typology provides us with a means by which two or more communities can be classified and systematically compared. Before the typology can be used in this way, however, we would have to collect and analyze a considerable amount of data pertaining to the two communities.

4. Assuming once more that the typology is valid, it is possible to predict some of the more significant changes which will occur as both communities undergo further urbanization. For example, if community A begins to grow in size and complexity, then the activities in which community members engage will become more heterogeneous, the family will less often be the context in which human activities occur, and human action will increasingly be guided by norms of rationality and expediency.

Ferdinand Tonnies (1855–1936)

The typological tradition is an extremly old one. Pitirim Sorokin points out, for example, that Confucius, Plato, Aristotle, St. Augustine, and Ibn Khaldun all authored constructed types.[4] For our purposes, however, the German scholar Ferdinand Tonnies can be considered the father of the typological tradition in sociology. First published in 1887, his famous *Gemeinschaft und Gesellschaft* was a predecessor to the works of Durkheim, Becker, Redfield, and the many other scholars who have developed type construction into a highly useful tool for the analysis of social systems. Hence, even though a brief review of the theory set forth by Tonnies poses a significant challenge for both reader and writer, the concepts of *Gemeinschaft* and *Gesellschaft* simply cannot be ignored.

We must immediately point out that Tonnies was not directly interested in the analysis of territorial communities. Rather, he sought to understand social relationships per se and to identify certain basic relationships which develop between human beings.[5] Nonetheless, it is important for the student of territorial communities to have some understanding of the basic elements which comprise Tonnies' scheme. Among other things, Tonnies has had a profound influence upon those who have used typological procedures in their attempt to understand territorial communities. Most of the writers who are considered in later sections of this chapter explicitly recognize this influence. Furthermore, much of what Tonnies says is reflective of differences between rural and urban communities and is helpful in the study of urbanization.

Before we explore the theoretical scheme set forth by Tonnies, a warning is in order. The theory developed by Tonnies is amazingly complex and multifaceted and defies sim-

---

[4] See Pitirim A. Sorokin, "Forward," in Ferdinand Tonnies, *Community and Society,* edited by Charles F. Loomis (New York: Harper & Row, 1963), p. vii.

[5] See Talcott Parsons, *The Structure of Social Action* (New York: The Free Press, 1949), pp. 686–94.

ple interpretation. In order to follow it one must know something of sociology, psychology, philosophy, economics, and jurisprudence, but one must also have the ability to see the forest for the trees. Hence, there is really only one satisfactory way to gain insight into the thinking of Ferdinand Tonnies. This is by reading *Gemeinschaft und Gesellschaft*.[6]

The Types of Will

At the very heart of Tonnies' theory is the assumption that all social relationships are willed, that is, they exist only because individuals want them to exist. However, the reasons individuals wish to associate with each other vary from person to person and from situation to situation. In some cases people associate with each other because they attach intrinsic significance to their relationships; in other cases individuals form relationships with each other for the sole purpose of pursuing a tangible goal. According to Tonnies, the first type of relationship has its basis in natural will whereas the second type of relationship has its basis in rational will.

Because the concepts of natural will and rational will are of central importance in understanding the concepts of *Gemeinschaft* and *Gesellschaft,* they must be explored in more detail. Although the first, natural will, has many different dimensions, its key components are understanding and unity. In a relationship resting on natural will each individual fully understands the other and takes a direct interest in his welfare. Furthermore, a unity of goals, values, and beliefs which rests upon sentiment and the memory of common traditions and experiences is achieved. All of this adds up to one thing: the relationship which springs from natural will becomes an end in itself rather than a means to some other end. The prototype of such a relationship is of course the family, wherein each member is valued for his own sake, but Tonnies also maintains that natural will

[6] The most convenient edition is that cited in footnote 4.

is dominant in the thinking of peasants and artisans, women and young people.

Rational will, on the other hand, entails the careful weighing of various means to a desired end. When two merchants deal with each other, for example, they have a definite end or purpose in mind and each one carefully plans and plots so that he can achieve his goals. Thus, the individual driven by rational will is concerned chiefly with his future well-being and bases his actions upon deliberation and discrimination. Although Tonnies implies that there is a subtle distinction between deliberation and discrimination, both concepts refer to the individual's ability to choose means and ends carefully and wisely. According to Tonnies, rational will, based as it is on deliberation and reasoning, is dominant in the thinking of businessmen, aged persons, scientists, and the educated classes. It would also seem to be characteristic of the urbanite.

Gemeinschaft and Gesellschaft

Hence, Tonnies assumes that social relationships may rest on two bases: they may rest upon understanding, unity, and sentiment (i.e., natural will) or upon the desire to reach some specific end (i.e., rational will). Once this is understood the two basic types of relationship delineated by Tonnies, Gemeinschaft and Gesellschaft, can be elaborated upon.

There are many different features of the Gemeinschaft-like relationship. Among other things, McKinney and Loomis maintain that relationships of this type are characterized by mutual aid and helpfulness, mutual interdependence, reciprocal and binding sentiment, diffuse or blanket obligations, and authority based upon age, wisdom, and benevolent force.[7] Furthermore, persons enmeshed in a Gemeinschaft-like relationship share sacred traditions and a spirit of brotherhood which grows out

[7] See John C. McKinney and Charles P. Loomis, "The Typological Tradition," p. 558.

of bonds of blood, common locality, or mind. Tonnies expresses this point clearly when he states that,

> The Gemeinshaft of blood, denoting unity of being, is developed and differentiated into Gemeinschaft of locality, which is based on a common habitat. A further differentiation leads to a Gemeinschaft of mind, which implies only co-operation and co-ordinated action for a common goal. Gemeinschaft of locality may be conceived as a community of physical life, just as Gemeinschaft of mind expresses the community of mental life. In conjunction with the others, this last type of Gemeinschaft represents the truly human and supreme form of community.[8]

The specific organizational forms in which *Gemeinschaft*-like relationships become manifested will be considered in more detail later.

In distinct contrast to this type of relationship is the *Gesellschaft*-like relationship. In *Gesellschaft*-like relationships, the participating individuals are separated rather than united and individualism reaches its zenith. Similarly, the individual rarely takes action on behalf of the *Gesellschaft* itself. Rather, all actions are taken in light of their potential benefit for the individual. Because of this the relationships which emerge between members of the *Gesellschaft* are contractual and functionally specific and frequently involve the exchange of goods, money, or credit and obligations. Tonnies puts the case well when he says that in *Gesellschaft*-like relationships "nobody wants to grant and produce anything for another individual . . . if it be not in exchange for a gift or labor equivalent that he considers at least equal to what he has given." [9] Because of this the *Gesellschaft* is supposedly characterized by a continual state of tension. Open conflict between its members is avoided only through the media of convention, legislation, and public opinion.

At this point we might well remember that Tonnies was in-

---

[8] Tonnies, *Community and Society,* p. 42.
[9] Ibid., p. 65.

terested only in the analysis of social relationships. However, it is obvious that the concepts of *Gemeinschaft* and *Gesellschaft* do have applicability in the study of various forms of social organization. Perhaps the best example of a truly *Gemeinschaft*-like relationship is the family and, more particularly, the relationship which develops between parent and offspring. This type of relationship rests almost entirely upon sentiment and understanding (i.e., natural will) and is devoid of the desire for tangible gain. Others forms of organization which involve *Gemeinschaft*-like relationships are neighborhoods, villages, and towns. According to Tonnies the town represents the most complex form of *Gemeinschaft*-like relationship and "both village and town retain many of the characteristics of the family; the village retains more, the town less." [10] In contrast to these *Gemeinschaft*-like organizations, the city, the national capital, and the metropolis are typically *Gesellschaft*-like organizations. In these communal types money and capital reign supreme and the emphasis is upon the production of goods, profit, and knowledge in a rational and efficient manner. In the city and metropolis the mentality of the capitalist and businessman prevails.

The Types of Law

During the era in which Tonnies wrote *Gemeinschaft und Gesellschaft,* there was much interest in law and the forms it assumes. It is not surprising therefore that Tonnies proposed that different types of law are associated with different types of organization. To be more specific, Tonnies argued that social control in the *Gemeinschaft*-like organization is based upon folkways, mores, and customs which, from the standpoint of members of the *Gemeinschaft,* possess eternal truth and never lose their binding force. Above all, the law of the *Gemeinschaft* involves the control of the whole over its parts, and the interests of the family, village, or town always come before those of the

[10] Ibid., p. 227.

individual. On the other hand, the form of law typical of the *Gesellschaft* is more rational and scientific and exists independently of superstition, faith, and tradition. As such, law represents a rational agreement between members of the *Gesellschaft* and its only purpose is to uphold the rights, duties, and obligations of these members. In short, law in a *Gesellschaft*-like organization is simply another form of contract. The members of the *Gesellschaft* abide by the law because it is to their benefit to do so.

Concluding Remarks

Before we leave Tonnies and his concepts of *Gemeinschaft* and *Gesellschaft,* a few concluding remarks are in order. First, Tonnies obviously viewed his work as an exercise in the articulation of ideal types which rarely, if ever, appear in the real world. In commenting on the concepts of rational and natural will, for example, Tonnies points out that,

> Between these two extremes all real volition takes place. The consideration that most volition and action resembles or is inclined toward either one or the other makes it possible to establish the concepts of natural will and rational will, which concepts are rightly applied only in this sense. I call them normal concepts. What they represent are ideal types, and they serve as standards by which reality may be recognized and described.[11]

The last sentence in this statement is of particular interest because it suggests that Tonnies regarded his ideal types as merely tools by which empirical phenomena may be classified and understood.

Secondly, there is every reason to think that Tonnies conceived of his theoretical system as a dynamic one. More than anything else, he presents a theory of social and cultural change. On various occasions, for example, Tonnies points out that as

[11] Ibid., p. 248.

time passes, *Gesellschaft*-like relationships replace *Gemein-schaft*-like ones and that natural will continually yields to the triumph of rational will. To be more specific, Tonnies offers what is, in essence, an economic interpretation of social and cultural change. He maintains that with the emergence of capitalism and the concomitant desire for monetary gain, the values and ideologies associated with *Gemeinschaft* fade away and are replaced by values associated with trade and commerce. Thus, "the merchants or capitalists . . . are the natural masters and rulers of the Gesellschaft." [12] It is they who stimulate the shift from a *Gemeinschaft*-dominated society to one dominated by *Gesellschaft*-like relationships.

Just how Tonnies evaluated this basic change in the nature of social relationships is open to question. On the one hand, Loomis correctly points out that "Tonnies continually reminded his readers that the process of change through which the individual who was controlled by natural or integral will in his Gemeinschaft was 'freed' and became the subject of rational will was 'healthy' and 'normal.' Although critics accused him of recommending Gemeinschaft as good and condemning Gesellschaft as bad, he disclaimed any such intention." [13] At the same time, Tonnies seems to betray a preference for *Gemeinschaft*-like relationships and a belief that *Gesellschaft*-like relationships are superficial and even unnatural. This preference is most clearly indicated when, in citing the political scientist Bluntschli, Tonnies states that,

Whenever urban culture blossoms and bears fruits, Gesellschaft appears as its indispensible organ. The rural people know little of it. On the other hand, all praise of rural life has pointed out that the Gemeinschaft among people is stronger there and more alive; it is the lasting and genuine form of living together. In contrast to Gemeinschaft, Gesellschaft is transitory and superficial. Accordingly Gemeinschaft should be

[12] Ibid., p. 83.
[13] Ibid., p. 3.

understood as a living organism, Gesellschaft as a mechanical aggregate and artifact.[14]

It is interesting to note that Tonnies' attitude toward *Gemeinschaft,* to the extent that it is reflected in this passage, is very similar to that of many Americans as they look back with nostalgia on "the good old days" when the United States was no more than a collection of rural villages and towns.

Communal Types: Major American Contributions

Following the publication of *Gemeinschaft und Gesellschaft,* the use of type construction as a basic methodological tool in the social sciences became rather popular. Needless to say, many of the best-known constructed types, including those of Max Weber, Emile Durkheim, and Howard Becker, have only an indirect bearing on the analysis of territorial communities. Hence, they are not considered by the present writer. However, three constructed-type theories of community which cannot be ignored are those developed by Robert M. MacIver, Carle C. Zimmerman, and Robert Redfield.

Robert M. MacIver

The wisdom of including Robert M. MacIver's concepts of communal and associational relations in a discussion of typological theories of community might be questioned. For one thing, the distinction that MacIver draws between communal and associational relations is not expressed in a highly formalized typology. Rather, the two concepts simply point to two fundamentally different types of relationships which can develop between men. Of more importance, however, is the fact that MacIver used the term *community* in a somewhat different way than it is used in this book. MacIver's concept of community is much more inclusive than that of the present author's. None-

[14] Ibid., p. 35.

theless, the two concepts which he has developed are meaningful ones and are applicable to the analysis of territorial communities.

The distinction which MacIver draws between communities and associations is a simple one. He begins with the assumption that all social relationships are an outgrowth of the common interests which prevail between men: many of the goals that men pursue can only be realized by working together, and as a result, human beings affiliate with each other because it is to their interest to do so. This brings us to MacIver's basic definition of the term *community*. Thus, when persons unite together to pursue "not this or that particular interest, but the basic conditions of a common life, we call that group a community. The mark of a community is that one's life may be lived within it, that all one's social relationships may be found within it." [15] In brief, it is within a community that an individual can satisfy all his physical, psychological, social, and economic needs. As such, a community may encompass a territorial area as small as a household or as large as a nation.

In contrast to the all-encompassing nature of communal relations are those of an associational nature. According to MacIver, an association consists of persons united together to pursue some particular interest or interests. Therefore, the difference between communities and associations is entirely clear, that is, "a community is a focus of social life, the common living of social beings; an association is an organization of social life, definitely established for the pursuit of one or more common interests. An association is partial, a community is integral." [16] More specifically, associations are a part of community structure itself and may be of a "political, economic, religious, educational, scientific, artistic, literary, recreative, philanthropic, and (or) professional nature." [17]

[15] Robert M. MacIver, *Society: A Textbook of Sociology* (New York: Farrar & Rinehart, Inc., 1937), p. 9.
[16] Robert M. MacIver, *Community: A Sociological Study* (New York: The Macmillan Company, 1931), p. 24.
[17] Ibid., p. 24.

Carle C. Zimmerman

The theory developed by Carle C. Zimmerman centers around his concepts of "localistic" and "cosmopolitan" communities. In reality, this theoretical scheme contains little that is new, and as a matter of fact, Zimmerman readily acknowledges that his concepts closely parallel Tonnies' concepts of *Gemeinschaft* and *Gesellschaft*.[18] Nonetheless, Zimmerman's scheme is of interest because it was one of the first constructed types which dealt directly and specifically with territorial communities, that is, with communities which have "a relatively definite and compact geographic base." [19] Furthermore, Zimmerman is the first theorist we have considered in this chapter whose conceptual scheme is based on empirical research. At one time his book was as valuable for its insightful case studies of various communities as it was for its theoretical framework.[20] Nonetheless, Zimmerman constantly maintains that the concepts of "localism" and "cosmopolitanism" are themselves ideal types and should be so regarded.

The Typology. The distinction between localistic and cosmopolitan communities is rather simple.[21] Conditions found in the localistic community dictate, among other things, that the individual enjoys strong, viable ties with his family and community and that the interests of both groups come before those of the individual. In fact, the bonds between the individual and his community become so strong that he thinks of his community as "my group." [22] Furthermore, in the localistic community almost all associational ties are of a face-to-face nature and

18 See Carle C. Zimmerman, *The Changing Community* (New York: Harper & Row, 1938), especially pp. 80–84.

19 Ibid., p. 15.

20 It should be stressed that only one facet of Zimmerman's theory of community is presented in this chapter. The student with a deep interest in community theory would be well advised to read *The Changing Community* in its entirety.

21 "The Distinctive Traits of Localism and Cosmopolitanism" are summarized in ibid., pp. 107–10. The present discussion closely follows that of Zimmerman's.

22 Ibid., p. 107.

there is much overlapping of group memberships. Thus, "Masons are also Odd Fellows; Eastern Star women belong to the Culture Club; family members participate in the same groups, etc." [23] Needless to say, the associational structure of the localistic community is rather simple and unspecialized, and the number of such associations is limited.

The localistic community is both secluded and isolated.[24] Its members place a strong emphasis upon neighborliness and friendliness and consciously seek to meet one another's needs. Because of this, Zimmerman argues that the localistic community tends to encourage the development of healthy, stable personalities in its members, that relatives take direct responsibility for the sick and the poor, and that police officers "show considerable pride in the fact that they prevent crime rather than punish it." [25] Likewise, the orientation which members of the localistic community have toward materialism, government, and social change are much different from those of the modern city dweller. According to Zimmerman, the localite is mainly concerned with the nonmaterial pleasures of life, tends to mistrust "big" government, and is generally fearful and suspicious of change. The attitude of the localite toward change is often summed up in such statements as "change is usually for the worse" and "we might be better off the way we are." [26]

The traits which characterize the cosmopolitan community are the opposite of those which typify the localistic community. To be more specific, the term *cosmopolitan* applies to communities in which (1) there is a general emphasis upon the individual and his ability to realize his essentially selfish desires; (2) there is little neighborliness and friendliness; (3) time-honored traditions and customs are shunned or even abandoned; (4) great emphasis is placed upon the pursuit of wealth and material goods; and (5) isolation and seclusion are obsolete. In

[23] Ibid., p. 107.

[24] It should be noted that with the development of mass communications this type of community virtually disappeared from the American scene.

[25] Ibid., p. 108.

[26] Ibid., p. 108.

the cosmopolitan community there is little fear of strong, centralized government and the typical cosmopolitanite has a very positive attitude toward social change. This attitude is sometimes reflected in such statements as "let's get on with it" and "we can't be worse off than we are now." [27]

A Concluding Remark. It should be remembered that Zimmerman's typology grew out of research he conducted between 1905 and 1929 and that American community life has changed dramatically since that time. Among other things, the localistic community has surely disappeared from the American scene. This accounts for the fact that Zimmerman's typology sounds old-fashioned. This should not, however, be construed as a criticism of Zimmerman or his work. He obviously recognized that the localistic community, with all its purported virtues, would gradually disappear and that the cosmopolitan community would become the order of the day.[28]

Robert Redfield: The Folk–Urban Continuum

Some of the most penetrating analyses of community life have come from those anthropologists who examine the lifeways of people who dwell in the more isolated regions of the world. Especially to be singled out in this respect is the late Robert Redfield. Not only did Redfield provide students of the community with a wealth of colorful and well-documented case material relevant to life in rural Mexico, but he also made brilliant use of theory, and especially type construction, in organizing and interpreting these materials.[29]

[27] Ibid., p. 110.

[28] Zimmerman clearly had doubts about the desirability of this trend. See especially ibid., pp. 652–53.

[29] In addition to the specific materials discussed in this chapter, some of Redfield's major works are *Topoztlan: A Mexican Village* (Chicago: University of Illinois Press, 1930); *The Little Community* (Chicago: University of Chicago Press, 1955); *Peasant Society and Culture* (Chicago: University of Chicago Press, 1956); and *The Primitive World and Its Transformations* (Ithaca, N.Y.: Cornell University Press, 1953). See also Robert Redfield and Alfronso Villa, *Chan Kom: A Maya Village* (Washington, D.C.: Carnegie Institution of Washington Publication 448, 1934).

Although Redfield acknowledges the inspiration that he drew from Tonnies and other typologists, his own constructed type differs in significant ways from those we have already discussed. Among other things, Redfield not only sought to delineate polar types but also to understand the changes which occur as a community goes through the transition from "folk" to "urban." More specifically, he raised some basic questions as to what happens to communities as they become increasingly urbanized.[30] Redfield's interest in the changes which occur as a community evolves from "folk" to "urban" can be explained, in turn, by the fact that his typology is based on data collected by himself and others. Indeed, Redfield is the first theorist we have considered in this chapter whose work approaches the ideal in terms of scientific endeavor. He alternates between the articulation of theory and the examination of data which potentially support the theory. Because of this we cannot fully understand Redfield's folk–urban typology until we examine briefly the four communities he studied.

Four Communities: A Thumbnail Sketch

The four communities that Redfield studied were all located on the Yucatan Peninsula. This body of land juts northward and eastward from the lower portion of Mexico and is divided into the Mexican states of Yucatan and Campeche, and the territory of Quintana Roo.[31] Redfield tells us that when he conducted his studies during the early 1930's the Yucatan Peninsula was both physically and politically isolated from the rest of Mexico and, above all, retained a distinctive regional culture.[32] Furthermore,

[30] This does not mean that Redfield lacked interest in the outer limits of his continuum. Perhaps the nearest he comes to articulating these outer limits is in his article "The Folk Society," *The American Journal of Sociology,* **52** (January, 1947), pp. 293–308.

[31] For Redfield's own description of the Yucatan Peninsula see *The Folk Culture of Yucatan* (Chicago: University of Chicago Press, 1941), especially pp. 1–18.

[32] Ibid., p. 2.

there were communities on the peninsula which represented the extremes of primitive and modern, folk and urban.

To be more specific, one of the communities that Redfield studied, Merida, was of interest because it was the only major urban center in the entire region.[33] As of 1930 the city had a population which was both large (96,660 inhabitants) and heterogeneous. Redfield reports that a wide variety of occupations was represented in the city, as were several different racial and ethnic groups, three major linguistic groups (Spanish, Maya, and English), and people of all social classes and income levels. Furthermore, Merida was by no means isolated. Because it was the capital of the state of Yucatan and the largest city in the region, its population was highly mobile and it exercised a great deal of influence over the economic, political, and cultural affairs of the entire peninsula. At the same time, it was closely integrated with and exposed to influences originating in other parts of Mexico and the world.

In distinct contrast to Merida was the tribal village of Tusik, tucked far away from the mainstream of Yucatan society. Located in central Quintana Roo, it was one of the nine settlements within the territory claimed by the X-Cacal subtribe of Maya indians. As such it represented the epitome of the folklike community. As of the 1930's the village had a population of 106 pesons,[34] almost all of whom were of Maya blood and background. Furthermore, the people of Tusik were homogeneous in regard to their occupations. The only adult male who was completely freed from the burdens of agriculture was the community's priestly leader, and specialization was almost unknown in Tusik, except for one man who occasionally repaired guns and sewing machines. Although Redfield does not specifically mention the activities of Tusik women, it is safe to assume that they too were limited to the traditional tasks of maintaining the household and caring for the young.

[33] The following description of Merida, and of the other three communities, are summarized from ibid., pp. 19–57.
[34] Ibid., p. 51.

In addition to its homogeneity, Tusik was also extremely isolated. Members of the community harbored feelings of suspicion and hostility toward their more urbane neighbors and toward the Mexican government, and hence avoided communication and contact with outsiders. As a result, Tusik had neither school teachers nor representatives of larger governmental units and the Tusik native rarely ventured into larger towns and cities. About the only contact community members had with outsiders was with traveling merchants, who stayed in Tusik for only as long as was required to conduct business. The amount of isolation found in Tusik and its sister communities is best expressed by Redfield when he points out that,

> Tusik hides itself in the bush; none of the nine villages are built on the roads that connect Santa Cruz del Brava with Valladolid and Peto, and the paths that lead to Tusik are deliberately concealed. The advent of a visitor is a cause for alarm, and the news of the appearance of a stranger within the territory of the group is an occasion to send out a party to reconnoiter.[35]

This strongly suggests that Tusik's success in maintaining its social and cultural isolation was partly due to its geographic and physical isolation.

The other two communities, Chan Kom and Dzitas, represented intermediate points along a continuum which began with the folk community of Tusik and ended with the thoroughly urbanized community of Merida. The first, Chan Kom, resembled Tusik in many important respects. Its population was small (250 inhabitants as of 1930), everyone was dependent upon agriculture, and the vast majority of people was of Mayan blood and background. However, Chan Kom differed from Tusik in one important respect: its people did not place any value upon isolation. Rather, they sought to become incorporated into the larger Yucatan society and to take on many of the ways of the city. Partly because of this Chan Kom had "a

[35] Ibid., pp. 52–53.

reputation in Yucatan for industry, determination, and ambition." [36] The final community, Dzitas (population 1,200), represented yet another stage in the transition from folk to urban. Because it was located at the junction of a major railway and was a seat of local government, Dzitas was far from isolated. Furthermore, although Dzitas obviously lacked the heterogeneity of Merida, its population was comprised of various racial and social groups. Although most of the men of Dzitas were agriculturalists, many other occupations were represented, including a district judge, a variety of merchants, and numerous artisians.[37] Redfield captured the spirit of Dzitas best when he stated that "it lies on the frontier between the urban and rural ways of life." [38]

These are the four communities upon which Redfield based his folk–urban typology. When these communities are arranged in proper order (Tusik, Chan Kom, Dzitas, and Merida), a natural continuum exists from the isolated, homogeneous tribal village to the mobile, heterogeneous city. Redfield uses isolation–mobility and homogeneity–heterogeneity as the key independent variables in his typology.

The Folk–Urban Continuum

It will be recalled that Redfield sought to analyze the changes which occur in communities as they evolve from folk to urban rather than to describe the outer limits of his continuum. Specifically, he maintains that three basic changes occur as a community becomes more urbanized. These may be summarized as follows:

1. The community undergoes a process of *cultural disorganization*. By this Redfield means simply that the rules and norms which guide human action become more complex, multifaceted, and at times inconsistent. To be more specific, cultural disor-

[36] Ibid., p. 50.
[37] Ibid., p. 38.
[38] Ibid., p. 43.

ganization involves four basic elements.[39] First, much of the unity that was once characteristic of the community's culture is lost. All the members of the Tusik and Chan Kom communities, for example, subscribed to one organized body of beliefs, values, and ideas, whereas in the larger communities there were numerous subcultures built around ethnic, religious, and class differences. Secondly, cultural disorganization implies that many cultural alternatives are open to the individual and that relatively few behavioral patterns are normatively defined. Because cultural disorganization is typical of the city, the urbanite has to make many more choices than the ruralite, and the likelihood that his neighbors will follow the same course of action is slight. For example, Redfield points out that in the villages there is only one acceptable way to cope with illness, whereas in Merida many ways exist. Thus, "if a conservatively thinking native of Chan Kom falls ill and does not soon recover, he calls the shaman-priest. A Meridiano of the working class in similar circumstances may call an herbalist, buy a patent medicine, see a spiritualist, or visit a doctor." [40] Thirdly, Redfield suggests that the path from cultural organization to disorganization entails a decrease in the amount of interdependence between various elements of which the culture is composed. In Tusik different facets of the local culture are so interrelated that one cannot, for example, understand the beliefs, values, and practices associated with illness without also understanding those associated with agriculture and the supernatural. In Merida this is not the case. One's occupational successes or failures have little to do with one's religious strengths or shortcomings, nor is illness interpreted as evidence of impiety. Finally, Redfield argues that cultural disorganization often entails conflict and inconsistency between various cultural standards. In the folk village every item of culture harmonizes with every other item, whereas in the urban community the individual faces behavioral expectations which are inconsistent.

[39] For a more complete discussion of cultural disorganization see ibid., pp. 346–52.
[40] Ibid., pp. 111–12.

Theories of Community

2. Another major change which occurs as communities evolve from folk to urban is that they become more *secularized*. Thus, Redfield suggests that almost all activities in the folk communities are imbued with religious connotations, whereas in the more urbanized communities most human action is guided by considerations of expediency and rationality. It must be stressed, however, that Redfield does not equate the concept of "sacred" with formalized religion.[41] Rather, the term *sacred* implies only that "there is reluctance, emotionally supported, to call the thing rationally or practically into question." [42] Hence, the shift from sacred to secular is well illustrated by the fact that in the fields of Chan Kom and other folklike communities the growing of maize is surrounded by a host of inviolable religious connotations and beliefs. Once the crop is taken to market, however, then the rule "show the man how to get a better price, and he will follow the suggestion" applies.[43]

3. The final basic change which accompanies the transition from folk to urban involves the degree to which *individualism* becomes a hallmark of human behavior. In the villages of Yucatan all of one's actions have implications for one's family and community and hence these become extremely powerful reference groups. One plans his activities with their welfare in mind. On the other hand, in the more urbanized communities the welfare of one's family and community does not depend as much on the actions of the individual. As a result, the individual is given more leeway to do what he wants to do and be what he wants to be. In the city the practice of one's occupation becomes less a matter of obligation to family and community and more a matter of individual choice. Likewise, the right of the individual to hold land and use it for his own benefit becomes recognized, and the selection of a marital partner becomes a matter of individual discretion.[44]

[41] Ibid., p. 354.
[42] Ibid., p. 353.
[43] Ibid., p. 354.
[44] Ibid., p. 355.

Summary

In Figure 4-2 a schematic drawing of Redfield's folk–urban continuum is presented. This figure helps to summarize the preceding discussion and to make the differences between folk

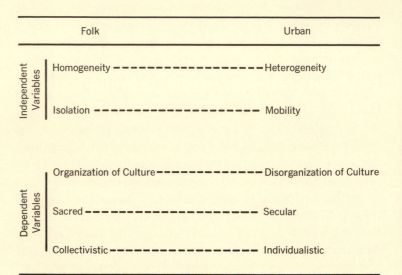

Figure 4-2. The folk–urban continuum.

and urban communities readily apparent. In essence, a folk community in its purest form is characterized by a highly homogeneous population that is both vicinally and socially isolated. As a consequence, its culture displays a considerable amount of organization (all of its parts are woven together in a consistent whole), emphasis is placed upon the sacred nature of things and activities, and members of the community are collectivistic in orientation. On the other hand, the urban community is characterized by cultural disorganization, secularity, and individualism. These three characteristics of course can be attributed to the heterogeneity of urban populations and to the high rates of mobility found within cities and between them and other places.

Redfield convincingly demonstrated that the communities of Tusik, Chan Kom, Dzitas, and Merida represented points along this continuum. This suggests that the typology itself has a measure of validity. To be more specific, the folk–urban continuum proved helpful to Redfield in his efforts to understand religious, familial, economic, and governmental activities in the four communities. Whether this typology also sheds light on community life in more advanced countries will be considered at a later point in this chapter.

Some Recent Innovations

During recent years the use of type construction in the analysis of communities has been overshadowed by the development of newer theoretical approaches. Nonetheless, the typological approach to community analysis is still used with effectiveness by several sociologists, including Gideon Sjoberg, George A. Hillery, Jr., and Roland L. Warren. Hence, we must conclude this chapter by examining recent innovations in constructed-type theories of community.

Before we examine the substantive contributions of Sjoberg, Hillery, and Warren something must be said about their methodological orientations. Among other things, all three theorists, especially Sjoberg and Hillery, link their theoretical schemes closely to empirical data. Indeed, Sjoberg and Hillery use type construction as a tool to derive generalizations from case studies and documents relating to specific communal forms. Because of this both theorists deny that their concepts are ideal types in the usual sense of the term. Rather, Hillery refers to his models of the *vill* and the *total institution* as empirical abstractions for the simple reason that all elements in the models are derived directly from an examination of actual community studies.[45] Presumably, there is nothing hypothetical about his work. Similarly, Sjoberg makes a distinction between ideal types

[45] See George A. Hillery, Jr., "Villages, Cities, and Total Institutions," *American Sociological Review,* **28** (October, 1963), p. 780.

and constructed types and maintains that his work falls into the latter category. According to him, a constructed type conforms much more closely to empirical reality than does an ideal type.[46] Furthermore, Sjoberg, Hillery, and Warren are all dedicated to the clarification of fuzzy concepts. Hillery's foremost goal is to bring some order to the chaos which surrounds the term *community,* whereas Sjoberg forces the reader to recognize that the "preindustrial city" is something quite different than the city as it is found in modern industrialized societies. Similarly, Warren argues that we must focus more clearly on the ties which exist between the local community and the larger society of which it is a part. We can no longer look at communities as though they are "independent islands, cut off from interaction with their geographical regions and with the larger culture." [47]

Gideon Sjoberg

After analyzing a wealth of literature pertaining to cities in various cultural settings, Gideon Sjoberg became disillusioned with urban sociologists who base their generalizations on observations drawn from modern, industrialized cities. In fact, he argues that there is a pressing need for comparative analysis in the study of cities. Furthermore, he advances the thesis that there are two distinctively different types of cities—the industrial and preindustrial—and that the differences between them can best be understood through the use of typological procedures. His main concern is with the latter, but one type of city cannot be understood without reference to the other.[48]

[46] Gideon Sjoberg, *The Preindustrial City: Past and Present* (New York: The Free Press, 1960), p. 21.

[47] Roland L. Warren, "Toward a Typology of Extra-Community Controls Limiting Local Community Autonomy," *Social Forces,* **34** (May, 1956), p. 338.

[48] Needless to say, the preindustrial city is quickly disappearing from the world scene. However, preindustrial cities are still found throughout India and the Middle East, as well as in parts of Latin America, Central Asia, Africa, and even Europe.

Theories of Community

Sjoberg's description of the preindustrial city and of the ways in which it differs from the industrial city is elaborate. Any attempt to offer a short sketch of these two communal types would be the height of folly. However, a few of the more striking features of the preindustrial city can be described under the headings of ecological, economic, and social organization.[49]

In regard to ecological organization, Sjoberg successfully demonstrates that the preindustrial city displays patterns of spatial organization that are considerably different than those found in cities in the industrial world.[50] To be more specific, four basic differences seem to stand out. First, the preindustrial city tends to be centered around edifices devoted to governmental and religious activities rather than around a "commercialized core," as is the case in the industrialized city. This is because commercial activities are not highly developed in preindustrial societies and are considered subordinate to activities of a governmental and religious nature. Secondly, in many preindustrial cities the spatial distribution of social classes is approximately the opposite of that found in the modern American city. The elitist upper-class clusters around the city center whereas the lower classes live on the outskirts of the city. Thirdly, there is usually a rigid segregation of persons in accordance with ethnic, occupational, and other differences. Most preindustrial cities have ethnic and/or religious ghettos and entire streets may be devoted to particular occupations and crafts.[51] Finally, even though spatial segregation is found in the preindustrial city, there is little specialization in terms of land use. The same plot of land is frequently used as one's home, work place, and commercial establishment, and public edifices may be used for worship, education, trade, and recreation.[52]

[49] This is the scheme used by Sjoberg in one of his earlier discussions of the preindustrial city. See Gideon Sjoberg, "The Preindustrial City," *The American Journal of Sociology,* **60** (March, 1955), pp. 438–45.
[50] For a more complete discussion see *The Preindustrial City: Past and Present,* especially pp. 91–103.
[51] Ibid., p. 101.
[52] Ibid., pp. 102–103.

The preindustrial city also differs from the industrial city in its economic organization. Needless to say, the most obvious difference lies in the lack of industrialization in the preindustrial city. This is due to the fact that preindustrial societies lack an advanced technological base which utilizes inanimate sources of energy and power. As a result, the preindustrial city displays a low division of labor in comparison to that found in urban industrial societies and one individual often has complete responsibility for the production and marketing of a particular item. Put differently, assembly-line production is simply nonexistent in the preindustrial city. This does not mean, however, that occupational specialization is absent. The preindustrial city does have its glass makers, goldsmiths, carpenters, merchants, teachers, and so forth. Many of these are organized into guilds which have numerous functions, including the minimization of competition and the recruitment and training of new members of the profession.[53]

Finally, the preindustrial city displays a number of interesting features in terms of its social organization. Two of these features are of particular importance. First, the preindustrial city tends to have a two-class system which consists of a small group of literate, upper-class leaders ("the elite") and a much larger group of lower-class and outcast persons; a middle class of any significant size does not exist. Secondly, kinship bonds are very strong and, contrary to the statements of many urban sociologists, the extended family system is held in much higher esteem than is the small, nuclear family. As Sjoberg puts it,

> The preindustrial urbanite functions within a family system and subordinates himself to it. One consequence is that, typically, marriages are arranged by families, not by individuals. The large extended family, with numerous relatives residing in a single "household"—i.e., one that is a functioning social unit—is the ideal toward which all urbanites strive, though a sizable, closely knit family is generally attainable only by the

[53] For further elaboration see ibid., pp. 190–96.

upper class. Economic circumstances prevent the urban poor and the peasantry alike from maintaining large households; for them the famille souche is more normal.[54]

Findings of this type led Sjoberg to doubt the universality of generalizations concerning city life that are based exclusively on studies conducted in industrialized societies.

It must be stressed that Sjoberg explains these and many other differences between the preindustrial and the industrial city in terms of differences in their technological base. In contrast to the modern city, the preindustrial city is totally dependent upon animate sources of energy, that is, energy supplied by human beings and animals. This explains many of the features of the preindustrial city. For example, the lack of modern transportation and communication facilities means that the outskirts of the city have little appeal to anyone, and especially to the elite. As a result, the upper classes cluster around the center of the city and the lowest classes are forced to inhabit the least accessible section of the city, i.e., that which lies the farthest distance from the center of activities. Similarly, the state of technological development which characterizes the preindustrial city helps to explain the existence of a rigid two-class system of stratification. A preindustrial city is complex enough to require a group of leaders and coordinators but, according to Sjoberg, the system of production still does not yield sufficient surpluses, including food, to support a large group of leisured or semileisured individuals.[55] Other ways in which the relatively simple technological base found in preindustrial cities influences their ecological, economic, and social organization could be cited, but perhaps we have made our point.[56]

[54] Ibid., p. 324.

[55] *The Preindustrial City,* p. 441.

[56] In all fairness it must be pointed out that Sjoberg is not a technological determinist. He recognizes that other factors influence urban development and that technology itself is to some extent a product of urbanization. See *The Preindustrial City: Past and Present,* especially pp. 13–18 and 67–77.

George A. Hillery, Jr.

Like many other conceptual and theoretical schemes, that of George A. Hillery has unfolded over time. Beginning with his attempt to give added meaning and precision to the term *community,* Hillery has since developed his methodological approach into an effective tool for constructing nonmathematical models of various units of social organization, including communities. The key to understanding Hillery's work is to understand his methodology.

Hillery uses case studies as his chief source of data. In reference to these studies Hillery points out that they "are in reality sources of data, sources which have greater value if they are taken in concert than if examined singly." [57] In order to tap these data systematically he "inventories" the various case studies and notes those traits typical of all villages, cities, total institutions, or whatever else he might be studying.[58] These traits are then articulated into a "model" which emphasizes those traits common to every example of the object being studied (i.e., villages, cities, total institutions, and so on). One question is always foremost in Hillery's mind: "What traits do all villages [or other types of organization] have, and which do they lack?" [59]

The Vill. The value of this approach can be conveyed by examining Hillery's concept of the vill. In his *Communal Organizations* [60] Hillery focuses upon villages and cities as organizational types and compares them to prisons and mental institutions. Hillery's source of data for this study are case studies

[57] George A. Hillery, Jr., "The Folk Village: A Comparative Analysis," *Rural Sociology,* **26** (December, 1961), p. 337.

[58] For a more detailed discussion of Hillery's methodology see ibid., pp. 34–42. See also George A. Hillery, Jr., *Communal Organizations: A Study of Local Societies* (Chicago: University of Chicago Press, 1968), pp. 11–25.

[59] "The Folk Village," p. 341.

[60] See footnote 58.

of ten folk villages, five cities, two prisons, and three mental hospitals. The villages, cities, and mental hospitals are located in different parts of the world so that the typology that is developed has cross-cultural applicability. Each case study is systematically compared with all the others in terms of nineteen different traits. We need not list and discuss these traits. It will suffice to say that they are elements that Hillery found, to a greater or lesser degree, to be characteristic of all ten folk villages.[61]

Basically, Hillery reports that the villages and cities are rather similar to one another in regard to the nineteen traits, as are the prisons and mental institutions. At the same time, the two sets of organizations differ rather sharply from each other. The folk villages and cities have much in common with each other but little in common with prisons and mental hospitals. It therefore follows that these two sets of organizations should be referred to by different names. Specifically, Hillery suggests that we use the term *total institution* as originally coined by Erving Goffman to refer to prisons, mental hospitals, and similar organizations. In an earlier article he also proposed that we use the term *vill* to refer to "folk villages and cities and *to nothing else*." [62] The reason for adopting the latter term is to avoid the confusion which currently surrounds the word *community*.

In elaborating further on his model of villages and cities, Hillery maintains that the elements of space, cooperation, and family are of central importance in differentiating vills from other organizational types. He also maintains that these three elements help to integrate and establish order among the remaining components of the model. The way in which this integration and order is achieved can be shown by means of an

[61] For an enumeration and description of these traits see *Communal Organizations,* Table 2.

[62] George A. Hillery, Jr., "Villages, Cities, and Total Institutions," p. 782.

example. Thus, Hillery tells us that in the folk village the family "is the basic economic, stratification, and socialization unit and the basis on which government, religion, and recreation operate." [63] Similar statements apply to space and cooperation and their relationship to other traits of which the model is composed. At the same time, Hillery does not maintain that a small, isolated folk village is, for all practical purposes, identical to a large city. The chief difference between these two types of vill is that the family is the key unifying element in the folk village whereas contractual cooperation is the key unifying force in the city. Nonetheless, villages and cities do array themselves along the same continua. The differences between them are a matter of degree. Hence, the same definition can apply to both folk villages and cities, i.e., "the vill is a localized system integrated by means of families and cooperation." [64] This definition obviously does not fit the total institution. These organizations are, in a sense, localized. However, they are not organized around the family and cooperation among members is not one of their essential properties.

Communal Organizations. Hillery's model of the vill represents an important contribution to the literature on community. In the final analysis, however, the distinction that he makes between communal and formal organizations and his typology of human groups may prove even more useful.[65] The value of this typology lies in the fact that it helps us (1) to explore the relationship between vills and other communitylike organizations, such as families, neighborhoods, and nations, and (2) to distinguish communitylike organizations from formal organizations, such as governmental units, service organizations (e.g., hospitals), and business concerns. The basic difference between formal organizations and communal organizations is, according to Hillery, very simple: the formal organization has one or more

[63] Ibid., p. 781.
[64] *Communal Organizations,* p. 65.
[65] See ibid., pp. 145–52.

specific goals that it seeks to attain.[66] On the other hand, the term *communal organization* "refers to a system of institutions formed by people who live together. The system has no specific goal. The reasons for living together are often no more than that of being born in the locality (for all communal organizations occupy a particular territory)." [67]

The relationship between communal organizations and vills is obvious once the two concepts are understood. The term *vill* is a very specific one which refers only to villages and cities. On the other hand, the concept of *communal organization* is much broader and applies not only to villages and cities, but to families, neighborhoods, nations, and other units of social organization which have no specific goal and which occupy a particular territory. Thus, the correspondence between the concept of communal organization and the concept of community as it is used in the present book is not direct. Rather, there is a perfect correspondence between what Hillery calls a vill and what the present writer calls a community.

Roland L. Warren

One criticism which can be levied at many students of community life is that they largely ignore the fact that most communities are a part of a larger society and culture. All too often sociologists seem to work on the assumption that communities are isolated, self-sufficient units of organization. Needless to say, nothing could be further from the truth. The modern community is profoundly influenced by events which occur and

[66] It should be noted that Hillery uses Talcott Parsons' definition of a "specific goal," i.e., "following Parsons we may describe a specific goal as having at least three characteristics: (1) the product of the goal is identifiable, such as automobiles, academic degrees, etc.; (2) the product can be used by another system—that is, the output of one system is an input for another system; and (3) the output is amenable to a contract, it can be bought and sold." See ibid., p. 147.

[67] Ibid., pp. 185–86.

decisions which are made in other communities and at the extracommunity (or societal) level. In the United States, for example, it sometimes appears that "communities are simply points of geographical contact of criss-crossing networks of different organizations like the Presbyterian Church, the Grange, Rotary International, Standard Oil Company of New Jersey, Atlantic & Pacific, and so forth." [68] This fact forces us to consider whether there is any value in studying the community as a *discrete, distinct* unit of social organization. Should we not simply study the community as a place where extralocal organizations converge because of their dependence on one another and because of their need to be accessible to a population which will "consume" the goods and services they offer?

An answer to this question is implied in the concept of *community autonomy* as it has been developed by Roland L. Warren.[69] Basically, Warren's concept of community autonomy reminds us that communities can be arrayed along a continuum in terms of the degree to which they have control over events and activities which occur within their boundaries. Some communities enjoy a high degree of autonomy; others do not. Likewise, the concept of community autonomy also applies to institutions and organizations that are found within a community. Some community-based institutions and organizations are almost completely autonomous in their operations, others are subject to a great deal of extracommunity control. Thus, the Baptist Church is often cited as an organization whose operations are almost totally controlled by members of the local congregation. On the other hand, the operations of the local branch of Bell Telephone Company may be entirely controlled by decision makers who have never visited the host community. Communities, as well as the institutions and organizations found within them, can presumably be classified in terms of the degree to which they have retained or lost their autonomy. The

[68] Roland L. Warren, "Toward a Typology of Extra-Community Controls Limiting Local Community Autonomy," p. 338.

[69] Ibid., especially p. 339.

student of community life would do well to bear this fact in mind when he studies the community, especially as it exists in the modern urban world.

Warren's discussion of community autonomy is closely related to his discussion of the community's horizontal and vertical axes. Put very simply, the term *horizontal axis* refers to the interrelationships which exist between the various institutions and organizations found within the community. As examples we might cite the relationships between local welfare agencies, between local churches, and so forth. In contrast, the community's vertical axis consists of "the relationship of the individual to a local interest group and of that local interest group to a regional, state, or national organization." [70] Of course it should be obvious that as the vertical axis becomes increasingly strong and well developed, there is a decrease in local autonomy. Warren's concept of "vertical axis" implies that many decisions affecting the local community, its groups, and its institutions are made at the extracommunity level.

Summary

There are several "tests" that can be used to evaluate the merits of a theoretical system. The theories developed by Tonnies, MacIver, Zimmerman, Redfield, Sjoberg, Hillery, and Warren meet some of these tests well. Among other things, each theorist has made his purposes clear, and the degree to which each has built upon the work of his predecessors is impressive. Nevertheless, two questions require further exploration. First, do the theories we have considered in this chapter represent *significant* contributions to the literature on communities? Our answer to this question can only be positive if the theories shed light on community structure and process. Secondly, the question of adequacy must also be raised. Do the theoretical systems con-

---

[70] Roland L. Warren, "Toward a Reformulation of Community Theory," *Human Organization,* **10** (Summer, 1956), p. 8.

sidered in this chapter represent valid analyses of the phenomena under scrutiny?

The first question, that of significance, can be approached from several different directions. Certainly the significance of the constructed type approach itself can hardly be questioned. To the extent that the core properties of different types of communities can be isolated, a step forward has been made. Obviously the theorists considered in this chapter have made progress in this direction, especially in identifying some of the characteristics of rural and urban communities. At the same time, the typologists are still a long way from agreeing upon the specific variables which best differentiate between these two communal types. This can be attributed partly to the fact that no two of them have focused upon communities in the same historical and cultural setting. Tonnies, for example, based his analysis on an intimate knowledge of medieval and nineteenth-century European society, Zimmerman focused on American communities as they were found during the first three decades of the twentieth century, and Redfield examined communities in a relatively underdeveloped region.

Herein lies a major criticism which applies to several of the constructed-type theories of community, and especially those of Redfield and Zimmerman. They fail to shed light on the type of community which predominates throughout the world today, that is, the community as it is found in mass society. With the development of modern means of transportation and communication, communities both large and small have been increasingly drawn into one all-encompassing orbit. The assumption that communities represent "subsocieties" and "little cultures" which was made explicitly by Redfield and Zimmerman and implicitly by some of the other typologists no longer holds. Rather, the differences between rural and urban communities have been reduced to a minimum and may be a matter of population size alone. This is why Warren's work is important. In essence, Warren seems to be telling us that the small American community simply cannot be described as socially and vicinally isolated, nor does it have a culture that is distinct from that of the larger society. The basic features of American society, such as its materialistic orientation and emphasis upon individualism, have penetrated into all communities. Under these conditions any attempt to identify fundamentally different types of communities may be quite misleading.

The question of how adequate the preceding theories are in terms of their explanatory power is something quite different. Certainly our review of constructed-type theories of community indicates a growing tendency to view empirical observation as an integral part of type construction. Thus, Tonnies' scheme is only loosely integrated with empirical data and, as a result, must be thought of as an exercise in the derivation of concepts. With increasing precision, however, Zimmerman, Redfield, Sjoberg, Hillery, and Warren provide concrete evidence which suggest that their typologies are valid. After reading Redfield's work, for example, one can hardly doubt that Yucatan communities do differ systematically from one another in terms of the variables which comprise the folk–urban continuum. That these same variables are probably not descriptive of differences between communities as they are found in mass society is another matter.

Up to this point we have said relatively little about the typologies that have been developed by MacIver, Sjoberg, and Hillery. This is because these theorists have had different purposes than Tonnies, Zimmerman, and Redfield. Specifically, MacIver, Sjoberg, and Hillery have been concerned largely with conceptual clarification and with adding increased precision to our knowledge of communities. With the exception of Hillery they have not attempted to construct polar typologies. MacIver, for example, simply draws a logical distinction between communities and associations, a distinction which seems both valid and significant. Likewise, the significance of Sjoberg's work is clear. The fact that urban sociologists have focused most of their attention on communities as they exist in highly industrialized societies has meant that many of our theories of the city have been limited both in scope and applicability. With the publication of the *Preindustrial City* a new dimension was added to our knowledge of the urban community. Finally, Hillery has made an outstanding contribution to the literature on communities by bringing the term *community* itself under close scrutiny. On the basis of Hillery's work one can only conclude that this word, with its many shades of meaning, is virtually useless for purposes of scientific communication. Even more importantly, however, the methodological innovations which have been made by Hillery must be applauded. It is the present writer's conviction that the most important task which faces sociology today is to pause a moment and take stock of what is *already* known. This is precisely what Hillery does when he uses case studies as sources of data.

Bibliography

Cahnman, Werner J. "Tonnies and Social Change," *Social Forces,* **47** (December, 1968), pp. 136–44.

Heberle, Rudolf. "The Sociology of Ferdinand Tonnies," *American Sociological Review,* **2** (February, 1937), pp. 9–25.

Hillery, George A., Jr. *Communal Organizations: A Study of Local Societies.* Chicago: University of Chicago Press, 1968.

————. "The Folk Village: A Comparative Analysis," *Rural Sociology,* **26** (December, 1961), pp. 337–53.

————. "Villages, Cities, and Total Institutions," *American Sociological Review,* **28** (October, 1963), pp. 779–91.

Jonassen, Cristen T. "Community Typology," in Marvin B. Sussman (ed.), *Community Structure and Analysis.* New York: Thomas Y. Crowell Company, 1959.

MacIver, Robert M. *Community: A Sociological Study.* New York: The Macmillan Company, 1931.

McKinney, John C. "Constructive Typology and Social Research," in John T. Doby et al., *An Introduction to Social Research.* Harrisburg, Pa.: Stackpole Company, 1954.

————. *Constructive Typology and Social Theory.* New York: Appleton-Century-Crofts, 1966.

————, and Charles P. Loomis. "The Typological Tradition," in Joseph S. Roucek (ed.), *Contemporary Sociology*. New York: The Philosophical Library, Inc., 1958.

Redfield, Robert. *The Folk Culture of Yucatan*. Chicago: University of Chicago Press, 1941.

————. "The Folk Society," *American Journal of Sociology*, **52** (January, 1947), pp. 293–308.

Sjoberg, Gideon. "The Preindustrial City," *American Journal of Sociology*, **60** (March, 1955), pp. 438–45.

————. *The Preindustrial City: Past and Present*. New York: The Free Press, 1960.

Tonnies, Ferdinand. *Community and Society*, edited by Charles P. Loomis. New York: Harper & Row, 1963.

Warren, Roland L. "Toward a Typology of Extra-Community Controls Limiting Community Autonomy," *Social Forces*, **34** (May, 1956), pp. 338–41.

Wirth, Louis. "The Sociology of Ferdinand Tonnies," *American Journal of Sociology*, **32** (November, 1926), pp. 412–22.

Zimmerman, Carle C. *The Changing Community*. New York: Harper & Row, 1938.

5

Social System Theory, Functionalism, and Community

Social system theory and structural functionalism have emerged as major types of sociological theory. Interestingly enough, sociologists have been slow in applying these theoretical approaches to the analysis of territorial communities.[1] As a result our understanding of the community has suffered. Thus, rather than focusing upon theories of community per se, in this chapter we examine the community in terms of concepts and theoretical systems borrowed from general sociology. Furthermore, the relationships between social system theory and structural functionalism are explored. Although the social system approach is "neither synonymous nor coextensive with structural-functionalism,"[2] the two theoretical systems are complementary. One's understanding of the community can be enhanced by bringing both approaches to bear upon its analysis.

The Community as a Social System

The term *social system* has been defined in many different

[1] Two notable exceptions are the textbooks by Sanders and Warren. See Irwin T. Sanders, *The Community: An Introduction to a Social System*, 2nd ed. (New York: The Ronald Press, 1966), and Roland L. Warren, *The Community in America* (Chicago: Rand McNally & Company, 1963). See also John E. Bebout and Harry C. Bredmeier, "American Cities as Social Systems," *American Institute of Planners Journal*, 29 (May, 1963), pp. 64–76.

[2] Joseph H. Monane, *A Sociology of Human Systems* (New York: Appleton-Century-Crofts, 1967), p. 11.

ways. For our purposes, however, a social system might be thought of as a *highly organized set of socially significant relationships between two or more persons or groups*. Seemingly, this statement fits every unit of organization which can be analyzed as a social system, including a family, a municipal government, the religious institution, or a community. To the preceding definition we might add the qualification that the relationship must endure through time. This would exclude fleeting, temporary relationships between two or more people from social system analysis. However, the phrase *endure through time* creates problems, and by pointing out that the relationship must be "highly organized" and "socially meaningful" we accomplish the same purpose. Everyone has fleeting relationships with salesmen, casual acquaintances, and so forth, but these relationships lack the highly organized quality which social systems possess. Likewise, they are not socially significant in the sense that they are the "bricks" upon which society is built.

The reader who is well versed in social system theory will immediately object that interaction is not mentioned in our definition. That interaction is of central importance in social system theory is evidenced when Loomis states that "the social system is composed of the patterned interaction of members." [3] This is a difficult idea to grasp, however, and the place of interaction in social system theory must be explored in great detail. It will suffice for now to point out that the terms *social system* and *interaction* are not necessarily synonymous, as Loomis' definition implies. Rather, interaction between its members is one of several properties that social systems possess.

Community Structure

One of the most significant contributions of social system theory is that it sheds light on the ways in which communities

---

[3] Charles P. Loomis, *Social Systems: Essays on Their Persistence and Change* (Princeton, N.J.: D. Van Nostrand Company, Inc., 1960), p. 4.

are structured and organized. In short, the community can be viewed as a system, the component parts of which are statuses and roles, groups and institutions. Furthermore, these components (or subsystems) are closely articulated with one another: roles and statuses are combined with other roles and statuses to form groups, groups are combined with other groups to form institutions, and finally, institutions are combined with other institutions to give rise to communities.

Status and Roles. To be more specific, sociologists often view statuses and roles as the basic building blocks of social organization. Indeed, the term *status* refers to the individual positions of which any social group, regardless of its size, is composed. The typical four-person nuclear family, for example, may be built around the statuses of husband and wife, mother and father, son and daughter, and brother and sister. This means that statuses are the most elementary units of social organization. Similarly, the term *role* refers to the manner in which the individual behaves as he occupies a status that has been assigned to him. Needless to say, the individual is free to decide for himself what patterns of behavior are appropriate to some of the statuses he occupies. At the same time, he may occupy other statuses which do not allow him a great deal of freedom in defining his role. The role behavior appropriate to his status may be rigorously defined for him by the larger group, community, or society.

Groups. It should be apparent that one's statuses and roles cannot exist in isolation. For instance, a man cannot have the status of father unless he has a child (another status), nor can he play the role of husband unless he has a wife. Hence, statuses become combined with other statuses and roles with other roles to give rise to groups. Groups constitute the second layer of organization that is found within a community.

There are several types of groups, not all of which are amenable to social system analysis. In his excellent introductory textbook, for example, Robert Bierstedt classifies groups according to a fourfold scheme which includes the statistical group, the societal group, the social group, and the associational group.[4] The term *statistical group* refers to such aggregates as all persons who voted for a particular political candidate, all persons who watch the same television program, all persons who purchase Brand X, *ad infinitum*. The members of these "groups" do not interact with each other and hence do not form a social system. Much the same thing can be said about societal groups, e.g., all persons of the same sex, race, occupation, and so forth. The members of this type of group may have a "consciousness of kind," but this does not inevitably mean that they interact with each other. On the other hand, it is appropriate to view Bierstedt's social and associational groups as social systems. The social group is characterized by consciousnes of kind and interaction and includes such diverse units of organization as kinship groups, cliques, friendship groups, and children's play groups. The members of an associational group also interact with one another and, in addition, the associational group has a formal structure.[5] By this we mean that the associational group is organized on a hierarchical basis and has leaders and followers, presidents and secretaries, full and associate members. Many groups of this type are found in a modern community. Bierstedt includes within this category such entities as a college or university, the community chest, the United States Steel Corporation, the Missouri Synod of the Lutheran Church, and the United States government, to cite a few of his examples.[6]

Institutions. Just as statuses and roles are the units of which groups are composed, so groups become the basic units out of which social institutions are formed. To be more specific, many of the groups that are found at the community level cannot exist in isolation from other groups which have complementary goals, functions, and purposes. For example, the local police department would be rather ineffective if it failed to

---

[4] Robert Bierstedt, *The Social Order: An Introduction to Sociology,* 2nd ed. (New York: McGraw-Hill Book Company, 1963), pp. 293–300.

[5] Ibid., p. 297.

[6] Ibid., p. 297.

receive the support and cooperation of the mayor's office, the city council, and the fire department. Because of the interrelatedness which exists between these groups, they are often analyzed as component parts of the same social system (i.e., the governmental system). The specific groups that are included in this system (the police department, mayor's office, and so on) are referred to as subsystems.

It is with some hesitancy that the present writer calls this the institutional level of communal organization. The term *institution* is rather ambiguous and has taken on many different shades of meaning. Nonetheless, most sociologists agree that all institutions share at least one essential property: they perform certain crucial functions which must be performed if the community (or society) is to persist through time. In order for an institution to carry out these functions, however, it must have an organizational structure. In the modern American community, for example, the function of governing is carried out by the governmental subsystem and the function of educating is carried out by the school subsystem. This is not to argue that the institutional structure of communities is the same in all societies. More will be said about this point when we consider the concept of *functional alternative*.

The Community. Our final task is to examine the structural features of the community itself. From the preceding discussion the reader can anticipate what we shall say. In short, a community is a system of systems, or more precisely, a system whose component parts are its various social institutions. Although the number of distinct institutional systems found at the community level varies from society to society, the most important ones found within the typical American community are the governmental, economic, educational, religious, and familial subsystems. Each of these can be broken down into a wide variety of social and/or associational groups. These in turn can be analyzed in terms of their component statuses and roles.

Although this approach to the analysis of community structure has obvious merits, it can also lead to serious misconceptions. First, the reader might well conclude that every group is totally integrated into the larger community through the media of institutions. This is not the case. Although most groups are subunits of larger institutions, such entities as play groups, friendship groups, and delinquent gangs are not. This suggests that a distinction must be made between those groups which are and those which are not a part of community structure itself. Secondly, the reader might mistakenly assume that the community possesses an extremely high degree of integration and conclude that all subsystems are closely articulated with all other subsystems. Again this is not always the case. There are groups or institutions within every social system which operate with a high degree of autonomy and independence. Indeed sometimes social system theory does lead one to the conclusion that every social system functions smoothly and as a well-integrated whole. This is one of the pitfalls inherent in this theoretical approach.

Interaction in Social Systems

There is interaction both within and between social systems. In fact, we indicated previously that a social system is essentially a network of interaction, although this point was not elaborated upon in any great detail. Thus, the nature of interaction and its place in social system theory must now be considered.

In relatively simple groups the term *interaction* implies that the actions of one person call for reciprocal action on the part of other persons. In the police department cited previously, for example, the chief may issue an order to one of his officers. This officer obviously will respond to the order, although we cannot always predict the nature of his response. Among other things, he may agree immediately to carry out the order or he may ask for further clarification (e.g., "Where did the accident occur?"). The important thing to note is that the officer's response in turn affects the subsequent responses of the police chief. Hence, interaction is a mutually adjustive, dynamic process in which person A responds to person B and person B responds to person A for as long as the parties are in contact. It is in this sense that a small, uncomplicated social system can be viewed as a network of interaction.

Unfortunately the concept of interaction is more difficult to apply to a complex system such as the community. Obviously the individual who belongs to a social system of this size does not interact with all other members of the system. Rather, face-to-face interaction is manifested *within* the subsystems of which the community is composed. Because of this the social system theorist sometimes analyzes the relationships between social systems in terms of systemic linkage. As defined by Loomis, this term refers to "a process whereby one or more elements of at least two social systems is articulated in such a manner that the two systems in some ways and on some occasions may be viewed as a single unit." [7] In essence, the concept of systemic linkage means that interaction occurs not only between individuals but also between groups and other groups, between groups and institutions, and even between two or more institutions.

That the linkages which develop between the subsystems of which a community is composed have much in common with face-to-face interactive relationships is obvious. For example, one can imagine a community in which an ecumenical council is formed to investigate the treatment of poor people by the local police department. It might well be found that police practices leave much to be desired. When this fact becomes known, members of the police department may react by attacking the ecumenical council, its leaders, and their motives. As a result the basic goal of the ecumenical council may well be diverted from improving the police department to defending its own position. The similarities between this chain of successive responses and the interaction which occurred in the police chief–officer relationship are clear.

[7] Loomis, *Social Systems*, p. 32.

Hence, a considerable amount of interrelatedness and linkage develops between the social systems of which a community is composed. Unfortunately, the specific mechanisms by which systemic linkage is achieved have not been clearly specified by social system theorists. Nonetheless there are several possibilities, including the following:

1. Units from within different systems may merge and in so doing give rise to a new system. It is in this way that the ecumenical council may have been formed: small groups from several different churches could have been drawn together to become the component parts of the council. Once in existence, however, the ecumenical council would represent a new subsystem within the community's religious system. Furthermore, the fact that various churches become linked together by councils of this type may strengthen the linkage between them on other fronts. One could expect an increase in good will between their members and greater cooperation and understanding between their pastors.

2. Leading members of the linked systems may interact on behalf of their respective systems. For example, delegates of the ecumenical council could directly confront the police chief, and vice versa. In confrontations of this type, the "delegates" normally act on behalf of their respective subsystems rather than for their own advantage as individuals.

3. A significant development at the community level during recent years has been the emergence of social systems which have the explicit purpose of coordinating relationships between other systems. Examples are community welfare councils which provide coordinative services for various welfare agencies and the Chamber of Commerce which attempts to link together and coordinate the activities of business establishments. Similarly, our fictitious ecumenical council may have been created as a means of furthering cooperation between local churches, especially in regard to helping the poor.

4. Finally, the interaction which occurs between two or more social systems can transpire in a very indirect manner. Among other things, messages can be carried between the systems by

the press, radio, or television. A short announcement in the local newspaper that the ecumenical council has found police procedures to be unsatisfactory may, for example, set off a whole series of responses and adjustments in the latter system.

Another method of studying interaction at the community level is in terms of the inputs and outputs which flow between its various subsystems.[8] As Roland Warren puts it, every subsystem in the community "will receive inputs of various types from other units in the locality: inputs which are a deliberate part of its operating needs, inadvertent inputs from the adaptive adjustments made by other local units, inputs involving the attitudes and behavior of those it employs or with whom it deals."[9] This classification of types of inputs, in the present writer's thinking, contributes much to our understanding of the relationships which can develop between two or more social systems. A local school system, for example, receives all of these inputs. In order for it to operate it must receive funds from its supporting agency, i.e., local government. The school is also affected by changes and adjustments which occur in other systems, and especially within the governmental subsystem. For instance, the latter system may be forced to reduce its budget greatly, with the inadvertent consequence that school programs must be curtailed. Finally, the school system is profoundly influenced by the attitudes and behavior of the persons with whom it deals. This includes the attitudes and behavior of the teachers it hires, the students it serves, and the public supporting it.

Yet another way of viewing the inputs and outputs which flow between social systems is presented in an article by John E. Bebout and Harry C. Bredmeier.[10] According to Bebout and Bredmeier, there are essentially four ways by which social sys-

[8] For an interesting example of this approach see Talcott Parsons, "General Theory in Sociology," in Robert K. Merton, Leonard Broom, and Leonard S. Cottrell, Jr. (eds.), *Sociology Today: Problems and Prospects* (New York: Basic Books, Inc., 1959), especially pp. 16–29.

[9] Roland L. Warren, *The Community in America,* pp. 294–95.

[10] See John E. Bebout and Harry C. Bredmeier, "American Cities as Social Systems," pp. 64–76.

tem A can get what it needs from other social systems. First, it can sometimes rely on *coercion* as a means of obtaining the input it desires. Coercion implies that system A is so powerful that it can narrow some other system's choices to the point that the latter system must comply with the demands made by system A. Secondly, system A can use *bargaining* as a means of obtaining the desired input. Bebout and Bredmeier use the term *bargaining* in its usual sense and thus we need not elaborate upon what it, as a means of obtaining a desired input, entails. The third way by which social systems obtain needed inputs is through *legal–bureaucratic mechanisms*. If system A receives inputs through legal–bureaucratic mechanisms, this implies that it is a member of a larger system and receives the input because it has a right to receive it and because the larger system "has a duty to hand it over." [11] For example, most governments have a duty to supply individual citizens with certain services (police protection, fire protection, and so on) upon demand. Finally, system A sometimes obtains needed inputs from other social systems through *identification or solidarity mechanisms*. Bebout and Bredmeier tell us that "what we have in mind here is the mechanism which causes you to give your children, parents, wives, husbands, or friends, what they want from you, and causes you to accept their outputs. You do so because you 'identify' with them, in the sense of seeing and feeling them as extensions of yourself; so that to have them indicate their needs to you is tantamount to your desire to satisfy them." [12]

Bebout and Bredmeier use this conceptual scheme to analyze the precarious position in which one type of social system, the central city, finds itself today. Specifically, they tell us that "most central cities must at present bargain with other units in their regions for the residents and industry they need; and their bargaining power is so weak as to threaten their viability unless aid from state and federal governments is supplied." [13]

[11] Ibid., p. 66.
[12] Ibid., p. 66.
[13] Ibid., p. 64.

Bebout and Bredmeier seriously question whether the city's bargaining power vis-à-vis other units (e.g., suburban communities) can ever be improved to the point that they can once more be self-supporting. Assuming that it can, however, a threefold effort will be required—land renewal, transportation renewal, and human development.[14] In the meantime other social systems, such as suburban communities and the state and federal government, must take responsibility for helping the central city to cope with the many crises it faces. It might be noted in passing that the poor bargaining position in which central cities find themselves today illustrates a basic principle of social system theory: *if a social system is to receive the inputs it requires, then it must also contribute to the other systems upon which it is dependent.* Otherwise it is unable to bargain for the input which it needs and must either wither away or rely on other social systems to supply it voluntarily with the required inputs.

Interrelatedness in Social Systems

It should be apparent that there is a high degree of interrelatedness between the various units of which a social system is composed. The nature of the ties which develop between social systems was briefly touched upon in our discussion of systemic linkage. However, we must also look at the external and internal patterns that all social systems possess and examine the concept of equilibrium as it has been developed by social system theorists.

External and Internal Patterns. To George C. Homans must go the credit for developing the concepts of external and internal pattern. Homans explains these concepts by stating that "We shall not go far wrong if, for the moment, we think of the external system [or pattern] as group behavior that enables the group to survive in its environment and think of the internal system [or pattern] as group behavior that is an expression of

[14] Ibid., p. 68.

the sentiments towards one another developed by the members of the group in the course of their life together." [15] To put the case differently, the external pattern consists of all the relationships which develop between one social system and another; the internal pattern consists of the relationships that members of a social system have with each other. It should be pointed out that whether the relationship between two or more systems is "external" or "internal" depends upon the perspective of the observer. For example, the relationships that a local department of public welfare has with the local police department are a part of that welfare department's external pattern. On the other hand, the ties between the welfare department and the police department are part of the same internal pattern when viewed from the perspective of the larger governmental system, of which both units are subsystems.

A closely related distinction is that which social system theorists draw between instrumental and expressive activities. Whereas the concepts of internal and external pattern refer to structural relationships within and between systems, the instrumental–expressive dichotomy focuses upon the activities that are carried on by social systems. Thus, on some occasions the members of a social system must direct their activities toward obtaining those things the system needs in order to persist through time: school officials must appeal to the local government for funds, must enlist the cooperation of parents, and otherwise must engage in "instrumental" activities. At other times the focus must be upon the needs of system members themselves. Among other things, approval and reward must be distributed to system members and potential conflicts between these members must be smoothed over.

Do these dichotomies, especially that relating to external and internal patterns, apply to the community itself? Clearly the answer to this question depends upon one's perspective. For example, local government is present as a social system in most

[15] George C. Homans, *The Human Group* (New York: Harcourt Brace Jovanovich, Inc., 1950), p. 110.

communities. By focusing upon the external and internal patterns of this particular system we can gain insight into the nature of community structure itself. However, the dangers of applying these concepts to the community as a whole are somewhat greater. Certainly we can refer to the ties between subsystems within a community as that community's internal pattern, i.e., a community's internal pattern consists of the numerous relationships which exist between the groups and institutions of which it is composed. Similarly, we might refer to the community's ties with other communities as its external pattern. However, the present writer agrees wholeheartedly with Roland Warren that it is not the community as a whole that is related to other communities. Rather, the relationships which do exist are between subsystems within one community and those in another. As Warren puts it,

> Most models of the community's relation to a larger region consider communities as units, relating them in their entirety to other communities in the region. Whether or not this type of analysis was adequate for preindustrial communities, it offers little help in analyzing contemporary American communities. . . . Putting this another way, the important contemporary link between the community and the outside world is not an undifferentiated link between the community as such and other communities of the surrounding region, but rather it is the link between the highly differentiated parts of the community and their respective extracommunity systems.[16]

In order to give substance to this important but subtle distinction, Warren differentiates between the community's vertical and horizontal patterns. The vertical pattern of a community includes "the structural and functional relations of its various social units and subsystems to extracommunity systems" whereas its horizontal pattern is found in "the structural and functional relations of its various social units and systems to each other." [17]

[16] Warren, *The Community in America,* p. 242.
[17] Ibid., pp. 161–62.

Theories of Community

Equilibrium. Another major concept in social system theory is that of equilibrium. In fact, this concept is of such central importance to social system theory that one of Talcott Parsons' definitions of "social system" is basically a definition of equilibrium. Thus, Parsons tells us that a social system consists of "two or more units, $x_1, x_2, \ldots x_n$, related such that a change in state of any x_1, will be followed by a change in the remaining $x_i \ldots x_n$ which is in turn followed by a change in the state of x_i, etc." [18] This statement is very similar to the definitions of equilibrium offered by other writers, and especially by George C. Homans and Kingsley Davis.[19]

To be more specific, social system theorists maintain that the various components of a social system must be closely integrated with one another. Without this integration the system itself could not meet the needs of its members. This integration is guaranteed by the tendency for subsystems to continually move toward a state of equilibrium. To paraphrase Parsons, the concept of equilibrium implies that when one unit of which a social system is composed undergoes change, then other units in the system also change. As a result, functional relationships between the units are maintained.

The nature of equilibrium as it is manifested at the community level can be illustrated by returning to our example of the interplay between the school system and governmental spending programs. Assuming that the governmental system does reduce the amount of money it allocates to the school subsystem, local school officials may be forced to eliminate supervised recreation programs. If the demand for recreational programs is great enough, however, there may be an increase in the number of recreational programs offered under commercial auspices.

---

[18] Morris Zelditch, "Note on the Analysis of Equilibrium Systems," in Talcott Parsons and Robert F. Bales, *Family, Socialization and Interaction Process* (New York: The Free Press, 1955), p. 402.

[19] See Homans, *The Human Group,* especially pp. 303–304; and Kingsley Davis, *Human Society* (New York: The Macmillan Company, 1948), pp. 633–36.

To state the case differently, the community may absorb changes in one of its subsystems (the school) through the mechanism of change in other subsystems.

The merits and deficiencies of social system theory will be considered at a later point in this chapter. However, there is no better time than the present to note that the concept of equilibrium has been vigorously criticized.[20] The gist of these criticisms is that the concept of equilibrium implies an over-mechanized view of social organization. Can it be assumed that the components of a social system are so closely interrelated that a change in one component dictates a change in some of the others? We could cite several examples which suggest that this question cannot always be answered in the affirmative. Unfortunately, the reciprocal relationships between social systems and the units of which they are composed are much more complex than is implied by the concept of equilibrium.

Boundary Maintenance

We have purposely emphasized the interrelatedness which develops within and between social systems. However, every social system must also encourage a sense of cohesiveness and loyalty among its members. Because of this, social systems develop boundaries and their members engage in various boundary-maintaining activities. We are given a clue to the nature of boundary maintenance when Loomis states that "this is the process whereby the identity of the social system is preserved and the characteristic interaction pattern maintained." [21] Furthermore, he suggests that both boundary maintenance and systemic linkage are essential properties of a social system, i.e., "without boundary maintenance, social groups would be indistinguishable among a mass of individuals and interaction would

[20] For example, see Walter Buckley, *Sociology and Modern Systems Theory* (Englewood Cliffs, N.J.: Prentice-Hall, Inc., 1967), especially pp. 23–31.

[21] Loomis, *Social Systems,* p. 31.

be haphazard; without systemic linkage an unthinkable parochialism would deny to groups any form of contact outside their own boundaries." [22]

A social system may possess three different types of boundaries. First, most social systems have *psychological boundaries*. By this we mean that some individuals are accepted as members of the system and enjoy the psychological rewards which accompany this acceptance, whereas others do not. An example of this is often seen in oldtimer–newcomer relationships, especially in a small community. On occasions the oldtimer may appear to be suspicious of new persons who migrate into *his* community and reluctant to accept these new persons as fellow community members. When this occurs the newcomer may complain that the "natives" are unfriendly, uppity, or whatever. It might be hypothesized that under these conditions, the newcomer will not identify with the community until he senses that the oldtimers accept him. Secondly, most social systems are characterized by a variety of *social boundaries*. Most communities, for example, are crisscrossed with a host of boundaries between various socioeconomic, racial, and ethnic groups. Finally, a few social systems have *physical or geographical boundaries*. Most communities, for instance, have legal boundaries beyond which their influence does not extend. Quite often these boundaries are of limited significance. They exist only on maps or in the minds of a few interested persons and have little meaning for the average citizen.

Functionalism and Community Analysis

Throughout our discussion of social system theory, we have emphasized the organizational and structural features of the community. Among other things, it was suggested that the community is a constellation of interrelated groups and institutions and that this interrelatedness is due to the fact that all social

[22] Ibid., p. 33.

systems have both internal and external patterns. It is only because of this interrelatedness that the community can be subjected to social system analysis.

Social system theory is often supplemented by functionalism, another basic type of modern sociological theory. Although social system theory and functionalism are closely related, there are differences between the two approaches. To be more specific, the social system theorist focuses upon units of social organization and upon the structural relationships which develop between them. Thus, the concept of external pattern tells us only that social systems are interrelated. It does not tell us why these relationships exist or what they entail. Functionalism, on the other hand, examines these relationships in terms of their content and consequences. In examining religion, for example, the functionalist is interested in why religious organizations are found in virtually all communities, what contributions the religious system makes to the total community system, and what the consequences for the community would be if the religious system disintegrated.

The Functional Approach

The term *function* is a central one in the theoretical system under consideration. Unless its meaning is understood, functional theory itself cannot be grasped. However, this term has numerous connotations and therefore gives rise to confusion.[23] Yet there have been clear statements of its meaning. One such statement is that offered by A. R. Radcliffe-Brown in the form of a biological analogy. As this pioneer in the functional analysis of primitive societies puts it,

> If we consider any recurrent part of the life process, such as respiration, digestion, etc., its *function is the part it plays in, the contribution it makes to, the life of the organism as a*

[23] For a discussion of some of the uses to which the word *function* has been put see Robert K. Merton, *Social Theory and Social Structure,* rev. ed. (New York: The Free Press, 1957), pp. 20–23.

         Theories of Community

whole. As the terms are here being used a cell or an organ has an activity and that activity has a *function*. It is true that we commonly speak of the secretion of gastric fluid as a "function" of the stomach. As the words are used here we should say that this is an "activity" of the stomach, *the function of which* is to change proteins of food into a form in which these are absorbed and distributed by the blood to the tissues.[24]

Hence, when we use the term *function* in sociology we mean the contribution that a unit of social organization makes to the larger system of which it is a part. For example, one of the functions of the family is to socialize the young so that they can take their place in society. Similarly, one of the functions of government is to restrain persons who by their actions threaten social order.

In addition to using the word *function* in several different ways, sociologists have at times failed to specify clearly the purposes of functional theory. However, functional theory seems to serve two basic purposes. First, functionalism gives the sociologist some insight into the "functional requisites" of social life, i.e., the functions which must be performed if a social system is to persist through time. To cite an example, the members of a society absolutely must reproduce if that society is to exist for any length of time. Secondly, the functionalist also determines what consequences, if any, a unit of social organization has for other units and for the total system of which it is a part. Thus one of the consequences of marriage and the family is that the population is reproduced, and one of the consequences of government is that a modicum of social control is assured.

It is apparent that these two purposes of functional theory are, in the final analysis, almost identical. Specifically, the functionalist assumes that *most* of the components of a social system engage in certain activities which must be performed if the

[24] A. R. Radcliffe-Brown, "On the Concept of Function in Social Science," *American Anthropologist*, **37** (July–September, 1935), p. 395. Italics added.

system is to persist through time. His task is to determine what these activities are and which subsystems are responsible for them.

Before we examine some of the basic concepts that are used in functional analysis, two cautions are in order. First, we must avoid falling prey to what Robert Merton calls the *postulate of universal functionalism*. As Merton explains it, "this postulate holds that all standardized social or cultural forms have positive functions." [25] He further quotes Bronislaw Malinowski, a leading anthropologist of the functionalist school, as saying that "the functional view of culture *insists* therefore upon the principle that in *every type of civilization, every custom, material object, idea and belief fulfills some vital function*. . . ." [26] Today most sociologists and anthropologists recognize that this is simply not the case. There can be components of a social system which perform no major functions for the system as a whole, and it is even possible that some of these components hinder other subsystems in the performance of their functions. Secondly, Malinowski's statement makes it clear that functionalism is not limited to the analysis of social systems. One can also study values and beliefs, ideals and material objects in terms of their functions. When pursued to its limits, the functional analysis of a system as complex as the community can become extremely detailed and elaborate.

Basic Concepts

A few of the basic concepts that are used in functional analysis have been alluded to in the preceding discussion. In order to round out our understanding of functionalism as a theoretical system, there are several other terms which must be considered.

The first of these is the concept of functional requisite. This concept dovetails with one of the major purposes of function-

[25] Merton, *Social Theory and Social Structure*, p. 30.

[26] Ibid., p. 30. Merton's reference is to B. Malinowski, "Anthropology," *Encyclopaedia Britannica,* First Supplementary Volume (London and New York, 1926), p. 132. Italics in original.

alism, to determine what functions must be performed if a social system is to persist through time. As has already been suggested, one of the major assumptions made by functionalists is that all social systems have certain "needs" which must be met if the system is to persist through time. These needs are referred to as functional requisites of the system.[27]

Although the concept of functional requisite is a useful one, it can also be misleading. This is partly because social systems do not literally have "needs" in the sense that individuals do. Although it is acceptable, for purposes of communication, to say that a system has needs, it should be realized that all we are really saying is that there are certain conditions which must be met if a social system is to maintain its viability. Furthermore, the concept of functional requisite increases the likelihood that the functionalist will offer explanations of a teleological nature, i.e., explanations which account for the existence of a unit of social organization in terms of its purpose. For instance, the statement that "religion is found in a particular society because it contributes to the survival of that society" is scientifically unacceptable. It may be true that religion is one of the functional requisites of society. Yet the question of why and how religion becomes a part of a particular society can only be answered through historical research.

A more serious difficulty inherent in the concept of functional requisite is that it suggests the *postulate of indispensability*. By this we mean that functionalists sometimes tend to regard all components of a social system as absolutely essential to its survival and persistence.[28] In the study of communities the greatest danger posed by this postulate is that it can lead to the conclusion that all communities *must* have discrete governmental, economic, educational, and religious subsystems. Although it is safe to assume that the functions performed by

[27] One of the most thorough discussions of functional requisites is contained in Marion J. Levy, Jr., *The Structure of Society* (Princeton, N.J.: Princeton University Press, 1952), especially pp. 71–76 and 149–97.

[28] For further discussion see Merton, *Social Theory and Social Structure*, pp. 32–36.

these systems must, in one way or another, be performed in all communities, this does not necessarily mean that every community has discrete systems which correspond to these functions.

This brings us to another major concept used by functionalists, that is, the concept of *functional alternative*. This concept simply draws our attention to the fact that the same functional requisite may be met in a variety of ways. We have, for example, pointed out that one of the major functions of government in modern society is to punish those individuals who persistently violate the norms. In many primitive societies, this same function is carried out by the family. A governmental system as Americans know it may be nonexistent.[29]

The final set of concepts that are central to functional theory are those of *manifest* and *latent* function. The first of these terms refers to the obvious, visible consequences and contributions of a social unit (group, institution, and so on), whereas the term *latent function* refers to the "unintended and unrecognized consequences" of the unit.[30] Thus, the manifest function of a religious organization is to bring the individual into unity with the supernatural and to provide means by which proper respect may be paid to higher beings. These functions of religion are recognized by everyone and are used as glib explanations for the existence of religious systems. On the other hand, it may be only the functionalist who recognizes that the religious system serves to reinforce communal and societal norms and to give persons a sense of security and well-being. The latter are latent functions of religion. More will be said about them later.

Functionalism and the Modern Community

Functionalism has not been tailormade for the student of community life. As a matter of fact, functionalists have had

[29] A description of one such society is contained in Kingsley Davis, *Human Society*, pp. 481–85.

[30] Merton, *Social Theory and Social Structure*, p. 62.

little to say about modern communities. Nonetheless, there is every reason to think that functional analysis will help us in the study of such entities. It is true that the institutions found in mass society are organized on a national basis. However, the behavior which leads to the performance of functions occurs at the local level: a mass society exists in and through the communities of which it is composed. Furthermore, there are certain conditions which must be met if a community is to survive as a viable, ongoing social system. Communities, like societies, have their functional requisites.

Needless to say, a full-fledged functional analysis of any community would be tedious indeed. Because of this the following analysis has been simplified and abbreviated. In the first place, our analysis is limited to the modern community. No attempt is made to analyze the primitive community nor to shed light on the suburb, rural neighborhood, or whatever. Secondly, because the central theme of this chapter has been that the community is a network of interrelated social systems, our analysis has been further limited by examining only the functional consequences of these systems. Although students of the community disagree upon many things, they do agree that the most important subsystems found at the community level are those that are concerned with governmental, economic, educational, religious, and familial activities.

Government. Local government is one of the most complex subsystems found in the American community.[31] Not only does the web of local government encompass a host of special districts (e.g., school districts, sewerage districts, port authorities, and so on), but municipal government itself may have dozens of branches and subunits. Included among these are such entities as the police department, the welfare department, the fire department, the parks and recreation department, and so

[31] For a brief discussion of some of the complexities of American local government see Committee for Economic Development, *Modernizing Local Government to Secure a Balanced Federalism* (New York: Committee for Economic Development, 1966), pp. 20–33.

on. One of the virtues of social system theory is that it provides a framework for analyzing the ways in which these many units are interrelated.

We can classify the functions of local government in a variety of ways. For example, a list of every unit of local government could be compiled and its functions identified. Thus, the function of the welfare department is to provide welfare services, that of the fire department is to fight fires, and so forth. However, this classificatory scheme would be needlessly long and detailed and of little relevance to the sociologist.

We need, then, to find a simplified, relevant classification of the functions of local government. Even if we confine our attention to the national level, there seems to be only two functions of government upon which sociologists agree. First, there is widespread agreement that government has the ultimate responsibility for social control.[32] This responsibility belongs to local government as well as to state and national government. Thus, local government can, through its police department, courts, and other regulatory agencies, forcefully restrain people who do not abide voluntarily by the norms. The high rates of crime and delinquency that are typical of many communities suggest that this function must be carried out if the community is to persist through time: it is a functional requisite of community life.

The other major function that most sociologists attribute to government is to oversee a society's relationships with other societies. However, to argue that local government has this function would be absurd. The governments of modern communities do not wage war, nor do they enter into treaties with other communities or societies. About the best that can be said is that local government represents one of the vertical links between the local community and government at the state and national level. The importance of this linkage cannot be ignored.

[32] See Davis, *Human Society*, pp. 486–88, and Bierstedt, *The Social Order*, pp. 505–506.

Whether or not a community receives its share of assistance from state and federal agencies depends partly upon local political officials.

This gives us some clues as to the functions of local government. There are, however, two other functions of local government that most sociologists seem to overlook. One of these is the provision of public facilities and services. During recent years all governments, especially those at the local level, have been forced to assume increased responsibility for furnishing roads, parks, sewage treatment plants, garbage collection services, and a variety of other facilities and services. Likewise, one of the most important developments during recent years has been the proliferation of social services provided by local government. The term *social services* should be construed broadly enough to include not only welfare services but also health services, recreational programs, and programs for the educationally disadvantaged. Whether the provision of these services should be viewed as an essential function of local government depends upon a variety of things. Certainly most of the facilities and services mentioned previously are essential if the city or metropolitan area is to survive in the twentieth century.

Economics. In modern societies the economic system is organized on a national rather than a communal basis. Indeed, no modern community produces every good and service that its members use. Nonetheless, it is legitimate to talk about economic systems at the community level. These systems encompass many and diverse units of social organization, including wholesale and retail outlets, banks and loan companies, factories, and labor unions.

Although production is organized on a national basis, there is one major function that local economic systems must perform. They must provide the mechanisms and means by which goods and services can be procured by the individual. It is in local communities that people find jobs, earn money, and make the majority of their purchases. This is one reason why human beings live together in communities and why they will always do so. Hence, the provision of jobs, goods, and services by local businesses and industries must be thought of as one of the functional requisites of community life. If business and industry become unable to do this, out-migration and consequent depopulation occur.

Education. Some readers of this book will object because we consider education to be a distinct communal subsystem. It is true of course that most schools are supported by local government, or if not, by a religious body or private foundation. Nonetheless, it is more accurate to consider local schools as a distinct subsystem at the community level, partly because they enjoy a great deal of autonomy from their sponsoring agencies. Furthermore, there has been a tremendous increase in the number of functions that schools are expected to perform. Today the school system is an active, functionally important part of virtually all modern communities.

Although the educational subsystem has many functions, one stands out above all others in importance: the school, along with the family, has a key role to play in socializing the young. If a community is to persist through time, it must develop human potentials, transmit cultural norms and values, and impart formal knowledge and skills. In a relatively simple society, the family can accomplish these tasks on its own. In a modern society, however, parents simply do not have the knowledge and skill, insight and experience required to teach the child everything that he must know in order to become a self-sufficient adult. As a result, a wide variety of educational systems has been created to assist in the complex and absolutely essential task of socializing the young. It is entirely possible that the extensive process of socialization through which the American child goes, involving as it does both family and school, is one of the most thorough ever devised by man.

In addition to its responsibilities as an agency of socialization, the school system performs many other functions. For example, some school systems play a part in the creation of new knowledge and values, are active participants in community recreation programs, and keep young persons out of the labor force. The latter is an excellent example of what the functionalist means by a latent function. It is an unanticipated consequence of the emphasis that we place upon school attendance.

Religion. There is no area in which functionalism has been more influential than in the study of religion.[33] Basically, functionalists see religion as a "societal necessity" and attribute two essential functions to it. First, they maintain that religion contributes to the system of which it is a part by encouraging people to adhere to norms and values that are "functional" for that system. Specifically, the injunctions against stealing, murder, adultery, and other transgressions that are advocated by most religious bodies are not only important as religious precepts but must be obeyed by the majority of community members if the community is to persist through time. Second, most functionalists also argue that religion helps the individual to develop and maintain a healthy, stable personality. This it purportedly does by providing persons with an "explanation" of the inexplicable (e.g., the premature death of a beloved spouse) and by promising the individual a more exalted status at some future time. It is true of course that man's world is one in which sorrow, failure, and gross inequalities are a reality. To the extent that religion can explain these uncomfortable realities, it contributes directly to personality integration and indirectly to the stability of the community itself.

Although this theory may fit the facts in simple, homogeneous societies, its applicability to the modern community is more problematical. Among other things, there have been several instances in which religion has not been an integrative force in community life. Rather, it has led to conflict among com-

[33] For a brief account of the influence of functionalism on sociological and anthropological theories of religion see J. Milton Yinger, *Sociology Looks at Religion* (New York: The Macmillan Company, 1963), pp. 121–28. One of the best explanations of the functional theory of religion is contained in Davis, *Human Society,* pp. 518–35.

munity members.[34] This conflict often arises when religious organizations champion norms and values that are at odds with those championed by other groups. One needs only to consider the controversies which often center around birth control programs and liquor-by-the-drink legislation. Similarly, some of the functional theories of religion do not allow for the fact that not all members of a modern community participate in the religious subsystem. Yet there is no solid evidence to suggest that these persons spurn basic norms and values or suffer from personality disintegration more frequently than persons who participate in formalized religious activities.

Because of these facts the value of functional theory as an explanation of religious phenomena within the modern community is questionable. About the most that can be said is that religion *may help some people* develop and maintain healthy personalities and *may encourage some people* to observe basic social norms and values. Obviously this statement cannot be extended to everyone for the simple reason that religion is not an integral part of everyone's life.

Family. It is extremely difficult to analyze the family as a structural component of the modern community. To be more specific, in communities in which the nuclear family predominates there is no such thing as *the* family subsystem in the sense that there is a governmental subsystem, a religious subsystem, or an educational subsystem. Rather, families have their structural embodiment in a multitude of small groups. Each of these can be analyzed as subsystems of the larger community but they do not become interrelated with each other in such a way as to form a discrete system.

Nonetheless, the family is a social institution. Those small groups that we refer to as families perform functions which

---

[34] For a description of two such cases see Gus Turbeville, "Religious Schism in the Methodist Church: A Sociological Analysis of the Pine Grove Case," *Rural Sociology,* **14** (March, 1949), pp. 29–39; and Kenneth W. Underwood, *Protestant and Catholic: Religious and Social Interaction in an Industrial Community* (Boston: The Beacon Press, 1957).

must be performed if the community is to maintain itself. In the first place, the family retains its age-old responsibility for reproduction. Although human beings can be reproduced outside of the framework of marriage, there are no societies which sanction this practice. Why this should be the case is not entirely clear, but it is probably because the presence of an adult male helps to assure that the child's needs will be fully met. Secondly, the family obviously has an important role to play in socialization. Among other things, the family has almost total responsibility for the child when he is young, when the vast bulk of socialization occurs.[35] Finally, the fact that the family is a primary group seems to dictate that it will retain its functional importance. Modern man does live in a world in which secondary groups predominate and in which the individual is subjected to a considerable amount of insecurity, instability, and frustration. The family, however, is one of the few remaining groups within which the individual potentially can meet his needs for affection, security, and emotional support. Because these needs must be met in one way or another, the family may become increasingly important as human societies become increasingly urbanized.

Summary

Social system theory and functionalism have often been criticized on the grounds that they are unduly complicated and difficult to grasp. This is neither a fair nor a valid criticism. Some of the theorists we have considered in this chapter, especially Kingsley Davis and Robert K. Merton, are elegant and articulate spokesmen for their theoretical systems. Furthermore, even though some writers do succeed in making social system theory and functionalism appear hopelessly complex, it is the present writer's contention that in reality both theoretical systems are relatively simple. This simplicity can be best conveyed

[35] For further discussion of the family's strategic importance in socialization see Davis, *Human Society*, pp. 405–407.

by briefly summarizing the basic principles of social system theory and functionalism as they apply to modern communities.

1. The community is a social system, the major subsystems of which are the institutions of government, economy, education, religion, and family. Each of these subsystems in turn is composed of a variety of social and/or associational groups. Finally, statuses are the basic building blocks out of which these groups are structured. The individual becomes a part of these groups, and hence a member of larger social systems, by playing the roles that are attached to these statuses.

2. There is a high degree of interrelatedness between the members of a given system and between one system and another. The concept of internal pattern refers to the relationships which develop within a system, whereas the concept of external pattern refers to the relationships which develop between one system and another. In studying the community it is helpful to supplement these concepts with Warren's concepts of horizontal and vertical pattern. A community's horizontal pattern includes the ties which develop between its various subsystems, whereas the vertical pattern encompasses the ties which exist between these subsystems and extracommunity systems.

3. There is a tendency for all social systems, including the community, to move toward a state of equilibrium. This means that a change in one component of the system stimulates changes in other units of which the system is composed. The result is adjustment, coordination, and integration among the various parts of a social system.

4. Even though there is much interrelatedness between the units of which a social system is composed, each subsystem still must establish itself as a discrete entity and command the loyalty of its members. Thus, the members of every social system consciously or unconsciously engage in various boundary-maintaining activities. As a result, social systems may have psychological, social, and/or geographic boundaries.

5. Some of the basic concepts that have been developed by the functionalists serve to enrich and give substance to social

system theory. The functional approach is based on the dual assumption that (a) certain activities must be carried out if a social system is to persist through time and (b) *most* units of social organization "contribute" to the system of which they are a part. These contributions make it possible for the larger system to persist through time.

The fact that social system theory and functionalism are relatively simple does not mean that they are above criticism. In reality, both theoretical systems have been the target of abundant criticism, and any attempt to summarize all the objections that have been raised against them would require that we add another chapter to this book.[36] However, many of these objections center around the contention that social system theory and functionalism represent overly mechanistic views of social organization. It is a fact that social system theorists and functionalists do tend to view a social system as a series of neatly articulated, well-coordinated parts which satisfy the "needs" (i.e., functional requisites) of the system and its members. Clearly this is not always the case. There can be a considerable amount of conflict between the units of which a system is composed. Furthermore, there is no guarantee that the members of any given subsystem will act in such a way as to assure that the subsystem does make positive contributions to the larger social system of which it is part.

The criticisms that have been levied at social system theory and functionalism should not blind us to the merits of these approaches. Thus, social system theory has given us many helpful clues as to how communities and other social systems are structured and organized. (See the preceding items 1 and 2.) Likewise, social system theory provides the sociologist with

[36] For a sampling of some of this criticism see Dorothy Gregg and Elgin Williams, "The Dismal Science of Functionalism," *American Anthropologist,* **50** (October–December, 1948), pp. 594–611; Wayne Hield, "The Study of Change in Social Science," *British Journal of Sociology,* **5** (March, 1954), pp. 1–10; and David Lockwood, "Some Remarks on the 'Social System,'" *British Journal of Sociology,* **7** (June, 1956), pp. 234–46.

concepts, tools, and propositions that he can use in the analysis of diverse units of social organization. Social system theory has been found helpful in the study of small groups, industrial and political bureaucracies, and entire societies, as well as in the study of territorial communities. Finally, both social system theory and functionalism force the sociologist to raise questions which, in the final analysis, are the substance of his discipline. Kingsley Davis, for example, argues that functional theory leads us to ask such questions as,

> What features of social organization or behavior appear in all or nearly all societies? Why are these features so nearly universal while others are more variable? What particular features characterize each type of society, and how do they mesh together in the operation of that type? [37]

Questions of this type must also be asked by the student of community life. Until they are answered our understanding of villages, cities, and metropolitan areas will be limited.

Bibliography

Adams, Bert N. *Kinship in an Urban Setting.* Chicago: Markham Publishing Company, 1968.

Bebout, John E., and Harry C. Bredmeier. "American Cities as Social Systems," *Journal of the American Institute of Planners,* **29** (May, 1963), pp. 64–76.

Committee for Economic Development. *Modernizing Local Government to Secure a Balanced Federalism.* New York: Committee on Economic Development, 1966.

Crain, Robert L., and Donald B. Rosenthal. "Community Status as a Dimension of Local Decision-Making," *American Sociological Review,* **32** (December, 1967), pp. 970–84.

Herriott, Robert E., and Nancy Hoyt St. John. *Social Class and the Urban School: The Impact of Pupil Background on Teachers and Principals.* New York: John Wiley & Sons, Inc., 1966.

[37] Kingsley Davis, "The Myth of Functional Analysis as a Special Method in Sociology and Anthropology," *American Sociological Review,* **24** (December, 1959), p. 762.

Loomis, Charles P. *Social Systems: Essays on Their Persistence and Change.* Princeton, N.J.: D. Van Nostrand Company, Inc., 1960.

Monane, Joseph H. *A Sociology of Human Systems.* New York: Appleton-Century-Crofts, 1967.

Turbeville, Gus. "Religious Schism in the Methodist Church: A Sociological Analysis of the Pine Grove Case," *Rural Sociology,* **14** (March, 1949), pp. 29–39.

Underwood, Kenneth W. *Protestant and Catholic: Religious and Social Interaction in an Industrial Community.* Boston: The Beacon Press, 1957.

Warren, Roland L. *The Community in America.* Chicago: Rand McNally & Company, 1963. See especially Chapter V.

————. "Toward a Reformulation of Community Theory," *Human Organization,* **15** (Summer, 1956), pp. 8–11.

6

Community Action and Community Leadership

Social system theory and functionalism provide the basic tools for a rather comprehensive analysis of community structure. These theoretical systems force us to focus our attention upon the units of which the community is composed and upon the relationships which develop between these units. However, during recent years there has been a growing interest in viewing the community from a more dynamic, "on-the-scene" perspective. Could we not gain much by using human action itself as a unit of analysis? Would not our understanding of community life be greatly enhanced by focusing upon local residents as they attempt to solve the problems which inevitably arise when man lives in proximity to his fellow man? Should we not examine patterns of leadership and decision making at the local level? Several students of the community have offered affirmative answers to these questions. Hence, it is to theories of community action and community leadership that we now turn.

Community Action Theory

One of the central problems in community action theory is to delineate the universe of community actions. Human beings are constantly acting: they work and play, get married and rear children, wage war and make peace, write books and burn them, seek solitude and fervently enter into group activities.

Obviously, not all of these activities are related to community living, nor are they of interest to the student of community life. Because of this the first task the community action theorist must face is that of determining what activities should be classified as communal in nature and how communal activities can be distinguished from noncommunal ones.

Communal Phenomena

At the heart of community action theory is a rather narrow and circumscribed, but nonetheless useful, concept of communal phenomena. The mere fact that an event or activity occurs in a specific locality does not mean that it is an integral part of community life. Rather, some events and activities which occur in a given locality do have a direct bearing on community life; other events and activities do not. Harold F. Kaufman makes this point clear when he states that "in the search for a more precise definition of community there is not only the question of differentiating localities as to their size and complexity, but within any given locality there is the problem of *distinguishing community phenomena* from those which might be considered noncommunity." [1]

To be more specific, Kaufman and other community action theorists view the community as but one of several interactional fields which exist in circumscribed, inhabited territories. Again, as Kaufman explains it, "the community field is not a Mother Hubbard which contains a number of other fields, but rather is to be seen as only one of the several interactional units in a local society." [2] From this it follows that the average citizen participates in the community field during only some of his waking hours. Sometimes he acts as a community member and participates in community relevant activities, but on other oc-

[1] Harold F. Kaufman, "Toward an Interactional Conception of Community," *Social Forces,* **38** (October, 1959), p. 9. Italics added.
[2] Ibid., p. 10.

casions he acts as a family member and engages in activities of family relevance, as an employee and engages in activities of an economic nature, and so forth.

From this it follows that the key to a successful theory of community action is to find criteria by which events and activities of communal relevance can be distinguished from those that are not relevant. How does one decide which actions are properly included within the community field? What does the sociologist focus upon when he studies community action? Indeed, what is the so-called universe of community actions?

There have been several attempts to answer questions of this type and to make the concept of community action operational. Among the most successful of these attempts is that made by Willis A. Sutton, Jr., and Jiri Kolaja.[3] According to Sutton and Kolaja, a sharp distinction cannot be drawn between events and activities that are properly included in the universe of community actions and those that are not. Rather, they maintain that locality-centered events and activities should be studied in terms of the degree of "communityness" they possess. Needless to say, "communityness" is a rather complex variable and has several components. These include (1) the degree to which the event or activity is locality related, (2) the degree to which the persons who are involved in or influenced by the event or activity are identified with the locality, and (3) the extent to which local people participate in the activity.[4]

Sutton and Kolaja discuss these components at length and offer several suggestions as to how they might be made opera-

[3] See Willis A. Sutton, Jr., and Jiri Kolaja, "Elements of Community Action," *Social Forces,* **38** (May, 1960), pp. 325–31; and Willis A. Sutton, Jr., and Jiri Kolaja, "The Concept of Community," *Rural Sociology,* **25** (June, 1960), pp. 197–203.

[4] Willis A. Sutton, Jr., and Jiri Kolaja, "Elements of Community Action," pp. 325–31. This is one of two approaches which Sutton and Kolaja have developed for measuring degrees of "communityness." Their other approach is discussed in Willis A. Sutton, Jr., and Jiri Kolaja, "The Concept of Community," especially p. 200.

tional.[5] They make one thing totally clear: the task of distinguishing between activities and events that are a part of the universe of community actions and those that are not is a difficult one. Nonetheless, because this chapter is built around a discussion of community action, perhaps the following guidelines for identifying events and activities that are of interest to the student of community life should be offered. (In developing these guidelines the present writer has leaned heavily on the work of Sutton and Kolaja.)

1. An activity or event is a part of the universe of community actions to the extent that the participants intend to solve some problem related to the locality in which they live. There are of course a number of problems with which local citizens may concern themselves. Examples would be raising money to repair city streets, setting the school budget for the year, coordinating the services offered by health and welfare agencies, and bringing racial tensions under control.

2. An activity or event is a part of the universe of community actions when most of the persons who are involved in or influenced by the action are members of the local community. If the persons who are involved in or influenced by the event or activity are outsiders, then the event or activity in most cases would not be a part of the universe of community actions. Furthermore, an event or activity is most likely to belong within the universe of community actions when the participants in the action episode enact roles that are of high communal relevance. Presumably, an event or activity which involves the mayor, school superintendent, or representatives of broad-based community associations (Chamber of Commerce, The Ecumenical Council, the PTA, and so on) would be more a part of the universe of community actions than would an event or activity which involves the leaders of a *particular* religious denomination, labor union, school, or whatever.

3. An activity or event is most likely to be a part of the uni-

[5] Willis A. Sutton, Jr., and Jiri Kolaja, "Elements of Community Action," pp. 325–29.

verse of community actions when a *large* number of community members participate in it. On the other hand, the number of participants in the event or activity does not matter if these participants come from elsewhere and exert no influence upon local affairs.

Types of Community Action

We have suggested that a great deal of effort has been spent in developing criteria by which the universe of community actions can be delineated. Unfortunately, much less time and effort has been devoted to a systematic analysis of the *specific types of activities and events* which fall within this universe. What kind of activities and events are properly included within the universe of community actions? How might these activities and events be classified? Some light can be shed on these questions by analyzing locality-related activities and events in terms of whether they are spontaneous, routinized, or planned.

Spontaneous Community Action. During recent years a number of American cities have been rocked by events and activities that were apparently spontaneous, unanticipated, and unorganized. Among the examples which might be cited are the race riots which have occurred with disturbing frequency, some of the student demonstrations which have disrupted not only college campuses but the surrounding community, and mob reactions to unpopular governmental policies. Subject to more positive evaluation on the part of most citizens are the spontaneous efforts of individuals and groups to render assistance when disaster strikes a community.[6]

Events and activities of this type are of interest to the student of community action, although the degree to which they are a part of the universe of community actions varies from case to

[6] A growing body of literature has emerged which relates to the influence of disaster on the community and upon human behavior. See William H. Form and Sigmund Nosow, *Community in Disaster* (New York: Harper & Row, 1958); and George W. Baker and Dwight W. Chapman, *Man and Society in Disaster* (New York: Basic Books, Inc., 1962).

case. Thus, riots and similar breakdowns of civil order are clearly a part of the universe of community actions: they apparently feed upon frustrations generated within the local community and, contrary to popular opinion, represent the efforts of local residents to cope with their problems. In its carefully documented analysis, for example, the 1967 National Advisory Commission on Civil Disorders points out that,

> Rioters are not only more likely than the noninvolved to have been born in the region in which the riot occurred, but they are also more likely to have been long-term residents of the city in which the disturbance took place. The Detroit survey data indicates that 59.4 percent of the self-reported rioters, but only 34.6 percent of the noninvolved, were born in Detroit. The comparable figures in the Newark survey were 53.5 percent and 22.5 percent.[7]

In addition, the Advisory Commission also reports that,

> Outsiders who temporarily entered the city during the riot might have left before the surveys were conducted and therefore may be underestimated in the survey data. However, the arrest data which is contemporaneous with the riot, suggest that few outsiders were involved: 90 percent of those arrested resided in the riot city, 7 percent lived in the same state, and only 1 percent were from outside the state. Our interviews in 20 cities corroborate these conclusions.[8]

These findings strongly suggest that the riots and civil disorders which have plagued Chicago, Newark, Detroit, Los Angeles, and a host of other cities obviously belong within the universe of community actions, at least in the sense that they represent collective responses to problems and frustrations encountered by community members. At the same time, one can also visualize an outbreak of violence which is stimulated by outside leaders whose goal is to put pressure on the federal government or on some other extracommunity system. An event of this type

[7] National Advisory Commission on Civil Disorders, *Report of the National Advisory Commission on Civil Disorders* (Washington, D.C.: U.S. Government Printing Office, 1968), p. 74.
[8] Ibid., pp. 74–75.

would obviously possess a much lower degree of "community-ness" than the events described by the National Advisory Commission.

Whether or not riots and similar breakdowns of social order are properly considered to be a part of the universe of community actions is of academic interest only. Regardless of where their specific interests lie, sociologists have a responsibility to bring their insights to bear upon the understanding of such problems. Until they do so their discipline will be rightly criticized on the grounds that it is esoteric. Fortunately, an increasing number of sociologists have awakened to this fact and are attempting to do something about it.

Routinized Community Actions. The universe of community actions also encompasses a variety of events and activities which occur on a routinized basis. In this context the term *routinized* must be defined in such a way that it includes any event or activity that is a normal, recurrent part of community life. Thus, in this day and age it is entirely possible to imagine a community in which there are more riots than charity drives. Nonetheless, a charity drive that is held on an annual basis would be an example of routinized community action; a riot would not. Among the other examples of routinized community action which might be cited would be the periodic meetings and deliberations of local governing bodies, annual parades, fairs, and other "social" events, as well as a host of other events and activities which happen on a recurrent basis. Some of these events and activities are of profound significance for the community and its members. Because of their routinized character, however, they often remain unanalyzed by community action theorists.[9]

Initiated Community Action. For one reason or another, com-

[9] It would be of considerable interest to know how many routinized activities and events occur in a typical community and how these are distributed by institutional type, i.e., how many are executed by the local government, by the local school system, by local churches, and so forth. Unfortunately, we simply do not have data which provides full and accurate answers to questions of this type. However, some of the research conducted by Willis A. Sutton, Jr., is suggestive of what might be found.

munity action theorists have focused much of their attention upon what might be referred to as initiated community action. Activities and events of this type, in contrast to those delineated previously, have as their main purpose the initiation of change at the community level through the mechanism of orderly group processes. Hence initiated community action can be viewed as an episode in the life of the community: a group comes into being, action is taken to bring about a desired change, and the group disbands or undertakes some other project. Obviously, some of these episodes may require only a few days for their completion; others may require a much greater period of time.

Although sociologists have generated a wealth of literature pertaining to initiated community action, the characteristics of this type of action have not always been clearly spelled out. However, initiated community action appears to have several characteristics, including (1) an emphasis upon problem solving or achieving a concrete goal, (2) the voluntary participation of local citizens, groups, and institutions, and (3) a democratic orientation. Each of these characteristics must be elaborated upon.

1. Initiated community action represents one method by which change in some facet of the community can be brought about. Therefore, one major characteristic of initiated community action is that emphasis is placed upon solving a problem or reaching some tangible, well-defined goal. To be more specific, the purpose of a community action episode may be to raise money for the United Fund, change attitudes toward mental illness,[10] or establish a community health council and

---

See Willis A. Sutton, Jr., "Toward a Universe of Community Actions," pp. 48–59. We should note that Sutton does not make a distinction between routinized and other types of community action. However, it is probably safe to assume that most of the actions observed by Sutton were of a routinized nature, i.e., they were a normal part of life in the community that he studied.

[10] For a description of a community action project of this type see Elaine Cumming and John Cumming, *Closed Ranks: An Experiment in Mental Health Education* (Cambridge, Mass.: Harvard University Press, 1957).

improve local health facilities.[11] We must stress, however, that initiated community action can also be used to impede progress. Persons whose interests are threatened may use initiated community action to prevent minority groups from gaining access to adequate housing, to block the expansion of services offered by local government, or whatever.

2. Another major characteristic of initiated community action is that participation in the action episode is on a voluntary basis. Specifically, each participant in community action episodes acts in his role as a community member rather than in his role as an employee of local government or of a local business firm: people supposedly do not enter into the action episode because it is a requirement of their occupation or because they receive financial remuneration. The only exception might be a professional person who is paid to help community members carry out successful community action programs.

The fact that local citizens voluntarily participate in community action programs does not mean that their motives are always completely pure. In fact, many people are openly suspicious of community action programs and of the individuals who become involved in them. For example, Kimball and Pearsall report that the citizens of Talladega, Alabama, seem to have a rather skeptical attitude toward proposals to broaden streets, extend sewers, fluoridate water supplies, and so forth. Thus,

> When action is proposed for the problems just mentioned, there is a traditional way of first responding to them. Talladegans always look behind proposals of citizens which call for public action to see what self-interest is being served. Thus, when an

[11] There are numerous accounts of community action projects of this type. See especially Floyd Hunter et al., *Community Organization: Action and Inaction* (Chapel Hill: University of North Carolina Press, 1956); Solon T. Kimball and Marion Pearsall, *The Talladega Story: A Study in Community Process* (University: University of Alabama Press, 1954); and Christopher Sower et al., *Community Involvement: The Webs and Informal Ties That Make for Action* (New York: The Free Press, 1957).

Ed Hyde wanted North Street widened, others suggested that he was motivated by the desire to have traffic flow past his hotel on that street. Similarly, it was implied that none of the city commissioners could benefit directly from extending sewerage to West End so they made no effort to meet the majority interest shown for this facility. When the dentists pushed for fluoridation of water, rumors were started which implied that the dentists would profit. Examples could be multiplied many times.[12]

It is undoubtedly true that on occasion the participants in community action programs are motivated by a desire for economic, political, or personal gain. This does not mean, however, that community action programs are undesirable or that they do not have a role to play in improving community life. The widening of a road may have economic rewards for an Ed Hyde, but it may also mean prosperity for other members of the community.

3. Most community action theorists also agree that the ideal community action program is one which has a democratic orientation. Specifically, community action programs should be free from control by vested interest groups and the participation of all interested, conscientious citizens should be welcomed. Likewise, one of the fundamental characteristics of the ideal community action program is that all members of the action group, and not just a "strong man," should be involved in setting goals, planning for action, and carrying the project through to completion. This is a feature of community action programs which must be borne in mind by professional persons whose job it is to assist local citizens in reaching their goals through initiated community action. The role of these persons is to educate and facilitate rather than to choose, plan, and carry out the action program.[13]

[12] Kimball and Pearsall, *The Talladega Story,* pp. 191–92.
[13] For a discussion of the role of professional consultants in community action and community development programs see Otto G. Hoiberg, "Contributions of the Social Scientist to Community Development," in Marvin B. Sussman (ed.), *Community Structure and Analysis* (New York: Thomas Y. Crowell Company, 1959), pp. 129–43.

It should be noted that several community action theorists have attempted to map the stages through which episodes of initiated community action pass as they move from initiation to completion. Although action episodes consist of a complex series of intertwined events, it nevertheless seems reasonable, for purposes of analysis, to break this flow of events down into a few basic stages or clusters of activity. It is to a consideration of these stages that we now turn.

Table 6-1 compares the stages through which community action episodes pass as they have been identified by several different sociologists. This table to some extent represents an oversimplification of the schemes developed by these men. Green and Mayo, for example, posit a series of substages within each of the four basic stages that they identify. Likewise, there is only a rough correspondence between the four schemes that are considered in Table 6-1. This is partly a matter of semantics and partly the result of the fact that each scheme sheds light on slightly different aspects of the total action process: Holland and his associates focus upon the mechanics of community action episodes, Kaufman as well as Green and Mayo delineate the specific steps that are required to carry a project through to successful completion, and Warren focuses upon the emergence and operation of action systems. Nonetheless, there is enough similarity in the four schemes that Table 6-1 can be used to describe briefly the stages through which community action episodes pass.

These stages can be summarized rather easily. Obviously, episodes of initiated community action begin when at least a few people become aware of a problem and express an interest in working toward its solution (Stage 1). This interest may arise in discussions among neighbors or among the leaders of voluntary associations, and it may even be stimulated by an outside change agent, such as a community consultant employed by a university or governmental body. At this stage in the action episode only a few people are involved. However, if a community action project is to move beyond the discussion stage,

Table 6-1. Stages in Community Action Episodes

	Holland et al.*	Kaufman †	Green and Mayo ‡	Warren §
Stage 1	Convergence of interest	Rise of interest	Initiation of action	Initial systemic environment
Stage 2	Establishment of an initiating set	Organization and maintenance of sponsorship	Goal definition and planning for achievement	Inception of the action system
Stage 3	Legitimation and sponsorship	Goal setting and the determination of specific means for their realization	Implementation of plans	Expansion of the action system
Stage 4	Establishment of an execution set	Gaining and maintaining participation	Goal achievement consequences	Operation of the expanded action system
Stage 5	Fulfillment of "charter" (ie., goal)	Carrying out the activities which represent goal achievement		Transformation of the action system

* John B. Holland, Kenneth E. Tiedke, and Paul R. Miller, "A Theoretical Model for Health Action," *Rural Sociology,* **22** (June, 1957), pp. 149–55.
† Harold F. Kaufman, "Toward an Interactional Conception of Community," *Social Forces,* **38** (October, 1959), pp. 9–17.
‡ James Green and Selz C. Mayo, "A Framework for Research in the Actions of Community Groups," *Social Forces,* **31** (May, 1953), pp. 320–27.
§ Roland L. Warren, *The Community in America* (Chicago: Rand McNally & Company, 1963), pp. 315–20.

a temporary action system must emerge which can "get the ball rolling" (Stage 2). In the typical episode of community action this stage involves the formation of an "initiating set." The initiating set usually involves many of the same people who originally became aware of the problem. Among other things, the persons who participate in the initiating set must define the goals of the action episode and map out specific strategies by which these goals may be achieved. Once these things have been accomplished, the initiating set must establish its right to take action, i.e., it must enlist the cooperation of persons who, by virtue of their position in the community, can make or break the project (Stage 3). There are essentially four groups which the initiating set must take into account, including "those whose approval gives sanction to the actions of the initiating set; those whose active sponsorship is essential for the mobilizing of community resources; those who remain neutral to the action; and those who may oppose the action." [14] Finally, a community action program of any consequence usually requires more than just the participation of members of the initiating set. Indeed, in most community action episodes the action system must be expanded in such a way that it includes members of the public who have not been previously involved (Stage 4). These persons may be needed to carry out the project, and widespread public involvement is one way of gaining broad-based support for the action program.

Once the goals and purposes of the action episode are achieved (Stage 5), two things may happen. First, the action system may be disbanded and its members may gradually lose contact with one another. However, in some cases the rewards of working together with other citizens to better one's community are so great that the participants in the action episode desire to tackle other problems and pursue other goals. When this occurs we can be sure that the community action program has been worth the effort invested in it.

[14] Holland, Tiedke, and Miller, "A Theoretical Model for Health Action," p. 154.

Leadership and Involvement

Any discussion of community action immediately brings to the forefront a wide variety of questions relating to community leadership and involvement. Who are the leaders in community activities and what are their characteristics? To what extent do community members become involved in local action episodes? Unfortunately, even though numerous investigators have focused upon questions of this type, their research has yielded relatively little in the way of basic generalizations. This is partly due to the fact that students of the community have used a variety of different research strategies in their study of community leadership and power—strategies which seem to yield different results.[15] It may also be partly due to the fact that these investigators have not always distinguished between different types of community events and activities. Surely a different group of persons will normally be involved in events and activities of a spontaneous type than will be involved in activities and events of a routinized nature.

Types of Community Leadership

Apparently community leadership is not something that is firmly placed in the hands of a few individuals. Rather, leadership tends to become diffused throughout the community, with one person or group exercising leadership in one situation and another person or group exercising leadership in another situation. Indeed, in his study of New Haven, Connecticut, Robert A. Dahl tells us that "probably the most striking characteristic of influence in New Haven is the extent to which it is specialized; that is, individuals who are influential in one sector of public activity tend not to be influential in another

[15] See especially Linton C. Freeman, Thomas J. Fararo, Warner Bloomberg, Jr., and Morris H. Sunshine, "Locating Leaders in Local Communities: A Comparison of Some Alternative Approaches," *American Sociological Review,* **28** (October, 1963), pp. 791–98.

sector."[16] Nonetheless, essentially three types of leaders may be identified at the local level. These three types of leaders and some of the more important facts about them are indicated in Table 6-2.

The first of these is the institutional leader. This person possesses the right to lead by virtue of the fact that he occupies a formal leadership position within the community. Included within this category are local political officials, such as the mayor and city councilmen, as well as school principals, influential ministers, labor union officials, and so forth. Even though these persons are official leaders in the sense that they are elected or appointed, their right to lead is usually circumscribed. A mayor, for example, does not have the right to make and execute decisions relating to all aspects of community life. Rather, his right to lead is limited to the affairs of municipal government.[17] This does not mean of course that the mayor never has influence which goes beyond that officially delegated to him. In addition to being the mayor, he may also be a part of the community's informal, but nonetheless influential, "power elite." Essentially the same observation applies to ministers, school superintendents, labor union officials, and other institutional leaders. In any event, the right of institutional leaders to exert influence and to make decisions is confined almost exclusively to activities and events of a routinized nature. Although they may become involved in nonroutinized community events and activities, it is usually not among their officially prescribed duties to do so.

There has been a considerable amount of debate as to how much decision-making power local institutional leaders actually possess. This debate has been spawned by contradictory findings from different communities. Thus, several studies have indicated

[16] Robert A. Dahl, *Who Governs?* (New Haven, Conn.: Yale University Press, 1961), p. 169.

[17] For a highly readable account of the mayor's role in exercising community leadership see Henry W. Mair, *Challenge to the Cities: An Approach to a Theory of Urban Leadership* (New York: Random House, Inc., 1966).

Theories of Community

Table 6-2. Types of Community Leaders

Type	Basis for Leadership	Area of Authority	Examples
Institutional	Occupies a formal leadership position in the community and is elected or appointed to his post.	Confined to routinized community actions.	Mayor, city councilman, school principal, ministers, labor union officials, etc.
Grassroots	Personal influence and the ability to get other people interested in a "cause."	Confined to community actions of a spontaneous and initiated nature.	Opponent of school desegregation, leader of campaign against water fluoridation, etc.
Power Elite	Wealth, economic power and/or personal influence.	Makes his influence felt in all areas of community action and decision making.	Wealthy businessman, top-echelon employee of commercial, banking, or industrial firm.

that in some communities institutional leaders are in fact the key decision makers.[18] On the other hand, an increasingly large body of research suggests that in many communities the formal leadership structure is very much influenced by a partially hidden "power elite." [19]

Another person who may make his influence felt at the local level is the grassroots leader.[20] This is the person who occasionally "pops" up from nowhere to assume leadership in some particular situation and then fades into the background, perhaps never to be heard from again. Among the examples that can be cited are the local citizen who leads a crusade for or against school desegregation or who becomes the main opponent of a proposed water fluoridation program. Unfortunately, little is known about leaders of this type. However, Kornhouser has garnered some evidence which suggests that these persons are likely to oppose those programs and policies that are championed by the official leadership structure.[21] In any event, the

[18] For example, see Robert A. Dahl, *Who Governs?;* Charles Freeman and Selz C. Mayo, "Decision Makers in Rural Community Action," *Social Forces,* 35 (May, 1957), pp. 319–22; Benjamin Walter, "Political Decision Making in Arcadia," in F. Stuart Chapin, Jr., and Shirley F. Weiss (eds.), *Urban Growth Dynamics* (New York: John Wiley & Sons, Inc., 1962), pp. 141–87; and Aaron Wildavsky, *Leadership in a Small Town* (Totowa, N.J.: Bedminster Press, 1964).

[19] The number of studies which focus upon the role of covert power elites in community leadership and decision making is legion. For a sampling of these studies see Robert S. Lynd and Helen M. Lynd, *Middletown* and *Middletown in Transition* (New York: Harcourt Brace Jovanovich, Inc., 1929 and 1937); Floyd Hunter, *Community Power Structure: A Study of Decision Makers* (Chapel Hill: University of North Carolina Press, 1953; Delbert C. Miller, "Industry and Community Power Structure: A Comparative Study of an American and an English City," *American Sociological Review,* 23 (February, 1958), pp. 9–15; and William V. D'Antonio et al., "Institutional and Occupational Representations in Eleven Community Influence Systems," *American Sociological Review,* 26 (June, 1961), pp. 440–46.

[20] Perhaps a better designation for this person would be the *meteor,* a term which was apparently coined by Aaron Wildavsky. See his *Leadership in a Small Town,* p. 336.

[21] See William Kornhouser, "Power and Participation in the Local Community," *Health Education Monographs,* No. 6 (Oakland, Calif.: Society of Public Health Educators, 1959), pp. 28–37.

opportunity to exercise leadership which these persons possess is confined almost exclusively to activities and events of a spontaneous or initiated nature. Community events and activities of a routinized nature fall into the province of institutional leaders.

More research has focused upon the role of the "power elite" or "ruling elite" in making decisions and exercising leadership at the local level. This research has suggested that in many communities there is a small group of men who, because of their wealth or economic position, largely determine the destiny of various community events and activities. One of the most thorough studies of such a power elite was that conducted by Floyd Hunter. In his study of the top forty leaders in a major Southern city, Hunter found that over one half were top-echelon employees of commercial, banking and investment, or industrial firms and that only four were governmental employees.[22] Similarly, in his study of 218 different community action programs aimed at obtaining better community health facilities, Paul A. Miller reports that 34 per cent of the "most active" participants were self-employed businessmen; that 28 per cent were professionals, and that 16 per cent were employed executives or managers.[23] On the other hand, only 8.2 per cent were civil officials.[24] These findings strongly suggest that the top leaders which were identified by both Hunter and Miller possess all the characteristics usually attributed to the "covert power elite," i.e., they are leaders who "do not hold political offices or offices in associations, they are not recognized by the community at large as key decision makers, they are active in a wide range of decision areas, and they work together as a group rather than independently or in opposition." [25]

The hypothesis that most American communities fit this "rul-

[22] Floyd Hunter, *Community Power Structure*, Table 4.

[23] Paul A. Miller, "The Process of Decision Making within the Context of Community Organization," *Rural Sociology*, **17** (June, 1952), p. 156.

[24] Ibid., Table 1.

[25] Charles M. Bonjean and David M. Olson, "Community Leadership: Directions of Research," *Administrative Science Quarterly*, **9** (December, 1964), p. 291.

ing elite" model of community leadership and power has been seriously questioned. During recent years there has been much research which suggests that an alternative perspective is called for in conceptualizing the power structure of American communities. In commenting on the critics of the ruling elite model of community power, for example, Willis D. Hawley and Frederick M. Wirt tell us that,

> This alternative perspective questions the existence of a single center of power, or a cohesive coalition of groups which wield power. Instead, the critics propose that there are usually (though not always) *multiple* centers of power, none of which is completely sovereign. In addition, these centers of power do not overlap or coalesce from issue-area to issue-area in any consistent way. In other words, *American cities are pluralistic.*[26]

Raymond Wolfinger adds further support to the pluralistic thesis when he points out that the findings of Hunter and others who subscribe to a ruling elite model of community power may be a product of their methodological approach.[27] In attempting to identify local influentials, most of these studies have utilized the reputational approach to the analysis of community power. Those who use this approach simply ask informed people in the community to name those persons whom they believe to be most influential in community affairs. Those persons who are named most frequently are assumed to be a part of the ruling elite. The difficulties inherent in this methodological approach are obvious. Among other things, one's informants may be familiar with the top leadership in only one area (schools, urban renewal, and so on) and the researcher's definition of *power* may be different from that of the informant.[28] Indeed, when we

[26] Willis D. Hawley and Frederick M. Wirt (eds.), *The Search for Community Power* (Englewood Cliffs, N.J.: Prentice-Hall, Inc., 1968), p. 89.

[27] Raymond E. Wolfinger, "Reputation and Reality in the Study of Community Power," *American Sociological Review,* 25 (October, 1960), pp. 636–44.

[28] Ibid., p. 638.

ask a person such questions as, "Who is the 'biggest' man in town?" or "who runs this town?" we may not get an accurate picture of who has the most influence on local affairs. Rather, we may in reality be getting answers to such questions as, "Who gets the most publicity in local newspapers?" "Who is the richest person in town?" or "Who forms the 'uppercrust' of this community?" In short, the basic assumption underlying the reputational approach is that there is a correlation between the influence an individual reputedly has and the amount of influence he actually exerts. This assumption is rather shaky. Furthermore, those persons who serve as informants for the researcher usually tend to move in the same circles, to know the same people, and even to know each other. It is not surprising that there is agreement among them as to who constitutes the most influential persons in the community.

The studies that we have discussed in the preceding pages, if not examined in concert, could lead the student to two distinctly different conclusions. First, one could conclude that every community has a covert power elite and that institutional leaders are merely pawns in the struggle for leadership at the local level. Secondly, one could adopt the opposite perspective, i.e., that in every community there is a pluralistic leadership structure: those who exercise leadership in relationship to one activity or event are not the same persons who exercise leadership in relationship to another activity or event. At the present time it would appear unwise to embrace fully either of these perspectives. About the only conclusion which can safely be drawn is that the nature of leadership structures varies from community to community. Some communities have a highly developed power elite; others do not. Bonjean and Olson are undoubtedly correct when they indicate that "apparently no single descriptive statement—not even a very general one—applies to community leadership in the United States today (unless the statement includes variability itself)." [29]

[29] Bonjean and Olson, "Community Leadership: Directions of Research," p. 290.

We have now identified three types of leaders who make their influence felt at the local level. Most communities have institutional leaders, grassroots leaders, and "behind-the-scenes" leaders, although their number and degree of influence varies widely from community to community. We should note, however, that our classification of community leaders is but one among many and that the literature on community leadership is vast. Although we cannot hope to review all the typologies of community leadership which have been developed, there are three which merit our attention.

One of these is Robert K. Merton's classification of the *types of influentials* which make their impact felt at the community level.[30] Specifically, Merton distinguishes between the "local" influential and the "cosmopolitan" influential. Put most simply, the local influential confines his interests to the local community and "is preoccupied with local problems, to the virtual exclusion of the national and international scene." [31] Presumably, his advice would be sought in regard to local politics, the activities of local service clubs, and other events and activities of a strictly local nature. It should be noted that the local influential gets his influence by cultivating a wide number of acquaintanceships and by participating in an elaborate network of social relations. Indeed, Merton tells us that "influentials in this group act on the explicit assumption that they can be locally prominent and influential by lining up enough people who know them and are hence willing to help them as well as be helped by them." [32] The cosmopolitan leader, on the other hand, is much more "worldly" in its attitudes and outlook. Although

[30] See Robert K. Merton, *Social Theory and Social Structure,* rev. and enlarged ed. (New York: The Free Press, 1957), pp. 387–420. It must be stressed that Merton's typology is not the product of armchair theorizing. Rather, it grew out of research that was conducted in "Rovere," a town of 11,000 persons located on the Eastern seaboard.

[31] Ibid., p. 393.

[32] Ibid., p. 397.

the cosmopolitan leader must show some interest in local affairs, he more often exercises influence over people's thinking on national and international issues. As such, the cosmopolitan leader claims his right to lead on the basis of his prestige, skills, and knowledge. At the same time, he has little interest in becoming enmeshed in an elaborate network of social relationships. As Merton puts it, "it is the prestige of his previous achievements and previously acquired skills which make him eligible for a place in the local influence-structure." [33]

There is another important fact about the localistic and cosmopolitan influential which should be noted. Thus, Merton maintains that the influence which the cosmopolitan influential wields is likely to be monomorphic, whereas the influence wielded by the local influential tends to be polymorphic.[34] By this Merton means simply that the cosmopolitan's ability to exert influence is often limited to a specific type of issue or event, whereas the localite may be able to exert influence in a variety of different situations. The cosmopolitan influential is, in effect, a *specialist;* the localite is a *generalist.* As a result, the cosmopolitan influential has influence in the realm of politics, fashion, *or* charitable activities. The local influential has influence in the area of politics, fashion, *and* charitable activities.

It should be apparent to the reader that Merton's typology carries on a grand tradition. He obviously drew his terms, as well as some of his thinking, from Carle Zimmerman and, ultimately, from Ferdinand Tonnies. Likewise, the relationship between Merton's typology and Roland Warren's concepts of the horizontal and vertical axis should not be overlooked. Indeed, further research might well reveal that the local influential operates almost exclusively on the horizontal axis and has an integrative function within the community, whereas the cosmopolitan influential undoubtedly operates along the vertical axis and links the local community to the larger world.

[33] Ibid., p. 400.
[34] Ibid., pp. 413–15.

Another typology of influentials of considerable interest to the student of community life is that developed by Nuttall, Scheuch, and Gordon.[35] The value of this typology lies in the fact that it sheds light on the dynamics of the decision-making process. The typology itself is shown in Figure 6-1. According to Nuttall and

		Perceived Access to Resource	
		Yes	No
Actual Access to Resource	Yes	(A) Manifest Influence	(B) Potential Influence
	No	(C) Reputed Influence	(D) Without Influence

Figure 6-1. A typology of influentials. [Source: Ronald L. Nuttall, Erwin K. Scheuch, and Chad Gordon, "On the Structure of Influence," in Terry N. Clark (ed.), *Community Structure and Decision-Making: Comparative Analyses* (San Francisco: Chandler Publishing Company, 1968), p. 351.]

his associates, a person's ability to exert influence in a given situation depends on two factors: (1) whether the person actually has access to the appropriate resources and (2) whether other participants in the decision-making process believe that he possesses the appropriate resources. Among the resources that the potential leader might possess would be the ability to reward persons who cooperate with him or to sanction those who do not. In the simplest case, the potential leader might be able to withhold from or deliver to another person a block of votes, depending upon whether the other person "helps" him reach his goals. Hence, in any episode of decision making, there are potentially four sets of actors: those with manifest influ-

[35] See Ronald L. Nuttall, Erwin K. Scheuch, and Chad Gordon, "On the Structure of Influence," in Terry N. Clark (ed.), *Community Structure and Decision-Making: Comparative Analyses* (San Francisco: Chandler Publishing Company, 1968), especially pp. 352–64.

ence, those with potential influence, those with reputed influence, and those with no influence. Once the decision has been made and the appropriate rewards or sanctions delivered, there may be of course a considerable reshuffling of actors in terms of their ability to exert influence. For example, the person with manifest influence may simply exhaust his resources and hence be left without influence when the next decision is made. Likewise, the person with potential influence, if he is wise and desires to do so, can often move into a position of manifest influence. On the other hand, those persons who have only reputed influence and those who have no influence at all are in a more precarious situation. For obvious reasons, persons with reputed influence will try to avoid decision-making situations in which a "payoff" will be demanded from them. If it is discovered that they lack the ability to reward or sanction, their position will become that of a person without influence. Likewise, the person without influence has two choices open to him, i.e., he can attempt to gain resources or he can attempt to shift the issue or the mode of decision making to the point that he has resources to use. For example, if a building contractor cannot muster enough support among members of the city zoning commission to get a "ruling" in his favor, he may turn to the local mayor in the hopes that he will intervene on the contractor's behalf. In return for the mayor's help, the contractor may promise to deliver his employee's votes to the mayor during a forthcoming election.

Rather than attempting to classify types of leaders, Agger, Goldrich, and Swanson classify power structures themselves according to types.[36] They do this by cross-classifying two variables: (1) the degree to which the ideologies of local political leaders are compatible or conflicting and (2) the degree to which political power is distributed among local citizens. The result of cross-classifying these two variables is shown in Figure

[36] Robert E. Agger, Daniel Goldrich, and Bert E. Swanson, *The Rulers and the Ruled: Political Power and Impotence in American Communities* (New York: John Wiley & Sons, Inc., 1964), pp. 73–78.

Distribution of Political Power Among Citizens

		Broad	Narrow
Political Leadership's Ideology	Convergent	Consensual Mass	Consensual Elite
	Divergent	Competitive Mass	Competitive Elite

Figure 6-2. Types of power structures. [Source: Robert E. Agger, Daniel Goldrich, and Bert E. Swanson, *The Rulers and the Ruled: Political Power and Impotence in American Communities* (New York: John Wiley & Sons, Inc., 1964), p. 73.]

6-2. In essence, there can be four types of power structure, the consensual mass, the consensual elite, the competitive mass, and the competitive elite. Basically, a power structure of the consensual elite variety would correspond to the "ruling elite" or "covert power elite" that we have discussed previously. On the other hand, a local power structure of the consensual mass type would correspond closely to the pluralistic system, i.e., it would be one in which A has power in one situation and B has power in another situation. The other two types of power structure are a bit more difficult to visualize. Presumably, a power structure of the competitive elite variety would exist when the "elitist" leaders have become fragmented into two or more competing groups. Much the same would be true in regard to the competitive mass, except that more citizens would be involved. Each of these citizens supposedly would align himself with one of the leadership factions.

Participation

It would be extremely interesting to know what percentage of the total population becomes involved in episodes of community action and what percentage occupy positions of leadership at the local level. Unfortunately, it is almost impossible to offer

Theories of Community

any ironclad generalizations concerning these questions. This is partly because adequate data relating to the extent of citizen participation in community action episodes are not available and partly because a number of contradictory statements have been made concerning the participation of Americans in community activities and associations. On the one hand, the idea has been propagated that Americans are pathological joiners. This idea can be traced back to a perceptive French observer of the American scene, Alexis de Tocqueville, who as early as the 1830's suggested that "in no country in the world has the principle of association been more successfully used or applied to a multitude of objects than in America." [37] On the other hand, one of the most common complaints voiced by community leaders is that local citizens will not participate in community activities nor will they assume positions of leadership when they are given the opportunity to do so. The truth probably lies somewhere between these two extremes. For example, a 1953 National Opinion Research Center Survey of 2,809 families found that in 31 per cent of the cases, at least one family member held an associational membership, and that in 21 per cent of the cases two or more associational memberships were held by family members. On the other hand, in 47 per cent of the cases no family members held an associational membership.[38] These data hardly suggest that Americans are pathological joiners. At the same time, they do not suggest that Americans are totally apathetic in regard to associational membership.

It is only in a very indirect manner that these data shed any

[37] Alexis de Tocqueville, *Democracy in America,* Volume I (New York: Alfred A. Knopf, 1953), p. 191.

[38] Cited in Charles R. Wright and Herbert H. Hyman, "Voluntary Association Memberships of American Adults: Evidence from National Sample Surveys," *American Sociological Review,* **23** (June, 1958), p. 287. Babchuk and Booth indicate that a much higher proportion of Nebraska's population join voluntary associations. See Nicholas Babchuk and Alan Booth, "Voluntary Association Membership: A Longitudinal Analysis," *American Sociological Review,* **34** (February, 1969), pp. 31–44.

light on the extent of citizen leadership and participation in community action episodes. They refer to associational memberships and not to participation in community activities. Nevertheless, on the basis of these data we might infer that citizen involvement in community action episodes is quite limited, a hypothesis which seems to be confirmed by the information that we do have at our disposal. Even in such emotion-packed episodes of community action as the 1967 riots which erupted in Detroit and Newark, our data indicate that approximately one half of those persons who were potentially involved (48 to 53 per cent) remained aloof and noninvolved.[39] Likewise, the apparent apathy of American citizens in regard to community activities and events of a routinized nature, such as voting in local elections and participating in local government, has been noted many times. Perhaps Harold Kaufman offers the most realistic appraisal of the situation when he says,

> The degree of involvement of a local population in the interactional community runs all the way from assuming a major role in policy making to no more than identification with the locality resulting from "residence and sustenance" activities. . . . It is likely that even in areas with the highest potential for community action, only a minority of the population is ever active at a given time.[40]

Summary

In this chapter we have reviewed some of the literature on community action, leadership, and involvement. The importance of this material lies in the fact that it forces us to ask some rather significant questions about the dynamics of community life. It is important to understand decision-making processes as they occur at the community level and to know who makes those decisions which affect the entire community. Likewise, it is important to know something about the nature and types of

[39] National Advisory Commission on Civil Disorders, *Report of the National Advisory Commission on Civil Disorders,* p. 73.
[40] Kaufman, "Toward an Interactional Conception of Community," p. 11.

community action and about the extent of citizen participation in episodes of community action.

It is hoped that this chapter has shed light on these matters. At the same time, it should be entirely clear that there are many unresolved problems in the study of community action, leadership, and involvement. For one thing, more adequate methods for delineating the universe of community actions must be developed. Until this is done, the concept of community that is championed by Harold F. Kaufman, Willis A. Sutton, Jiri Kolaja, and others will remain vague and ambiguous. Similarly, students of community life must continue to refine their methods of studying community power and leadership. At the present time, it appears that the findings of those who do research on community power and leadership are at least partly a product of their methodology: the reputational approach yields findings different from the issue area approach. Fortunately, technicalities of this type seem to work themselves out if the basic research problem is sound. Indeed, one can only hope that research on community action, leadership, and involvement will continue. The students of community life whom we have considered in this chapter have raised important questions and developed some significant ideas, concepts, and hypotheses. Future researchers will benefit greatly from their successes and their failures.

Bibliography

Aiken, Michael, and Paul E. Mott. *The Structure of Community Power: An Anthology.* New York: Random House, 1970.

Agger, Robert E., Daniel Goldrich, and Bert E. Swanson. *The Rulers and the Ruled: Political Power and Impotence in American Communities.* New York: John Wiley & Sons, Inc., 1964.

Babchuk, Nicholas, and Alan Booth. "Voluntary Association Membership: A Longitudinal Analysis," *American Sociological Review,* **34** (February, 1969), pp. 31–44.

Bonjean, Charles M., and David M. Olson. "Community Leadership: Directions of Research," *Administrative Science Quarterly,* **9** (December, 1964), pp. 278–95.

Bruyn, Severyn T. *Communities in Action: Pattern and Process.* New Haven: College and University Press, Inc., 1963.

Clark, Terry N. (ed.), *Community Structure and Decision-Making: Comparative Analyses.* San Francisco: Chandler Publishing Company, 1968.

Cumming, Elaine, and John Cumming. *Closed Ranks: An Experiment in Mental Health Education.* Cambridge, Mass.: Harvard University Press, 1957.

Dahl, Robert A. *Who Governs?* New Haven: Yale University Press, 1961.

D'Antonio, William V., et al. "Institutional and Occupational Representations in Eleven Community Influence Systems," *American Sociological Review,* **26** (June, 1961), pp. 440–46.

Freeman, Linton C., et al. "Locating Leaders in Local Communities: A Comparison of Some Alternative Approaches," *American Sociological Review,* **28** (October, 1963), pp. 791–98.

Freeman, Charles, and Selz C. Mayo. "Decision Makers in Rural Community Action," *Social Forces,* **35** (May, 1957), pp. 319–22.

Form, William H., and Sigmund Nosow. *Community in Disaster.* New York: Harper & Row, 1958.

Green, James, and Selz Mayo. "A Framework for Research in the Actions of Community Groups," *Social Forces,* **31** (May, 1953), pp. 320–27.

Hawley, Willis D., and Frederick M. Wirt (eds.). *The Search for Community Power.* Englewood Cliffs, N.J.: Prentice-Hall, Inc., 1968.

Holland, John B., Kenneth E. Tiedke, and Paul A. Miller. "A Theoretical Model for Health Action," *Rural Sociology,* **22** (June, 1957), pp. 149–55.

Hunter, Floyd, et al. *Community Organization: Action and Inaction.* Chapel Hill: University of North Carolina Press, 1956.

————. *Community Power Structure: A Study of Decision Makers.* Chapel Hill: University of North Carolina Press, 1953.

Kaufman, Harold F. "Toward an Interactional Conception of Community," *Social Forces,* **38** (October, 1959), pp. 9–17.

Kimball, Solon T., and Marion Pearsall. *The Talladega Story: A Study in Community Process.* University: University of Alabama Press, 1954.

Kornhauser, William. "Power and Participation in the Local Community," *Health Education Monographs,* No. 6 (Oakland, Calif: Society of Public Health Educators, 1959), pp. 28–37.

Lowry, Richie P. *Who's Running This Town?* New York: Harper & Row, 1965.

Mair, Henry W. *Challenge to the Cities: An Approach to a Theory of Urban Leadership.* New York: Random House, Inc., 1966.

Merton, Robert K. *Social Theory and Social Structure,* rev. and enlarged ed. New York: The Free Press, 1957. See especially pp. 387–420.

Miller, Delbert C. "Industry and Community Power Structure: A Comparative Study of an American and an English City," *American Sociological Review,* **23** (February, 1958), pp. 9–15.

Miller, Paul A. "The Process of Decision Making Within the Context of Community Organization," *Rural Sociology,* **17** (June, 1952), pp. 153–61.

Polsby, Nelson W. *Community Power and Political Theory.* New Haven: Yale University Press, 1963.

Sower, Christopher, et al. *Community Involvement: The Webs and Informal Ties that Make for Action.* New York: The Free Press, 1957.

Sutton, Willis A., Jr., "Toward a Universe of Community Actions," *Sociological Inquiry,* **34** (Winter, 1964), pp. 48–49.

————, and Jiri Kolaja. "The Concept of Community," *Rural Sociology,* **25** (June, 1960), pp. 197–203.

————. "Elements of Community Action," *Social Forces,* **38** (May, 1960), pp. 325–31.

Vogt, Evon Z., and Thomas F. O'Dea. "A Comparative Study of the Role of Values in Social Action in Two Southwestern Communities," *American Sociological Review,* **18** (December, 1953), pp. 645–54.

Walter, Benjamin. "Political Decision Making in Arcadia," in F. Stuart Chapin, Jr., and Shirley F. Weiss (eds.), *Urban Growth Dynamics.* New York: John Wiley & Sons, Inc., 1962.

Wildavsky, Aaron. *Leadership in a Small Town.* Totowa, N.J.: Bedminster Press, 1964.

Wolfinger, Raymond E. "Reputation and Reality in the Study of Community Power," *American Sociological Review,* **25** (October, 1960), pp. 636–44.

7

Community Change and Community Problems

There are many unknowns in community study. However, two things may be said with absolute certainty. First, during recent years most communities have been undergoing continuous and rapid social change. These changes have entailed, among other things, modification in their demographic characteristics, ecological layout, economic structure, and organizational patterns. Secondly, most modern communities, like their ancient predecessors, have been plagued by a host of economic, demographic, ecological, and social problems. Included among these problems have been overcrowding, blight, poverty, and unrest in urban areas and depopulation and economic decline in rural areas. Communities of all sizes share problems of crime and delinquency, mental illness, and racial conflict.

There is a two-way relationship between social change and social problems. On the one hand, social problems result from social change, especially when it is rapid and incessant. Robert Dentler, for example, reminds us that "vast social change produces vast social problems and these get magnified at the level of local communities." [1] Of more importance, however, is the fact that community problems can only be solved through yet further social change. Indeed, the word *solve* implies that conditions are changed to the extent that the problem disappears

---

[1] Robert A. Dentler, *American Community Problems* (New York: McGraw-Hill Book Company, 1968), p. 94.

or subsides in importance. Thus, a few of the problems that are faced by American communities will solve themselves with the passage of time. Most of them will be solved only through concerted, rational efforts to correct the problematic situation.

Types of Community Change

We have inferred that there are two types of community change. Thus, one type of community change results from conscious efforts to modify one or more facets of community life. One example would be the efforts of a city planner to improve patterns of traffic flow in a congested city. The term *planned change* encompasses these types of activity. On the other hand, many of the changes which occur at the local level are not purposefully instigated. Sometimes man may indeed be the "victim" rather than the instigator of community change. We refer to the latter as *unplanned change*.

In distinguishing unplanned from planned community change, we are not suggesting that it is only the latter which results from human activity. Rather, we are suggesting that some types of change (i.e., planned) result from a deliberate effort to modify community life whereas other types of change are the unanticipated by-product of human activity and interaction. The only type of change which fits neither of these categories is that caused by events beyond man's control, such as natural disasters. All other types of change are a product of human activity, regardless of whether the activity is intended to bring about change or not.

This is not to deny that a two-way relationship sometimes exists between planned and unplanned change. We have already suggested that unplanned change frequently gives rise to problems which can only be solved through carefully executed programs of planned change. Likewise, planned change can be an independent variable which brings in its wake a wide array of changes that were not anticipated when the planned change was instigated. The construction of superhighways, for example, sometimes has an adverse impact upon the economic prosperity of the small communities that are by-passed. However, it is obviously not the goal of state highway departments to put small roadside establishments out of business.

Unplanned Change and the Modern American Community

Almost every observer of American community life has his favorite list of changes which have occurred at the local level.[2] Among those most frequently mentioned are the growing impersonality and bureaucratization of community life, the growing complexity of the community as an ecological entity, and the continued spread of industrialization to virtually every village, city, and metropolitan area. However, if we were forced to identify the one change which has had a greater impact on American community life than all others it would have to be the continued spread of urbanization. One hundred years ago most Americans lived on farms or in small agricultural villages. Today the city or the metropolitan area is home for most Americans.

That urbanization has been the key change process that has occurred at the community level, at least in the United States, may be so clear as to require no further elaboration. For example, if one defines urbanization as the clustering of large numbers of people in small areas, then the last 100 years have obviously marked the entrance of the United States into the urban world. Thus Table 7-1 presents an overview of the extent to which the U.S. population has become urbanized since 1860; Figure 7-1 presents these same data in graph form. The meaning of these data is entirely clear. Today, in contrast to years past, the "statistically average" American is an urbanite who lives in a community that is both large and complex.

[2] For example, see Irwin T. Sanders, *The Community: An Introduction to Social System,* 2nd ed. (New York: The Ronald Press, 1966), pp. 464–66; and Roland L. Warren, *The Community in America* (Chicago: Rand McNally & Company, 1963), pp. 53–94.

Table 7-1. Percentage of the Total U.S. Population Living in Urban (over 2,500 population) and Rural (under 2,500) Places, 1860 to 1970

	Urban	*Rural*
1970	73.5	26.5
1960	69.9	30.1
1950 *	64.0	36.0
1940	56.5	43.5
1930	56.2	43.8
1920	51.2	48.8
1910	45.7	54.3
1900	39.7	60.3
1890	35.1	64.9
1880	28.2	71.8
1870	25.7	74.3
1860	19.8	80.2

* In 1950 the U.S. Bureau of the Census modified its definition of urban. This accounts for 5 per cent of the increase between 1940 and 1950.
Source: U.S. Bureau of the Census, *Census of the Population: 1960*, Pt. I, *U.S. Summary* (Washington, D.C.: U.S. Government Printing Office, 1964), Table 3. Figures for 1970 taken from U.S. Bureau of the Census, *1970 Census of Population*, Vol. I, *Final Population Counts: U.S. Advanced Report* (Washington, D.C.: U.S. Government Printing Office, 1971), Table 2.

These data refer only to the clustering of population in cities and metropolitan areas. However, William E. Cole has pointed out that "the term *urbanization* is sometimes used to denote much more than a population concentration. It denotes a process of urban culture dominance in the making." [3] This same idea is expressed by Nels Anderson when he tells us that,

> There is also the nonmigration aspect of urbanization; one can be urbanized by going to the city, but urbanization can also

[3] William E. Cole, *Urban Society* (Boston: Houghton Mifflin Company, 1958), p. 7. Italics in original.

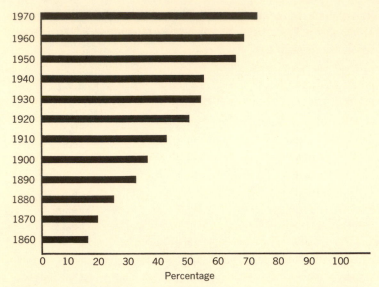

Figure 7-1. Percentage of total U.S. population living in urban places, 1860–1970. [Source: U.S. Bureau of the Census, *Census of Population: 1960*, Pt. I, *U.S. Summary* (Washington, D.C.: U.S. Government Printing Office, 1964), Table 3. Figures for 1970 taken from U.S. Bureau of the Census, *1970 Census of Population*, Vol. I, *Final Population Counts: U.S. Advanced Report* (Washington, D.C.: U.S. Government Printing Office, 1971), Table 2.]

come to him in a non-urban place. In this sense, urbanism is outward reaching. People may be urbanized without migrating to cities and without changing from agricultural to non-agricultural work.[4]

That the type of urbanization to which Cole and Anderson refer has swept the United States should be obvious. Today the American "ruralite" has become thoroughly urbanized in his attitudes, values, and patterns of behavior. The differences between the ruralite and the urbanite are slim indeed, and it no longer makes sense to talk about American rural, as opposed to American urban, culture.

[4] Nels Anderson, "The Urban Way of Life," *International Journal of Comparative Sociology*, **3** (September, 1962), pp. 176–77.

Although urbanization seems to be the most important type of change affecting American community life today, the present writer is not blind to other types of community change. What one defines as significant in terms of social change depends a great deal upon his frame of reference. Thus, a human ecologist might argue that the most significant change which has occurred recently in American communities has been the increased segregation of racial groups from one another,[5] but an industrial sociologist would maintain that industrialization is the most fundamental type of change occurring at the local level. However, it must be remembered that our interest lies in the community as a social system rather than in the groups of which it is composed or in the larger society of which it is a part. Seemingly, the increased segregation of racial groups from one another is properly studied by a specialist in human ecology, whereas industrialization is properly studied by industrial sociologists and by economists. Furthermore, it might be noted that one type of change can only be explained by reference to another type of change.[6] Is it not safe to assume that urbanization itself has stimulated many of the changes which have occurred on the intracommunity level, including increased racial segregation? Likewise, can it not also be assumed that urbanization has been a by-product of various changes which have occurred at the societal level? One of these changes certainly has been the industrialization of American society.

[5] For evidence that this has occurred see Donald O. Cowgill, "Trends in Residential Segregation of Non-Whites in American Cities, 1940–1950," *American Sociological Review*, **21** (February, 1956), pp. 43–47; Davis McEntire, *Race and Residence* (Berkeley: University of California Press, 1960), pp. 40–46; and John H. Strange, "Racial Segregation in the Metropolis," in Michael N. Danielson (ed.), *Metropolitan Politics: A Reader* (Boston: Little, Brown and Company, 1966), pp. 41–52.

[6] Thus, William F. Ogburn reminds us that "whenever a result occurs, something has varied." See his "How Technology Causes Social Change," in Francis R. Allen et al., *Technology and Social Change* (New York: Appleton-Century-Crofts, 1957), p. 12.

Why Urbanization Has Occurred

If urbanization is in fact the most fundamental change affecting American community life, then our next task is to explain why it has occurred. Thus, it is widely agreed that the urbanization of American communities, as well as of communities throughout the world, has been stimulated by *the dual factors of improvement in agricultural technology and improvement in transportation and communication facilities.* The role these two factors have played in stimulating urbanization must be examined in greater detail.

Agricultural Technology. Several writers have observed that the emergence of cities and metropolitan areas had to await a revolution in agricultural productivity.[7] Throughout most of human history surplus agricultural commodities could not be produced in sufficient quantity to feed a large nonagricultural population. This meant that the majority of people had to work the soil. By March of 1968, however, 4.6 per cent of the total U.S. labor force (1.8 per cent of the total population) could produce enough to feed both the entire population of the United States and millions of people in other countries.[8] It is only under conditions similar to these that urbanization can occur.

Our increased ability to produce food and hence to support a large nonagricultural population can be traced to the dramatic modernization of agricultural technology that has occurred during recent years. In his analysis of the influence of technology on agriculture, for example, Delbert C. Miller points out that,

Through countless centuries, agriculture was carried on by hand labor, with only a few simple tools supplemented to a

---

[7] See National Resources Committee, *Our Cities: Their Role in the National Economy* (Washington, D.C.: National Resources Committee, 1937), p. 29; and Gideon Sjoberg, *The Preindustrial City: Past and Present* (New York: The Free Press, 1960), pp. 28–30.

[8] Calculated from U.S. Bureau of the Census, *Statistical Abstract of the United States: 1968* (Washington, D.C.: U.S. Government Printing Office, 1968), Tables 2 and 310.

slight extent by animal power. The New England farmer of colonial times was dependent upon tools of the most primitive sort. His chief tools were the harrow, a spade, and a fork, all made of wood and clumsily constructed. Few could afford a plow, and a town often paid a bounty to anyone who would buy a plow and keep it in repair. One plow would be used to do the work for a large territory.[9]

Obviously, urbanization cannot occur when methods of farming are this primitive: most able-bodied men have to be engaged in cultivating the soil. This means, in turn, that the population must be dispersed over the land and that living in large cities is completely impossible. However, the nineteenth century ushered in an era of innovation in agricultural technology. Among the most significant breakthroughs were the mechanization of farm equipment, the improvement of plants and animals through selective breeding, and the development of scientific methods of insect control and soil replenishment.[10] Once these and related developments had occurred, the urbanization of America could also occur. Millions of people were released from agricultural endeavors and eventually found their way to the city.

To determine why dramatic changes in agricultural technology began to take place during the nineteenth century may be taking us too far afield. Very briefly, however, the revolution in agricultural productivity which occurred during the nineteenth century was but one facet of the larger industrial revolution which began a century earlier. Noticeable increases in agricultural productivity had to await the invention of steam, electric, and gasoline engines as sources of power for agricultural machinery and the development of applied chemistry, horticulture, and agronomy. Likewise, a modern factory system was required before tractors, harvesters, plows, and other tools

[9] Delbert C. Miller, "Impact of Technology on Agriculture," in Francis R. Allen et al., *Technology and Social Change*, p. 327.

[10] For further discussion of these and related developments see ibid., pp. 326–35.

could be produced in sufficient quantity to meet the needs of modern agriculture.

Hence, urbanization in the United States was the end result of a long, complex chain of developments: the urbanization of American communities was stimulated by a revolution in agricultural technology, and this revolution in agricultural technology was a part of the larger industrial revolution. It might be noted in passing that this account of urbanization reflects the general approach to the explanation of social and cultural change which was developed by William F. Ogburn.[11] Basically, Ogburn argued that social and cultural changes, especially those which involve a technological variable, occur in such a way that change 1 stimulates change 2, change 2 stimulates change 3, and so on. This, of course, is essentially what we have said about urbanization, i.e., the processes of urbanization that are sweeping the world today had their roots in the industrial revolution.

Transportation and Communication. Our increased ability to produce agricultural commodities accounts for one facet of urbanization in the United States, i.e., the growth of large cities. Nonetheless, our explanation of urbanization still suffers from two serious deficiencies. First, other factors had to be combined with increases in agricultural productivity before the concentration of population in large cities became possible. One of these factors was the development of efficient methods of transportation.[12] Obviously, increased agricultural productivity is of little

[11] William F. Ogburn, "How Technology Causes Social Change," in Francis R. Allen et al., ibid., p. 20. The student who is particularly interested in technology and its bearing on social and cultural change should become acquainted with Ogburn's work. See especially his *Social Change* (New York: B. W. Huebsch, 1922). A 1950 edition of this work with a supplementary chapter has been published by the Viking Press of New York. For a compilation of his more significant articles see William F. Ogburn, *On Culture and Social Change,* edited and with an introduction by Otis Dudley Duncan (Chicago: University of Chicago Press, 1964).

[12] An excellent discussion of the relationship between transportation and urban development is contained in Harlan W. Gilmore, *Transportation and the Growth of Cities* (New York: The Free Press, 1953).

consequence in hastening urbanization unless there are means by which agricultural products can be transported to the city.[13] Secondly, as it now stands our explanation of urbanization accounts only for the movement of people to cities. It does not tell us why rural people themselves have, in a real sense, become urbanized. In this connection it seems clear that the degree to which rural people become urbanized depends upon the development of transportation and communications facilities; if transportation and communication facilities become highly developed, the differences between rural and urban people tend to disappear. In reality this is a simple and rather obvious generalization about a specific type of social change. It suggests that changes in the social and cultural patterns which characterize rural areas result from innovation in systems of transportation and communication.

There are numerous shreds of evidence which support this generalization. Thus, in discussing the influence of the highway and, by implication, the automobile on rural life, Firey, Loomis, and Beegle suggest that,

> Now more than ever before the farm family can participate in "the larger society" which is borne by metropolitan newspapers, urban recreational facilities, urban libraries and schools, and many other points of contact unknown to the nineteenth-century country dweller. Organizations and activities once the prerogative of the urbanite are now just as accessible to the ruralite. . . . Highways, in short, have made the rural population more cosmopolitan.[14]

[13] Thus, Gilmore points out that "even if area A has sufficient surplus to support the population of area B, unless the transportation system can transport these goods, as far as B is concerned, the surplus of A does not effectively exist." Ibid., p. 137.

[14] Walter Firey, Charles P. Loomis, and J. Allan Beegle, "The Fusion of Urban and Rural," in *Highways in our National Life: A Symposium,* ed. by Jean Labutut and Wheaton J. Lane (Princeton, N.J.: Princeton University Press, 1950), p. 160. See also Francis R. Allen, "The Automobile," in Allen et al., *Technology and Social Change,* p. 126, who reminds us that "interaction with urban dwellers, coupled with an extension of the radio, TV, and other inventions to the rural scene, has tended to urbanize some of the rural dweller's attitudes."

Of even greater importance has been the development of motion pictures, radio, and television. With the emergence of these media of communication, the rural dweller has become a full participant in the urban society which now engulfs the United States. The era when the United States was characterized by two societies, one rural and one urban, has long since passed.

Urbanization and Its Derivations

Enough has been said to make it clear that the urbanization of American communities has been made possible by increased agricultural productivity and by the development of modern transportation and communication facilities. At the same time, it is equally clear that urbanization has had its own derivative effects and has itself brought about change in other facets of community life. Some of the effects of urbanization on community life were discussed in Chapter 2, where we considered Wirth's analysis of urbanism. Unfortunately, however, the changes which occur as a community undergoes urbanization are not always positive. Urbanization often brings in its wake problems of congestion and overcrowding, a wide variety of conditions which adversely affect human welfare, and difficulties in providing adequate governmental, educational, health, and welfare services. Many of these problems can only be solved through further change. Hence, we must now examine the types of planned community change and determine how they can be used to solve community problems.

Type of Planned Community Change

City planning, community organization, and community action and development are three terms which frequently crop up in discussions of planned community change. Although these terms are sometimes used interchangeably, they refer to different processes of planned change which are used to cope with different types of problems.

City Planning

The city planner pursues several different goals. Therefore, the nature of city planning is somewhat difficult to specify. Nevertheless, the term *city planning* usually refers to the process by which cities and metropolitan areas are rehabilitated and renovated, as well as guided in their future development, as physical entities.[15] As a result, problems of traffic congestion and inadequate transportation facilities, urban deterioration and blight, slum housing and suburban sprawl all come within the purview of the city planner. In attempting to cope with these and related problems, most city planners are not only concerned with the improvement of existing conditions but with preventing new problems from arising as the urban area continues to grow. In addition, city planners from time to time may design entirely new communities, such as Radburn, New Jersey, and Greenbelt, Maryland.[16]

Although city planning focuses upon the physical and ecological dimensions of urban problems, a growing number of city planners have voiced the idea that their activities are but a means to a larger end. In reviewing the assumptions upon which city planning has traditionally rested, for example, Melvin M. Webber points out that,

> For generations it has been generally understood that the physical environment was a major determinant of social behavior

[15] Lloyd Rodwin says essentially the same thing when he indicates that, "The city planner is the professional advisor and diagnostician on the physical environment of the city—and especially on the problems and on the methods of making plans and of establishing a framework for public and private decisions affecting the physical environment." See his article "The Roles of the City Planner in the Community," in Charles R. Adrian (ed.), *Social Science and Community Action* (East Lansing: Michigan State University Press, 1960), p. 48.

[16] For a discussion of planned communities in the United States, including Radburn and Greenbelt, see Paul K. Conkin, *Tomorrow a New World: The New Deal Community Program* (Ithaca, N.Y.: Cornell University Press, 1959), especially Part III; and Arthur Hillman, *Community Organization and Planning* (New York: The Macmillan Company, 1950), especially pp. 111–20.

and a direct contributor to individuals' welfare. Having accepted professional responsibility for the physical environment, the city planner was thus accorded a key role as agent of human welfare: the clearly prescribed therapy for the various social pathologies was improvement of the physical setting. If only well-designed and well-sited houses, playgrounds, and community facilities could be substituted for the crowded and dilapidated housing and neighborhoods of the city's slum, then the incidence of crime, delinquency, narcotics addiction, alcoholism, broken homes, and mental illness would tumble.[17]

It is now recognized that the improvement of the city as a physical entity will not by itself solve all the problems faced by urban dwellers. As a result, modern city planners see themselves as members of one among several professions which can contribute to the solution of urban problems. This has led to a renewed interest in the bearing of physical planning on the achievement of the nation's broader health, welfare, and educational goals.[18] *A Brief History of City Planning.*[19] City planning of one kind or another is probably as old as the city itself. As mankind began to cluster in cities there were certain conditions which had to be met if life in an urban milieu was to be both safe and pleasant. Among other things, streets had to be designed so as to allow access to public facilities and gathering places, and provisions had to be made for defending the city against armed attack: the latter requirement gave rise to the walled city and to the hilltop city built around a citadel. Likewise, more than

[17] Melvin M. Webber, "Comprehensive Planning and Social Responsibility," *Journal of the American Institute of Planners,* **29** (November, 1963), p. 233.

[18] See ibid., pp. 232–41; and Harvey S. Perloff, "Common Goals and the Linking of Physical and Social Planning," in American Society for Planning Officials and the Community Planning Association of Canada, *Planning, 1965* (Chicago: American Society of Planning Officials, 1965), pp. 170–84.

[19] The following summary is necessarily very brief. For a beautifully prepared history of city planning in the United States see John W. Reps, *The Making of Urban America: A History of City Planning in America* (Princeton, N.J.: Princeton University Press, 1965).

one ruler ordered the construction of temples and other public buildings which stood as monuments to his own power, beneficence, and foresight. As a result, many of the great cities of antiquity were characterized by carefully planned buildings, parks, monuments, and plazas. Some of these cities retain their magnificence to this day.

The colonial period of American history was marked by a healthy interest in city planning.[20] Perhaps the most noteworthy attempt to create a fully planned city in the United States was that proposed by Major Pierre Charles L'Enfant for Washington, D.C. L'Enfant visualized nothing less than a city of beauty and magnificence. It would be marked by spaciousness, broad garden-lined avenues radiating from central squares, and the balanced placement of public buildings, statues, fountains, and waterways.[21] Unfortunately, L'Enfant's ambitious plan did not reach maturation [22] nor did similarly ambitious plans for Buffalo, Detroit, Indianapolis and several other cities. There were several reasons for this, but the most important one seems to have been the failure of government to curb the ambitions of greedy landowners and speculators. To these individuals land and its development represented a means by which one could acquire private wealth rather than a precious commodity to be developed and used for the public good. Glabb explains the situation very well when he states that "in the struggle between the speculator and the architect, the planner, or the visionary, the speculator ordinarily won." [23] As a result, by the middle of the nineteenth century American cities did not bear the marks

20 See ibid., especially Chapters 2–7.

21 Charles N. Glabb and A. Theodore Brown, *A History of Urban America* (New York: The Macmillan Company, 1967), pp. 251–53.

22 See Lewis Mumford, *The City in History: Its Origins, Its Transformations, and Its Prospects* (New York: Harcourt Brace Jovanovich, Inc., 1961), pp. 403–409. For an on-the-spot assessment of the difficulties encountered in making L'Enfant's plan a reality see "Modifications of the Washington Plan (Nicholas King to Thomas Jefferson, September 25, 1803)," in Charles N. Glabb, *The American City: A Documentary History* (Homewood, Ill.: The Dorsey Press, 1963), pp. 38–42.

23 Ibid., p. 34.

of planned beauty, efficiency, and order. Rather, they bore the marks of a society which had allowed considerations of private gain to determine the architecture of its buildings, the quality of its housing, the location of its public facilities, and the layout of its transportation routes.

Modern city planning emerged as a response to the deterioration and decay that had been allowed to engulf our cities. Although the history of modern city planning is long and involved, there are several landmarks which should be mentioned. One of these, the emergence of city planning as a professional endeavor, is usually traced to 1917. It was during this year that the American Institute of Planners, the major professional organization to which city planners belong, was founded. At the time of its inception, this organization had twenty-four members: as of 1965 it had a membership af approximately 4,000.[24] This is an impressive rate of growth but even today the demand for professionally trained planners far exceeds the supply. Another significant development has been the growing involvement of the federal government in attempts to cope with the urban crisis. Two pieces of legislation are important in this regard. The first was the Housing Act of 1949 which authorized the federal government to provide grants and loans to cities for the purpose of acquiring and redeveloping blighted residential areas.[25] This act, which was an outgrowth of earlier legislation, also made federal loans available to cities for the purpose of developing previously unused land. Another potentially significant step was the passage of the Demonstration Cities and

[24] American Institute of Planners, *A Challenging Career for You: Urban Planning* (Washington, D.C.: American Institute of Planners, 1965).

[25] For a discussion of urban renewal and the 1949 housing act see Lawrence M. Friedman, *Government and Slum Housing: A Century of Frustration* (Chicago: Rand McNally & Company, 1968), especially Chapter IV. The interested reader might also consult Herbert J. Gans, "The Failure of Urban Renewal: A Critique and Some Proposals," *Commentary* (April, 1965), pp. 29–37.

Theories of Community

Metropolitan Development Act of 1966. According to officials of the U.S. Department of Housing and Urban Development, this legislation

> provides for a new program designed to demonstrate how the living environment and the general welfare of people living in slum and blighted neighborhoods can be substantially improved in cities of all sizes and in all parts of the country. It calls for a comprehensive attack on social, economic and physical problems in selected slum and blighted areas through the most effective and economical concentration and coordination of Federal, State, and local public and private efforts.[26]

Whether the Demonstration Cities and Metropolitan Development Act will eventually fulfill its promises depends upon the degree to which it is adequately funded and the degree to which imaginative, creative planning occurs at the local level.

Problems and Procedures in City Planning. That city planning represents a means of bringing about planned change should be obvious. The competent city planner seeks through purposeful action to create a more satisfactory physical environment in which urbanites can live, work, and play. It is because of this that city planning is often viewed as a problem-solving profession along with social work, psychiatry, medicine, and the other helping professions.

To be more specific, there are several major problem areas of concern to city planners. First, they must wrestle continually with problems centering around transportation and traffic congestion. The private automobile is supreme in our society; as a result, our cities have become nerve-wracking asphalt jungles. This means that the city planner, along with traffic engineers, must engage in an endless search for new and more efficient methods of accommodating the ever-increasing volume of traf-

[26] U.S. Department of Housing and Urban Development, *Improving the Quality of Urban Life: A Program Guide to Model Neighborhoods in Demonstration Cities* (Washington, D.C.: U.S. Government Printing Office, 1966), p. 1.

fic.[27] Closely related to this problem is that of urban sprawl. William H. Whyte, for example, points out that "already huge patches of once green countryside have turned into vast, smog-filled deserts that are neither city, suburb, nor country, and each day—at the rate of 3,000 acres a day—more countryside is being bulldozed under."[28] That urban sprawl and problems of traffic congestion are closely related should be obvious. It was the automobile which made possible the suburbanization of American cities and it is the automobile-driving suburbanite who both morning and night clogs our city streets and highways. Thirdly, there is not a major city in the United States that has been completely exempt from problems of blight and deterioration. This blight and deterioration manifests itself in shabby slum housing, decayed buildings, and patches of unused land which become trash-strewn eyesores. Finally, there are many cities within which public facilities are woefully inadequate. Public buildings are inaccessible and overcrowded, parks and playgrounds fail to meet the needs of their users, and other public facilities are unsafe and/or outmoded.

There are several tools that city planners can use in their efforts to solve some of these problems. Usually the first step in city planning is to develop a comprehensive master plan. Very briefly, the master plan represents the planner's window to the future. Ideally, it is based upon population projections, economic forecasts, and other estimates which give the planner some clue as to what will happen to the city as it continues to grow. The master plan of course should make specific proposals for the orderly development of unused land within the city. In addition, plans should be made for the improvement of transportation systems, the development and improvement of public

---

[27] For further discussion see Francis Bello, "The City and the Car," in The Editors of *Fortune, The Exploding Metropolis* (Garden City, N.Y.: Doubleday & Company, Inc., 1958), pp. 53–80; and Lewis Mumford, *The Highway and the City* (New York: Mentor Books, 1963), especially Chapter 22.

[28] William H. Whyte, Jr., "Urban Sprawl," in The Editors of *Fortune, The Exploding Metropolis,* p. 133.

facilities, and the rehabilitation of blighted areas. Last but not least, the master plan might well contain some proposals for beautifying the city, in addition to providing for the renovation of blighted and unsightly areas.[29]

Even the most carefully developed master plan is absolutely worthless unless some of its provisions can be implemented. However, the tools that the planner can use to achieve the goals outlined in the master plan are rather limited. About the most common method by which municipal governments attempt to assure the orderly development of land within their jurisdiction is through the enactment of zoning ordinances.[30] These ordinances simply specify the uses to which various tracts of land within the city may be put. One tract may be reserved for commercial development, another for light industry, a third for single-family dwelling units, and so forth. Ordinances of this type can be effective in achieving desirable community goals when they are used in conjunction with rigorously enforced building codes. Today many municipal governments have the power to set structural and safety standards for new buildings, and even to regulate architectural styles. These codes are enforced by requiring builders to obtain a building permit and by on-site inspections while construction is in progress. When zoning ordinances and building codes are used in combination, they allow the city and its planners (1) to control the uses to which urban lands are put and (2) to regulate the quality and appearance of buildings that are constructed within each zoning area.

Direct action is the other major tool that municipal governments can use in making the master plan a reality. American cities will become bearable places in which to live only if local

[29] For a description of the typical master plan and a discussion of some of the limitations of master planning see Herbert J. Gans, "Regional and Urban Planning," in David Sills (ed.), *International Encyclopedia of the Social Sciences* (New York: The Macmillan Company, 1968), Vol. XII, pp. 129–37.

[30] For a thorough analysis of zoning in the United States see Richard F. Babcock, *The Zoning Game: Municipal Practices and Policies* (Madison: The University of Wisconsin Press, 1966).

governments, with the help of government at the state and federal level, channel billions of dollars into massive programs of slum clearance and the construction of public housing, modern transportation systems, and a variety of other public facilities. One tool which makes it possible for local government to carry out projects of this type is its right of eminent domain. Very briefly, this means that the city can requisition privately owned land, providing that its owner is paid a fair price. It is only through the exercise of this right that city government can acquire land for new highways, housing projects, parks, and other public facilities.

Obstacles to City Planning. We have said that there are two basic ways by which the goals of the city planner can be made a reality. First, local government can place controls on the use of land and regulate building practices. Second, if funds are available and if the political climate is right, the municipal government can use direct action to change the city as a physical entity. Nonetheless, there are many obstacles that the city planner must overcome. The task of assuring the rational, orderly development of our cities and metropolitan areas is a difficult one.

A thorough discussion of all the obstacles that are encountered by city planners is beyond the scope of this chapter. However, two of the most important ones must be briefly mentioned. First, the city planner must constantly deal with vested interest groups. In most cities there are at least a few individuals who stand to lose if the master plan is implemented fully. This is particularly true in respect to slum clearance. Slum housing is frequently owned by private investors who are able to charge high rents while doing little to maintain or improve their property. Irwin T. Sanders is undoubtedly correct, however, when he points out that vested interest groups are not always motivated by a desire for personal gain.[31] Sometimes well-intentioned citizens demand programs and projects that are desirable in

[31] Irwin T. Sanders, *The Community: An Introduction to a Social System,* 2nd ed. (New York: The Ronald Press, 1966), p. 501.

themselves but that do not dovetail with the master plan. For example, a group of citizens may urge the city government to locate a park on a plot of land that is earmarked for industrial development. When situations of this type arise, the city planner must exercise his public relations skills and present the master plan to the public in an open-minded but nonetheless persuasive manner.

The existence of vested interest groups is only one obstacle to intelligent city planning. An even greater problem lies in the fact that the area over which the city planner has authority is frequently smaller than the area which requires unified planning. In short, the city planner's authority usually ends at the city limits, whereas the city as a physical entity does not. Rather, the city often merges into numerous suburban communities that are politically independent and that refuse to participate in any effort at metropolitan planning. Richard L. Meier points out some of the problems that this entails when he suggests that,

> Most of the best ideas for improving the city, including the siting of a new industry, the levying of a new tax, or the establishment of an institution for higher education, can be blocked by a handful of small communities that feel they would get nothing from a project for themselves, or fear that it might "hurt" them at some time in the future.[32]

So far efforts to cope with problems of this type have had only limited success. One of the most hopeful approaches has been the merger of various local governments into one over-all metropolitan government. This in itself can be a tremendously difficult task. Very often the proposed consolidation is vigorously opposed by groups who fear an increase in taxes and a decrease in local autonomy at one and the same time.[33]

[32] Richard L. Meier, *Developmental Planning* (New York: McGraw-Hill Book Company, 1965), p. 390.

[33] There is a vast reservoir of literature relating to metropolitan government and the difficulties which confront it. Some of this literature is reprinted in Philip B. Coulter (ed.), *Politics of Metropolitan Areas: Selected Readings* (New York: Thomas Y. Crowell Company, 1967), and in Michael N. Danielson, *Metropolitan Politics: A Reader.*

Community Organization

Community organization is another approach to planned community change which we must briefly consider. The nature of this type of planned change is made clear by C. F. McNeil when he states that "community organization has been defined as the process of bringing about and maintaining a progressively more effective adjustment between social welfare resources and social welfare needs within a geographic area or functional field." [34] This definition suggests that community organization is an activity that is carried on by social workers and by persons in closely related fields. These persons may be employed by the United Fund, community welfare councils, religious and other private agencies, and a variety of social action groups. In addition, many of the duties that experts in community organization perform on a full-time basis are among the part-time activities of caseworkers and group workers. Likewise, McNeil's definition also suggests that the goals of community organization are usually achieved by bringing community resources to bear upon its unmet needs. It is safe to assume that every community has some gaps in the health and welfare services that it provides for its citizens. At the same time, most communities have at least a few resources that can be used to fill these gaps.

With these preliminary comments in mind, we may examine some of the more concrete goals that the expert in community organization may pursue.[35] In so doing we must remember that

[34] C. F. McNeil, "Community Organization for Social Welfare," in *Social Work Yearbook,* 1951 ed. (New York: American Association of Social Workers, 1951), p. 123. For further discussion of definitions of community organization see Ernest B. Harper and Arthur Dunham, *Community Organization in Action: Literature and Critical Comments* (New York: Association Press, 1959), pp. 54–59, 63–64.

[35] The analysis presented below is similar to that offered by Murray G. Ross. See his *Community Organization: Theory and Principles,* 2nd ed. (New York: Harper & Row, 1967), pp. 203–24. For a different approach see Jack Rothman, "An Analysis of Goals and Roles in Community Organization," *Social Work,* 9 (April, 1964), pp. 24–31.

community organization, like city planning, is a type of instigated social change. It represents a way of modifying and improving health and welfare services at the local level.

To be more specific, the expert in community organization
may define his goals in essentially three ways. First, he may see
his task as that of pursuing a very specific limited objective. If
he is the director of the local United Fund, he may define his
job as that of raising a certain amount of money during the
annual fund-raising campaign. Similarly, he may be aware of
the need for a mental health center in his community and direct
his efforts toward convincing other people that a facility of this
type should be created. More generally, the expert in community organization may define his goal as that of strengthening community health and welfare systems by creating a new
agency, adding to the services rendered by a specific agency,
or by bringing about a specific reform in social work practice.
However, he never does this by forcing the public or its social
agencies to accept the proposed innovation. Rather, he attempts
to involve the public and its social agencies in the decision-
making process and in bringing about the desired change.

Secondly, the expert in community organization may see his
job as that of coordinating and strengthening social agencies
which already exist. In larger communities, one often finds that
there are several agencies which provide identical services and
which therefore compete for clients. For example, it is quite
common to find that a department of child welfare, a guidance
clinic, and a mental health center all furnish psychiatric services
for children. At the same time, there may be other needs that
are left unmet or that are not adequately met because the area
of competence and responsibility of the various agencies has
not been clearly defined. If this is the case, the community organization worker can encourage the competing agencies to develop a more satisfactory division of labor. The department of
child welfare might agree to refer all children with severe behavioral disorders to the guidance clinic, the guidance clinic

could refer its adult clients to the mental health center, and so forth. This simple reshuffling of clients can free each agency to render superior service in its area of competence.

The coordinative goals of community organization of course may flow in other directions. Instead of focusing upon the waste and inefficiency caused by a duplication of services, the expert in community organization may encourage several agencies to pool their resources in order to solve a particular problem. In short, he might initiate a concerted interagency attack on a growing community problem such as juvenile delinquency, mental illness, or whatever. Needless to say, if the worker is to achieve this type of coordination, he must elicit the support and participation of the appropriate agencies. The coordination of welfare services is something which can only be done by the agencies themselves. The most that the worker can do is to encourage and facilitate the process of interagency cooperation.

Finally, about the most significant task of the expert in community organization is to foster public involvement in solving social problems and in improving welfare services. There seems to be two reasons why the "public involvement" component of community organization is becoming increasingly important. First, most welfare agencies must receive financial and other types of support from the communities in which they are located. It is safe to assume that taxpayers will only tolerate the expenditures of public agencies if they are convinced that these agencies are rendering valuable services. The same thing is true in respect to supporting private agencies. The expert in community organization can help to elicit this support by encouraging public participation in setting welfare goals and in ameliorating social problems. Secondly, it is now recognized that some programs of social and economic rehabilitation demand mass public involvement if they are to be successful. Indeed, many of the new federal programs such as the Model Cities Demonstration Act and some of those authorized by the Economic Opportunity Act of 1964 require public participation in initiating, planning, and carrying the project through to completion. The community organization worker has skills that can be used to secure this participation.

Community Action and Community Development

The terms *community action* and *community development* refer to the voluntary efforts of local citizens to achieve a goal they desire for themselves, their neighborhood, or their community. Because we discussed community action theory in the preceding chapter, it need not be considered further. However, programs of community action and community development may be of several types. Two of these are directly relevant to planned community change. Because they represent types of planned change, something must be said about the approach to community action and development that is advocated by Saul Alinsky and about the community action program authorized by the Economic Opportunity Act of 1964.

Saul Alinsky and the "Power Bloc" Approach. There is probably no name more closely associated with a "radical" approach to community action than that of Saul Alinsky.[36] Basically, Alinsky argues that in a democracy the poor and the disadvantaged will only be heard if they organize themselves into effective "power blocs." His basic assumption is that the local power structure (i.e., "the establishment") will do little for the poor unless it is forced to do so. Therefore, the poor must become organized to the point that they can confront, negotiate, and bargain with this power structure on equal terms.[37] However, the poor usually cannot do this on their own. Rather,

> The mean and difficult job of building the organization must
> be handled by professionals who know how to deal with the
> apathy of the slum and who can find a way of bringing its

[36] Alinsky outlines his basic approach in his *Reveille for Radicals* (Chicago: University of Chicago Press, 1946). For a very brief review of Alinsky's "power bloc" approach see Robert A. Dentler, *American Community Problems,* pp. 84–87.

[37] See Dentler, ibid., p. 84.

disparate fragments together into a working whole for more often than not, the indigenous leaders of the slum area are out of touch with one another, and only very rarely do they possess the skills to set up a large organization and keep it running.[38]

This is where Alinsky and his associates enter the picture. It is their task to search out indigenous leaders, to help them create power organizations, and to teach them the skills entailed in the politics of confrontation. At the same time, Alinsky does not consider himself to be an outside agitator. Rather, he is convinced that the essence of democracy lies in a confrontation between the strong and the weak. He would maintain that when he encourages the use of direct action techniques such as picketing, rent strikes, and demonstrations, he is helping to make democracy more responsive to the needs of the people.

That the politics of confrontation can be an effective method of inducing change is indisputable. One needs only to read Charles E. Silberman's account of Alinsky's work in Woodlawn, an apathy-filled, problem-ridden Chicago slum, to be convinced of this.[39]

Nonetheless, the use of direct action techniques by the poor has both advantages and limitations. On the positive side, one cannot ignore the sense of purpose and accomplishment that active involvement can give disadvantaged people. At the same time, there is a constant danger that the militant or pseudo-militant use of power by the poor will deepen the distrust and misunderstanding which already exists between the rich and the poor, the white and the nonwhite. This is a risk which may have to be taken, however, because many communities refuse to extend assistance to their disadvantaged citizens on a voluntary basis. All too often the only way the Negro and other disadvantaged groups can obtain help with their problems is through the strong and effective application of power.

[38] Charles E. Silberman, "Up from Apathy: The Woodlawn Experiment," *Commentary,* **37** (May, 1964), p. 54.
[39] Ibid., pp. 51–58.

The Community Action Program. On August 20, 1964, Congress passed the Economic Opportunity Act. This act supposedly provided for an all-out war on the poverty which touches the lives of millions of Americans. Among the more important programs that Congress approved were the Job Corps, the Neighborhood Youth Corps, and Volunteers in Service to America (VISTA). In addition, the Act also authorized the president to establish the Office of Economic Opportunity, which would have responsibility for coordinating the anti-poverty efforts of all federal agencies.[40] One of the most significant features of the Economic Opportunity Act was that it authorized federal participation in community action programs.

The purposes of and the philosophy behind the community action program are best captured in President Johnson's "Message on Poverty," which he delivered to Congress on March 16, 1964.

> through a new community action program we intend to strike at poverty at its source—in the streets of our cities and on the farms of our countryside among the very young and the impoverished old.
>
> This program asks men and women throughout the country to prepare long-range plans for the attack on poverty in their own local communities.
>
> These are not plans prepared in Washington and imposed upon hundreds of different situations.
>
> They are based on the fact that local citizens best understand their own problems, and know how to deal with these problems.
>
> These plans will be local plans striking at the many unfilled needs which underlie poverty in each community, not just one or two. Their components and emphasis will differ as needs differ.
>
> These plans will be local plans calling upon all the resources

---

[40] For a more thorough discussion of the programs authorized by the Economic Opportunity Act see Walter A. Friedlander, *Introduction to Social Welfare,* 3rd ed. (Englewood Cliffs, N.J.: Prentice-Hall, Inc., 1968), pp. 324–32.

available to the community—Federal and State, local and private, human and material.

And when these plans are approved by the Office of Economic Opportunity, the federal government will finance up to 90 per cent of the additional cost for the first two years.

The most enduring strength of our nation is the huge reservoir of talent, initiative, and leadership which exists at every level of our society.

Through the community action program we can call upon this, our greatest strength, to overcome our greatest weaknesses.[41]

This statement contains a hint of what many persons hoped would become the two principal components of the Community Action Program. First, the legislation which authorized federal participation in community action programs called for the use of a variety of tools in attacking poverty at the local level. Among other things, participating communities were encouraged to create their own community action boards. These boards, in turn, would enlist the cooperation of schools, welfare agencies, and other community resources in waging a grassroots war on poverty. Secondly, the act also required the "maximum feasible participation" of the poor in planning and executing programs financed by the Office of Economic Opportunity. Although no fixed standards were established, "a developing consensus, both within the agency (OEO) and in Congress, settled on a pattern by which at least one-third of the seats on a community action agency's governing board were to be held by directly selected representatives of the poor." [42] It is only because citizen involvement is required that we can consider federally sponsored community action projects to be a form of community action as it has been defined in this book.

[41] *Message to the Congress of the United States on the Economic Opportunity Act of 1964,* by President Lyndon B. Johnson (March 16, 1964).

[42] David A. Grossman, "The Community Action Program: A New Function for Local Government," in Barnard J. Frieden and Robert Morris (eds.), *Urban Planning and Social Policy* (New York: Basic Books, Inc., 1968), pp. 441–42.

Although the community action program supposedly encourages each community to design programs uniquely suited to its own needs, most of the funds expended on this phase of the war on poverty have gone into "national emphasis programs." The most popular of these has been Head Start. This is a program which gives preschool children from impoverished families an opportunity to enrich their academic and social skills before they enter grade school. Likewise, much of the money that Congress has allocated to the Office of Economic Opportunity has been earmarked for national programs of health care, adult education, and legal aid services. As a result, little money has been left for the funding of programs conceived of at the local level.[43]

It is too soon to render a final verdict on the community action program.[44] However, it seems to be widely agreed that it has not been as successful as might be hoped. Part of this is due to the fact that Congress, in passing the Economic Opportunity Act, simply promised too much and part of it has been due to technical problems such as a lack of adequate budgets and budgeting procedures and the profound misunderstanding which has been generated by the provisions that local community action boards must enlist the maximum feasible participation of the poor in planning and implementing programs. In any event, it seems rather obvious that the Community Action Program as it is presently constituted does not have the potential for actually eliminating poverty in the United States. If this is a goal the United States wishes to pursue, some program of income redistribution must be instigated. This might take the form of a guaranteed annual income and/or massive programs through which federal, state, and local governments create socially useful jobs for the employable poor. At the same time, the critics

[43] Ibid., p. 444.

[44] A number of efforts have been made to evaluate the community action program and the war on poverty. For example, see Louis A. Forman (ed.), "Evaluating the War on Poverty," *The Annals of the American Academy of Political and Social Science,* **385** (September, 1969), pp. 1–156.

of the community action program might be reminded that the war on poverty is only a few years old. In these few years the community action programs have met with some success in bringing needed services to the poor and in developing indigenous leadership capacities.

Community Development in Foreign Countries. The terms *community action* and *community development* mean essentially the same thing. Sometimes, however, the latter term is used to refer specifically to those efforts that are made to assist people in the underdeveloped countries of the world to improve the conditions under which they live. Thus, many of the underdeveloped countries lack even the most basic resources that are required to solve community problems. Neither money nor equipment are available for use in community projects and the capacities of potential community leaders have never been developed. In these resource-barren communities, people represent the only tool that can be utilized in an effort to instigate community change. Community development focuses upon the long-range development of this one resource.

A well-conceived community development program always has at least two goals. Certainly the overriding goal of community development is to encourage people to mobilize whatever resources they may have in an effort to improve conditions at the local level. In a real sense, community development represents a process by which community members are taught to carry out their own programs of planned change. There are many skills which must be learned, but the most important are those of working with other people for the common good, learning to utilize the abilities of indigenous leaders, and learning to make creative use of the meager resources available to the community. The "instructor" in this learning process is either a specialist in a particular field (e.g., agriculture, engineering, and so on) or a generalist who has a broad knowledge of the processes and techniques involved in community development. He may be an employee of the national government under whose jurisdiction the community falls, the government of another country, or a private philanthropic organization.

In addition to its basic goal of encouraging community members to work together in order to solve common problems, community development programs usually have a more specific objective: to build a road or a schoolhouse, to improve the community's water supply, to modernize agricultural practices, and so on. However, these concrete objectives are always subservient to the goal of developing human capacities. The reason that experts in community development place such a strong emphasis upon human capacities is made clear by Curtis and Dorothy Mial when they suggest that "since the job of building better communities is not likely ever to be finished, the real goal of community development cannot be the solution of any specific problem but the development of people who can continue to take leadership responsibly and wisely.[45]

Summary

We began this chapter by assuming that there is an intimate relationship between community change and community problems. Indeed, all community problems have a cause, and sometimes this is a change in some aspect of community structure. That many of the problems which plague modern communities are the result of rapid change should be obvious. Among the more important types of change which have given rise to community problems are rapid population growth, industrialization, and the mass movement of people into large metropolitan areas.

From the welter of changes which have occurred at the community level, we have identified urbanization as being the most important. Not too many years ago most Americans lived in small communities and were uniformly rural in their values, attitudes, and patterns of behavior. Today the majority of Americans live in large cities and metropolitan areas and the lives of all Americans are touched by what might be called a

[45] Curtis and Dorothy Mial, "Community Development—USA," *International Review of Community Development*, No. 4 (1959), p. 14. Irwin T. Sanders sheds further light on the nature of community development. See his "Theories of Community Development," *Rural Sociology*, **23** (March, 1958), pp. 1–12.

metropolitan culture. Much the same is true in countries throughout the world. We have argued of course that urbanization is best viewed as a derivative effect of other changes, the most important of which have been the agricultural revolution and the improvement of methods of transportation and communication. These changes can be traced to yet other types of change.

Finally, we have suggested that the only solution to most community problems is to stimulate yet further change. Indeed, the term *solve* implies that change is purposefully used to alleviate a problem. Sometimes the required change occurs spontaneously and the problem solves itself. However, most community problems do not simply disappear with the passage of time. If most of the problems which plague modern American communities are to be solved, the required changes must be instigated. Because of this, three different types of planned community change have been discussed in this chapter. Not all students of the community will agree with the distinctions the present writer has drawn between city planning, community organization, and community action and development. Although there is wide agreement as to the nature of city planning, the other three terms are often used interchangeably. Nonetheless, one of the purposes of this book is conceptual clarification and the terms *city planning, community organization,* and *community action* and *development* supposedly do refer to different types of planned community change. At the same time, the rather rigid distinctions that have been drawn between these three types of planned change are useful for conceptual purposes only. In attempting to solve their problems, success will come only to those communities which utilize a proper blend of city planning, community organization, and community action and development.

Bibliography

Alinsky, Saul. *Reveille for Radicals.* Chicago: University of Chicago Press, 1946.

Allen, Francis R. *Socio-cultural Dynamics: An Introduction to Social Change.* New York: The Macmillan Company, 1971.

—————— et al. *Technology and Social Change*. New York: Apple-ton-Century-Crofts, 1957.

Babcock, Richard F. *The Zoning Game: Municipal Practices and Policies*. Madison: University of Wisconsin Press, 1966.

Clinard, Marshall. *Slums and Community Development: Experiments in Self-help*. New York: The Free Press, 1966.

Conkin, Paul K. *Tomorrow a New World: The New Deal Community Program*. Ithaca, N.Y.: Cornell University Press, 1959.

Coulter, Philip B. (ed.). *Politics of Metropolitan Areas: Selected Readings*. New York: Thomas Y. Crowell Company, 1967.

Cowgill, Donald O. "Trends in Residential Segregation of Non-Whites in American Cities: 1940–1950," *American Sociological Review*, **21** (February, 1956), pp. 43–47.

Dentler, Robert A. *American Community Problems*. New York: McGraw-Hill Book Company, 1968.

Editors of *Fortune*. *The Exploding Metropolis*. Garden City, N.Y.: Doubleday & Company, Inc., 1958.

Franklin, Richard (ed.). *Patterns of Community Development*. Washington, D.C.: Public Affairs Press, 1966.

Forman, Louis A. (ed.). "Evaluating the War on Poverty," *The Annals of the American Academy of Political and Social Science*, **385** (September, 1969), pp. 1–156.

Friedman, Lawrence M. *Government and Slum Housing: A Century of Frustration*. Chicago: Rand McNally & Company, 1968.

Gans, Herbert J. "The Failure of Urban Renewal: A Critique and Some Proposals," *Commentary* (April, 1965), pp. 29–37.

——————, *People and Plans: Essays on Urban Problems and Solutions*. New York: Basic Books, 1968.

——————. "Regional and Urban Planning," in David Sills (ed.), *International Encyclopedia of the Social Sciences*. New York: The Macmillan Company, 1968.

Gilmore, Harlan W. *Transportation and the Growth of Cities*. New York: The Free Press, 1953.

Glabb, Charles N., and A. Theodore Brown. *A History of Urban America*. New York: The Macmillan Company, 1967.

Goodman, Percival, and Paul Goodman. *Communitas: Means of Livelihood and Ways of Life*. Chicago: University of Chicago Press, 1947.

Hoiberg, Otto G. "Contributions of the Social Scientist to Community Development," in Marvin B. Sussman (ed.), *Community*

Structure and Analysis. New York: Thomas Y. Crowell Company, 1959.

Jacobs, Jane. *The Death and Life of Great American Cities.* New York: Random House, 1961.

Kramer, Ralph M. *Participation of the Poor: Comparative Case Studies in the War on Poverty.* Englewood Cliffs, N.J.: Prentice-Hall, Inc., 1969.

Loewenstein, Louis K. (ed.). *Urban Studies: An Introductory Reader.* New York: The Free Press, 1971.

McEntire, Davis. *Race and Residence.* Berkeley: University of California Press, 1960.

Mumford, Lewis. *The City in History: Its Origins, Its Transformations, and Its Prospects.* New York: Harcourt Brace Jovanovich, Inc., 1961.

————. *The Highway and the City.* New York: Mentor Books, 1963.

Ogburn, William F. "How Technology Causes Social Change," in Francis R. Allen et al. *Technology and Social Change.* New York: Appleton-Century-Crofts, 1957.

————. *On Culture and Social Change,* edited and with an introduction by Otis Dudley Duncan. Chicago: University of Chicago Press, 1964.

————. *Social Change.* New York: B. W. Huebsh, 1922.

Perloff, Harvey S. "Common Goals and the Linking of Physical and Social Planning," in American Society for Planning Officials and the Community Planning Association of Canada, *Planning, 1965.* Chicago: American Society of Planning Officials, 1965.

Reps, John W. *The Making of Urban America: A History of City Planning in America.* Princeton, N.J.: Princeton University Press, 1965.

Rodwin, Lloyd. "The Roles of the City Planner in the Community," in Charles R. Adrian (ed.), *Social Science and Community Action.* East Lansing: Michigan State University Press, 1960.

Ross, Murray G. *Community Organization: Theory and Principles,* 2nd ed. New York: Harper & Row, 1967.

Sanders, Irwin T. "Theories of Community Development," *Rural Sociology,* **23** (March, 1958), pp. 1–12.

Silberman, Charles E. "Up from Apathy: The Woodlawn Experiment," *Commentary,* **37** (May, 1964), pp. 51–58.

Strange, John H. "Racial Segregation in the Metropolis," in Michael N. Danielson (ed.), *Metropolitan Politics: A Reader*. Boston: Little, Brown and Company, 1966.

Webber, Melvin M. "Comprehensive Planning and Social Responsibility," *Journal of the American Institute of Planners*, **29** (November, 1963), pp. 232–41.

three
Research and Community Study

In the preceding chapters we have considered essentially the same kind of information that is presented in most courses of the community. If there is anything new and unique about these chapters, it lies in the way they are organized. The remaining two chapters, however, deal with topics that are not always covered in courses on the community. Specifically, an effort is made to introduce the student to some of the most significant empirical studies of community life and to show him how the sociologist does research on the community. This is done in the belief that instruction in research methods, if it is to be meaningful, must be incorporated into every course the student takes.

It is hoped that Chapter 8 will encourage the student to think things, we examine the relationship between research and theory about why research on communities is important. Among other building as two components of community study and consider the role that scientifically trained researchers might play in helping a community to solve its problems. Some attention is also focused upon the question of whether a community, if it is selected carefully, can serve as a "sample" of the society and culture of which it is a part. Furthermore, in this chapter the reader is also introduced to some of the most widely heralded studies of community life. It must be stressed that these introductions are brief. The only satisfactory way to get acquainted with these studies is to read them on one's own.

In the concluding chapter of this book we explore some of the methods by which community studies have been conducted, i.e., through the use of participant observation, social surveys, and records and documents. Our emphasis is not on the techniques that each of these methodological approaches entail. Rather, consideration is given to the basic characteristics of each of these methods, what types of data they yield, and where their advantages and limitations lie. It is hoped that this chapter will be useful to students who wonder how social scientists "know what they know" and to those students who would like to begin exploring their own communities on a scientific level.

Research on Community Life

The construction of theories has a very important role to play in our quest for knowledge about communities. Without human ecology, social system theory, and the other approaches to community analysis we have discussed, our knowledge of community structure and process would consist of little more than a chaotic assortment of findings and observations. If these raw data are to constitute a meaningful whole, they must be organized into a coherent explanatory system. This is the function of theory, i.e., to make clear the relationship between what might at first appear to be unrelated bits of information. At the same time, the mere construction of theoretical systems does not yield scientific knowledge. Rather, scientific knowledge results when our data are collected and processed in certain clearly prescribed ways. Because of this we must turn our attention to research as a component of community study.

Research and Community Study

During the hours in which they are awake, human beings constantly acquire information or "data." We read about community affairs in the newspaper, on Sunday drives we observe how "the other half" lives, and we communicate with our neighbors about topics of mutual interest. This does not mean, however, that all our knowledge is scientific or that anyone can do research. Thus, the unique features of research as a method of acquiring knowledge must be explored.

The Nature of Research

Sometimes the meaning of a term seems so obvious that nobody takes time to define it. The term *research* apparently falls into this category. Most textbooks on methods of social research simply do not delve into the question of what research is or how it differs from other methods of gaining knowledge. One exception is a textbook by Wilson Gee.[1] Although Gee does not offer his own definition of research, he does provide us with a sampling of those definitions that have been developed by other writers. Even though each author's definition is somewhat unique, there seems to be unanimous agreement that research involves "a searching, investigation, or inquiry, presumably of a careful nature, for new knowledge, or at least a new arrangement and interpretation of existing knowledge." [2] This is implied, for example, in Frederic A. Ogg's assertion that "man learns a good many things by accident—by simply stumbling upon them. In the main, however, he adds to his knowledge by definite, deliberate inquiry—by coming up against a question or a problem and casting about for an answer or solution. This process of conscious, premeditated inquiry we call research." [3]

We shall not attempt to derive our own definition of research. To do so would take us too far away from our main concern, i.e., *the bearing of research on community study*. Perhaps it will suffice to say that research entails the systematic collection of raw data that are, in turn, converted into findings and principles. We should also note that from an analytical standpoint, research has two different facets. First, research involves the use of a

---

[1] See Wilson Gee, *Social Science Research Methods* (New York: Appleton-Century-Crofts, Inc., 1950). Chapter IV of Gee's book is entitled "The Meaning of Research."

[2] Ibid., p. 128.

[3] Cited in ibid., p. 127.

wide variety of methods, procedures, and techniques. These are the tools that the researcher utilizes in his quest for empirically grounded knowledge. As such, they include the processes by which he collects, analyzes, and presents data. Secondly, the researcher is also expected to incorporate certain values and ethical standards into his work. Persons who engage in any type of scientific research must attempt to be objective, to remain neutral on ethical and moral issues, and to evaluate their findings in a skeptical, critical manner.

The Functions of Research

Before we look at some of the methodological details of conducting research on community structure and process, there are some questions which must be raised. What benefits can be expected to flow from research on community life? Why do social scientists spend time and money on studies of both rural and urban communities? These questions can be answered by examining the role that research plays in the construction of theoretical systems and the contributions it can make to the solution of community problems. We must also consider the proposition that research on particular communities can yield generalizations which apply to the larger society.

Theory and Research in Community Study. It is absolutely essential that we have good theories if meaningful research is to be conducted. Among other things, theory helps the researcher choose relevant problems for investigation and to organize and interpret his data. At the same time, careful research is essential if one is to arrive at scientifically valid theories. There are several reasons why this is the case.

Thus, perhaps the chief function of empirical research is that it helps us to differentiate between scientifically valid theories and other explanations of reality. Without research, for example, there would be no way to determine if cities do display a characteristic ecological structure, nor would it be possible to determine whether many other propositions which have been made about community life are valid. Sjoberg and Nett express essentially the same idea when they suggest that "theory, as a system of concepts or ideas, is of course, not unique to science but is basic to all systems of philosophy and religious thought." [4] However, they further explain that "an essential difference, perhaps the only one, between theories in science and in other belief systems lies in the method of validation employed. Scientific theories are necessarily subject to validation through empirical observation, not by fiat or on the basis of tradition." [5] This is not to imply that all or even most of our theories of community structure and process have been subjected to empirical test. Indeed, some of the most popular theories of community are too broad and loosely articulated to be put to such a test.

In addition to helping the student of community life decide which of his ideas can stand the test of science and which cannot, Robert K. Merton has suggested that research has several other implications for the theorist.[6] In the first place, any piece of research can potentially display what Merton refers to as a serendipity pattern. By this he means that the research may unearth findings that are both unanticipated and strategic and that call for the development of new theory.[7] To cite one example, it has been generally assumed that property values are permanently reduced when nonwhites move into an all-white neighborhood. However, research conducted by Gillette has suggested that this simply is not the case. If anything, the migration of nonwhites into a previously segregated neighborhood serves in the long run to increase property values.[8] Findings of this type not only raise questions concerning the validity of "common-

[4] Gideon Sjoberg and Roger Nett, *A Methodology for Social Research* (New York: Harper & Row, 1968), p. 28.

[5] Ibid., p. 28.

[6] Robert K. Merton, *Social Theory and Social Structure,* rev. ed. (New York: The Free Press, 1957), pp. 102–17.

[7] Ibid., pp. 103–108.

[8] See Thomas L. Gillette, "A Study of the Effects of Negro Invasion on Real Estate Values," *The American Journal of Economics and Sociology,* 16 (January, 1957), pp. 151–62.

sense" knowledge, but they also create a demand for new theory. The fact that the movement of nonwhites into a previously segregated neighborhood increases property values must be explained. Similarly, research findings often force the theorist to modify and improve his theories. Findings which are not incorporated into the theory may keep cropping up. When this happens, the theory eventually must be reformulated.[9]

In addition to the fact that research may compel the social scientist to extend and modify his theories, innovations in research methodology sometimes bring new theoretical problems and previously neglected areas of inquiry to our attention. During recent years, for example, it has once more become popular to do research on the ecological structure of cities and metropolitan areas. This renewed interest in human ecology can be attributed partially to the development of social area analysis as a methodological tool for studying the spatial structure of urban areas. Likewise, empirical research often forces the social scientist to define his concepts carefully. As Merton puts it,

> the clarification of concepts, commonly considered a province peculiar to the theorist, is a frequent result of empirical research. Research sensitive to its own needs cannot easily escape this pressure for conceptual clarification. *For a basic requirement of research is that the concepts, the variables, be defined with sufficient clarity to enable the research to proceed,* a requirement easily and unwittingly not met in the kind of discursive exposition which is often miscalled sociological theory.[10]

Perhaps one reason why many of the concepts that are used by the student of community life are so fuzzy is that much of what has been written about community life consists of "discursive exposition."

Research and Community Problems. In Chapter 7 we considered some of the methods by which community problems can be

[9] Merton, *Social Theory and Social Structure,* p. 108.
[10] Ibid., p. 115. Italics in original.

solved. However, the question of whether sociologists *can* and *should* bring their research skills to bear on the solution of community problems was ignored. That research can be used to find solutions to community problems should be obvious. Among other things, the researcher can supply data upon which intelligent decisions can be based and he can locate and analyze resistance to any changes that the problem-solving activity might entail. That sociologists should use their research skills to help solve community problems is somewhat more debatable. Indeed, we have ignored the proposition that research should be utilized to cope with practical problems until now because it is controversial. Opinions on this issue range all the way from those of sociologists who feel that it would be unprofessional for them to get involved in the nitty-gritty of community problem solving to those who feel that it would be unprofessional for them not to become so involved.

Perhaps one reason sociologists are sometimes reluctant to use their research skills to help a community solve its problems lies in our failure to distinguish between "fact-gathering" and research. Thus, in one instance with which the writer is familiar, a group of citizens asked a sociologist to assist them in pursuing a goal to which they were deeply committed. In this case the citizens sought to further school integration through a busing program and had a pressing need for information on the following questions:

1. How many students must be bused in order to assure that school A will have the same percentage of nonwhite students in its total student body as schools B, C, and D?

2. From which parts of the city should students be selected for busing? (Here the guiding criterion might be to keep at a minimum the average mileage students must travel between home and school.)

3. What will be the per pupil cost of instigating a busing program? For example, how many new buses will the school district have to buy?

Obviously, the sociologist cannot spend the hours that he devotes to professional activities on questions of this type, simply because they hold no promise of extending our knowledge of human society.[11] At the same time, there are questions centering around school desegregation that are both sociologically relevant and that have a bearing upon the practicalities of the problem itself. For example, it might well be asked whether rates of juvenile delinquency and mental illness among nonwhite students would decrease if local schools were integrated. That is, would school integration reduce the magnitude of other community problems? Likewise, the sociologist should be able to answer the question that is asked again and again by middle-class parents: will the presence in the classroom of nonwhite, culturally deprived children eventually lower the quality of education?

It is only by asking questions of this type that the sociologist can make a meaningful contribution to the solution of community problems. Any intelligent citizen can learn to gather facts and answer questions similar to those raised in regard to busing. However, only a professionally trained person knows how to explore the larger implications of community problems and to see them in all their complexity. Furthermore, by viewing problems in a wide perspective, the sociologist can often forge a link between his personal concern for community problems and his professional obligation to engage in research which expands our knowledge of human society.

The Community as a Sample. That research is an essential component of community study should be obvious. Among other things, careful research must be conducted if sociologists are to derive accurate theories of community structure and process. Likewise, the present writer firmly believes that sociologists have some obligation to bring their research skills to bear upon the solution of community problems. However, there is an even more important reason why sociologists select particular communities for intensive study. In short, it has sometimes been assumed that if the sociologist chooses his study communities

[11] Of course he may want to deal with such questions in his role as an interested and conscientious citizen.

with care, then they can serve as a mirror of the society and culture of which they are a part. If this is the case, then the community becomes in effect a sample from which the sociologist can derive generalizations which apply to the larger society and culture. One of the leading spokesmen for the "community as sample" approach, Conrad M. Arensberg, makes this same point when he states that "the community has served as a sample or unit of observation for the study of a culture or society, as a locus or local embodiment of a wider or general social problem or phenomenon, as a testing ground for plans of change, amelioration, or development." [12]

Oddly enough, the merits of the "community as sample" approach have not been vigorously debated. Most students of the community seem to agree that their findings can be generalized to the larger society and culture, assuming that the study community is carefully chosen. Presumably, some communities are more valid "samples" of their society and culture than others. "Communities are," according to Julian H. Steward, "parts of regions and nations. If the formulation of a problem studied in one community is to have significance for other communities or larger groups, the community must be selected on the basis of explicit criteria." [13]

Steward does not discuss the criteria that should be used in selecting a community to serve as a sample of the larger society and culture. However, Conrad M. Arensberg devotes an entire paper to this question. [14] According to Arensberg, a community should possess four basic properties if it is to serve as a sample of the larger universe (i.e., the society and culture). Although these properties are rather complex, they can be summarized as follows:

    1. If a community is to serve as an adequate sample of the

[12] Conrad M. Arensberg, "The Community as Object and as Sample," *American Anthropologist,* **63** (April, 1961), p. 241.

[13] Julian H. Steward, *Area Research: Theory and Practice* (New York: Social Science Research Council, Bulletin 63, 1950), p. 44.

[14] See Arensberg, "The Community as Object and as Sample," pp. 241–64.

larger society and culture, then to some degree it must be *representative* of that society and culture. If the larger society is built around several racial groups and several social classes, then members of each of these racial groups and social classes must be represented in the community. Likewise, if the society is characterized by a high division of labor, then the community must also have a high division of labor. More generally, if a community is to serve as a sample of the larger universe, there must be found within it all the roles and the statuses, the types of actors and the types of groups, that are found in the larger society.

2. If a community is to be an accurate mirror of the larger society, it must display a certain degree of *completeness*. At first glance it may appear that this requirement is almost identical to item 1. This, however, is not the case. Rather, when Arensberg states that the community must display a degree of completeness, he apparently means that it must be distinguishable from other communities. In addition, it must also possess, at least to some extent, all the units of organization typically found in the other communities of which the larger society is composed. If the "typical" community has both slums and suburbs, then both slums and suburbs must be present in the study community.

3. If the results of studies pertaining to a particular community are to be generalized to the larger society, then the study community must display a degree of *inclusiveness*. By this Arensberg means that the study community must possess many of the institutions and cultural traits typical of the larger society. If members of the study community tend to be much more urbane and cosmopolitan than other members of the society, then the community will not do as a sample. Likewise, a community should not be selected as a sample of the larger whole if it lacks an institution which predominates in the larger society. Only a community which displays most of the cultural and institutional traits which characterize the larger society can serve as a microcosm of that society.

4. Finally, if a community is to serve as a valid sample of the larger universe, it must display a degree of *cohesiveness* similar to that of the larger society. If the society is well integrated and closely knit, then the community must display these same traits. At the same time, those cleavages and disunities which characterize the larger society must be reflected in the study community. "A sample community must," according to Arensberg, "reflect both the unities and the fissions . . . of the whole society it mirrors." [15]

Presumably, the researcher who takes these four criteria into account in selecting his study community can assume that his findings will have applicability to other communities and to the larger society. By doing research on carefully selected communities, he can learn about the patterns of interaction and association, the cultural traits, and the personality types which characterize the whole society. At the same time, Arensberg does not argue that the study community must be an exact replica of the larger society. Numbers and proportions are not as important as the fact that the roles and statuses, cultural traits and social cleavages which typify the larger society are, to some extent, reflected in the study community.[16]

We have already pointed out that the community as sample approach has not been vigorously debated. However, it seems clear that the future of community study hinges almost entirely upon whether a carefully selected community can serve as a sample of the larger society. If we conclude that each community is completely unique, then one of the primary reasons for studying the community is lost. Nothing can be learned about other communities or about the larger society by studying community A. On the other hand, if community A is in fact a microcosm of the larger society, then it represents an ideal setting in which to conduct research. A balanced view probably

[15] Ibid., p. 260.
[16] See ibid., pp. 255–60.

lies somewhere between these two extremes. Every community is unique to some extent. To maintain that any community faithfully and without distortion mirrors the larger society would seem to be foolhardy. On the other hand, it seems reasonable to assume that communities, like personality types, are to some extent a reflection of the society and culture of which they are a part. If the researcher uses a particular community to sample the larger society, his first task is to distinguish between those features that are unique to the local community and those that are local manifestations of the larger society and culture.

The Varieties of Community Research:
A Review of Literature

Before we examine some of the methods by which communities can be studied, a few of the more notable studies of community life should be examined briefly. This review is necessary for one reason: it will introduce the reader to the types of research problems which have engaged the attention of students of the community. Until we can visualize some of the questions which can feasibly be explored at the community level, our knowledge of research methods will do us little good. Space prevents us from considering all the community studies that have been published. *It also prevents us from dealing in great detail with the studies that we do consider.* The only fully satisfactory way to become acquainted with these studies is to read them on one's own. However, the reader who wishes to supplement the present review should consult the articles and chapters that have been written by Hollingshead, Steward, and Simpson.[17]

---

[17] See August B. Hollingshead, "Community Research: Development and Present Conditions," *American Sociological Review*, **13** (April, 1948), pp. 136–46; Julian H. Steward, *Area Research*, pp. 20–43; and Richard L. Simpson, "Sociology of the Community: Current Status and Prospects," *Rural Sociology*, **30** (June, 1965), pp. 127–49.

Research on Community Structure and Dynamics

One important type of community research focuses upon community structure and dynamics. Because this type of research asks what life is like and how it is organized in particular communities, it might be argued that only those studies which fall into this category are representative of community research in the strictest sense of the word. Indeed, these studies do tend to be holistic, i.e., they "have in common the effort to understand the community as a totality." [18] There are of course several different types of study which fall into this broad category.

Ethnographic Research. Ethnographic research represents one major approach to the study of community structure and dynamics. Indeed, the term *ethnographic* implies that the investigator attempts to describe the community as a totality and to see the manifold and complex interrelations between its parts. One of the best examples of an American community study which takes an ethnographic approach is the Lynds' study of Middletown, which, according to the researchers, "proceeds on the assumption that all the things people do in the American city may be viewed as falling under one or another of the following six main-trunk activities: Getting a living, making a home, training the young, using leisure in various forms of play, art, and so on, engaging in religious practices, engaging in community activities." [19] The fact that the Lynds devote several chapters to an analysis of each of these activities as they were carried out in an Indiana community during the mid-1920's makes it clear that they did seek to understand their study community as a whole. Other famous investigations which take an essentially ethnographic approach are James West's study of

18 Simpson, ibid., p. 129.

19 Robert S. Lynd and Helen Merrell Lynd, *Middletown: A Study in American Culture* (New York: Harcourt Brace Jovanovich, Inc., 1929), p. 4. The Lynd's second study, conducted during the mid-1930's, is also ethnographic in its approach and should not be ignored as a seminal contribution to community research. See *Middletown in Transition* (New York: Harcourt Brace Jovanovich, Inc., 1937).

Plainville, a small Missouri farm community, and Redfield's studies of communities located on the Yucatan Peninsula.[20] Even though they focus upon subcommunities rather than upon an entire city, Wirth's study of *The Ghetto,* Whyte's *Street Corner Society,* and Herbert J. Gans' study of the *Urban Villagers* are definitely ethnographic in nature.[21]

Research on Social Stratification. Another set of studies which focus upon community structure and dynamics is made up of those which investigate patterns of social stratification at the local level. The best known of these are three studies conducted by Lloyd Warner and his associates: a study of a New England town with a population of about 17,000 (Yankee City), a study of a Southern town of about 10,000 population (Old City), and a study of a Midwestern town with a population of about 6,000 (Jonesville).[22] The most striking feature of these studies is the thoroughgoing manner in which the investigators describe and explore the class system of each community. Among other things, Warner maintains that the six classes he identifies (upper-upper, the lower-upper, the upper-middle, the lower-middle, the upper-lower, and the lower-lower) are real entities to which local residents themselves attach significance [23] and

[20] See James West, *Plainville, U.S.A.* (New York: Columbia University Press, 1945); and Robert Redfield, *The Folk Culture of Yucatan* (Chicago: University of Chicago Press, 1941). We reviewed Redfield's work in Chapter 4.

[21] Louis Wirth, *The Ghetto* (Chicago: University of Chicago Press, 1928); William Foote Whyte, *Street Corner Society* (Chicago: University of Chicago Press, 1955); Herbert J. Gans, *The Urban Villagers* (New York: The Free Press, 1962).

[22] The Yankee City studies include, among others, W. Lloyd Warner and Paul S. Lunt, *The Social Life of a Modern Community* (New Haven: Yale University Press, 1941), and W. Lloyd Warner and Paul S. Lunt, *The Status System of a Modern Community* (New Haven: Yale University Press, 1942). The results of the Old City study are presented in Allison Davis, Burleigh B. Gardner, and Mary R. Gardner, *Deep South* (Chicago: University of Chicago Press, 1941); and of the Jonesville study in W. Lloyd Warner and Associates, *Democracy in Jonesville* (New York: Harper & Row, 1949).

[23] Warner and Associates, *Democracy in Jonesville,* p. xiv.

that these classes exist throughout the country.[24] Furthermore, Warner and his associates are responsible for developing two methods for determining the social rank an individual holds.[25] Both of these indexes draw our attention to significant aspects of social ranking, but both have been subjected to heavy criticism.[26]

There have been a number of other studies which investigate various aspects of stratification at the local level. One study often hailed as a classic is August Hollingshead's analysis of Elmtown.[27] In summarizing the findings of this study, Hollingshead states that,

> On the basis of the data presented, certain tentative conclusions appear to be warranted. First, each of the five strata, as delimited by the procedures used, has a distinct subculture. Second, identification with a given class or stratum is dependent upon the possession of a constellation of appropriate traits. Third, the members of each class participate in community activities in significantly different ways from the members of other classes.[28]

A more recent analysis of stratification at the local level is Arthur Vidich and Joseph Bensman's study of Springdale, a small community in upstate New York.[29] This study is signifi-

---

[24] Ibid., pp. xiv–xv.

[25] W. Lloyd Warner, Marchia Meeker, and Kenneth Eels, *Social Class in America* (Chicago: Science Research Associates, 1949).

[26] For example, see Harold W. Pfautz and Otis Dudley Duncan, "A Critical Evaluation of Warner's Work in Stratification," *American Sociological Review,* **15** (April, 1950), pp. 205–15, and Oswald Hall, "Review of Social Class in America," *American Journal of Sociology,* **56** (January, 1951), pp. 366–68.

[27] August B. Hollingshead, *Elmtown's Youth* (New York: John Wiley & Sons, Inc., 1949). Warner's Jonesville and Hollingshead's Elmtown are the same community.

[28] August B. Hollingshead, "Selected Characteristics of Classes in a Middle Western Community," *American Sociological Review,* **12** (August, 1947), p. 395.

[29] Arthur J. Vidich and Joseph Bensman, *Small Town in Mass Society* (Princeton, N.J.: Princeton University Press, 1958).

cant for two reasons. First, the authors improve upon earlier studies by recognizing that various groups of approximately equal social rank may still differ markedly from each other in values and behavior. College professors, for example, may have little in common with local businessmen, even though both groups may earn about the same income, live in the same neighborhood, and be ranked in about the same way by other members of the community. The Springdale study, unlike earlier ones, takes this horizontal dimension of social differentiation into account. Secondly, Vidich and Bensman recognize that Springdale is profoundly influenced by decisions made at the societal level and that local residents are in no way the "masters" of their own fate. One of the major weaknesses of earlier community studies lies in their failure to take into account the fact that modern communities are not isolated, self-contained entities. Rather, they are small nodes in that infinitely complex web of relationships we call mass society.

Research on Race Relations. A final type of study which focuses upon community structure and dynamics is that which considers race relations at the local level. Among the most famous of these are John Dollard's *Caste and Class in a Southern Town* [30] and the study of Old City we referred to previously. Although both of these studies are concerned with social stratification, focusing as they do upon caste and class structures in small Southern communities, their greatest contribution lies in the thoroughgoing analysis of Southern race relations that they provide. To be more specific, *Deep South* presents an in-depth picture of the manner in which mechanisms of social control can be used to perpetuate a caste system of race relations, even though this entails the violation of values that are basic to a democratic society. This study also suggests that a caste system can only be maintained in an essentially rural setting and that the caste system of race relations found in the Deep South will

[30] John Dollard, *Caste and Class in a Southern Town* (New Haven: Yale University Press, 1937).

probably erode away as this region becomes more urbanized. The years which have passed since Davis and the Gardners collected their data suggest that they were prophets in a sense. Dollard's study is of particular interest in that it attempts, through the use of psychoanalytic techniques, to determine the psychological costs and consequences of racism. That these costs are great should be obvious. In his discussion of Dollard's work, for example, Maurice Stein tells us that this "study also deepens our concept of community disorganization in that it shows how an overtly orderly community can exact tremendous emotional penalties from its members. Actually, Southerntown dehumanizes both whites and Negroes so that members of the two castes respond to each other categorically instead of concretely." [31]

The Community as a Variable

About the most common research design in the social sciences is that which analyzes the relationship between two or more variables. It is usually assumed that a change in one variable is the cause of change in another variable. Community studies which utilize this research design are extremely common and therefore we must give some attention to them. There are, for example, a prodigious number of studies which investigate the influence of community size on behavior, attitudes, and values. Similarly, there have been studies which examine the community as it is influenced by changes in other facets of modern society. Studies which exemplify each of these research designs must be examined.

Before we do this, however, it should be noted that some of the studies which examine the correlation between community size and other variables should not be called community studies. They may not shed much light on community structure, and the researchers who conduct them are frequently more interested

[31] Maurice R. Stein, *The Eclipse of Community: An Interpretation of American Studies* (Princeton, N.J.: Princeton University Press, 1960), p. 174.

in the dependent variable than they are in the community. A person who examines the correlation between fertility rates and community size, for example, is usually interested in demographic behavior rather than the sociology of community life. Nonetheless, studies of this type must necessarily be based on the assumption that there is something about communities which causes them to influence human behavior, attitudes, and values. Moreover, it behooves the student of community life to know how people who live in different types of communities think and act and, more importantly, to determine why community size does influence their behavior, attitudes, and values. These comments, of course, do not apply to studies which examine the impact of other variables upon community structure and process. These studies are obviously of relevance to the student of community life because they help us to understand the causes of community change.

The Community as an Independent Variable. The ideal way to study the influence of community size on a dependent variable would be to record changes in the latter as a particular community increases in size or undergoes the transition from rural to urban. Unfortunately, this could take decades and it would probably be impossible to determine whether change in community size really caused the change in the dependent variable. The latter change could be due to the effects of yet a third variable. Hence, those investigators who wish to explore the relationship between community size and other social phenomena are forced to compare communities of varying sizes in terms of the dependent variable. Of course we cannot assume always that differences in community size really explain the observed differences in the dependent variable. It is always possible that the relationship is completely spurious.

In any event, literally hundreds of studies have utilized this research design, so many in fact that we cannot hope to review them all. However, a few examples can be cited. Thus, the National Opinion Research Center has collected data which indicate that persons who live in rural areas are on the whole less likely to join voluntary associations than are persons who live in urban areas.[32] Furthermore, their children may display higher levels of personality adjustment than do the children of urban residents,[33] but they also tend to display lower levels of educational aspiration.[34] In a rather different vein, Alfred Kinsey and his associates have even collected data which suggest that farm boys engage in sexual activities with slightly less frequency than nonfarm boys.[35] Other dependent variables that are frequently the subject of studies of this type are attitudes toward various governmental programs and the incidence of mental illness, crime, and juvenile delinquency. One of the important functions of studies of this type is that they do expose myths. For example, everyone "knows" that rural people are more conservative than urban people. However, a study by John L. Haer suggests that this is not always the case.[36]

Because they generate a certain amount of interest, studies of this type will probably continue to appear. There is reason to suspect, however, that studies which examine the relationship between community size and other social phenomena will become quite meaningless with the passage of time. Research conducted during recent years is making it increasingly evident that many of the hypothesized relationships between community size and other variables do not exist today. This is not surprising. Studies of this type are based on the assumption that rural people are surrounded by a cultural milieu that is quite different

[32] Charles R. Wright and Herbert H. Hyman, "Voluntary Association Membership of American Adults: Evidence from National Sample Surveys," *American Sociological Review,* **23** (June, 1958), pp. 289–91.

[33] A. R. Mangus, "Personality Adjustment of Rural and Urban Children," *American Sociological Review,* **13** (October, 1948), pp. 566–75.

[34] For example, see Archie O. Haller and William H. Sewell, "Residence and Levels of Educational and Occupational Aspiration," *American Journal of Sociology,* **62** (January, 1957), pp. 407–11.

[35] Alfred C. Kinsey, Wardell B. Pomeroy, and Clyde E. Martin, *Sexual Behavior in the Human Male* (Philadelphia: W. B. Saunders Company, 1948), pp. 449–64.

[36] John L. Haer, "Conservatism–Radicalism and the Rural–Urban Continuum," *Rural Sociology,* **17** (December, 1952), pp. 343–47.

from that within which urban people function. This assumption simply does not fit the facts of modern American society. The fusion of rural and urban, at least in the United States, is a *fait accompli*.

The Community as a Dependent Variable. Only a handful of studies have examined the influence that other variables can have upon community life. However, the few studies which do utilize this research design are of utmost interest in that they shed light on some highly significant questions. For example, studies have been conducted which help us to understand what happens to small communities when they undergo rapid industrialization and experience heavy in-migration. Likewise, specialists in business and economic research have attempted to assess the impact which the construction of new highways has on the economic life of communities. Some of these studies must now be examined.

A good place to start is with Lowell J. Carr and James E. Stermer's study of Willow Run, Michigan. In this study the authors indicate some of the things which can happen to a small community when it undergoes extremely rapid industrialization.[37] In 1941 Willow Run was chosen by the Ford Motor Company as the site of "the biggest mass-production bomber plant in the world."[38] Within several months Willow Run was deluged by tens of thousands of factory workers and faced the prodigious task of coping with this gigantic influx of population. The picture which Carr and Stermer paint is a bleak one in which our ability to induce technological change far outstrips our ability to adjust to such changes. Thus, the writers tell us that,

> Willow Run demonstrated that the industrial culture's devices for creating social changes had far outrun its devices for readjusting to these changes. A bomber factory was certainly

[37] Lowell Julliard Carr and James Edson Stermer, *Willow Run: A Study of Industrialization and Cultural Inadequacy* (New York: Harper & Row, 1952).
[38] Ibid., p. 8.

twentieth century. Political answers for technological questions and business as usual in the face of a crisis were both antediluvian, and prescientific. Eighteen hundred trying to master the 1940's was the portent of Willow Run. It was a portent that boded no good for America in the atomic age.[39]

A closely related piece of research was Havighurst and Morgan's study of Seneca, Illinois, another war-boom community.[40] Apparently the people of Seneca reacted to the rapid changes that were thrust upon them in much the same way as the people of Willow Run. This raises the possibility that the findings of these two studies can be generalized to other communities that are exposed to a similar pattern of change. In a somewhat different vein, Rudolf Haberle has analyzed the effects of industrialization on the organization of Southern cities.[41] Although Haberle's paper does not present the results of field research, it makes it clear that industrialization has played a key role in bringing about change in the ecological and class structure of cities in the Southern United States.

Sociologists have conducted relatively little research pertaining to the impact of new, multiple-lane highways upon community life. However, this has been a favorite area of inquiry for specialists in business and economic research. Generally speaking, these studies suggest that new freeways have a favorable impact upon property values and upon the volume of business in the communities through which they pass.[42] The practice of bypassing communities with these freeways does not inevitably spell disaster for local businessmen. For instance, in analyzing the effects of bypassing four Kansas communities with

[39] Ibid., p. 8.

[40] Robert J. Havighurst and H. Gerthen Morgan, *The Social History of a War-Boom Community* (New York: Longmans, Green and Co., 1951).

[41] Rudolf Haberle, "Social Consequences of the Industrialization of Southern Cities," *Social Forces,* **27** (October, 1948), pp. 29–37.

[42] For a summary of relevant findings see H. Kirk Dansereau, "Some Implications of Modern Highways for Community Ecology," in George A. Theodorson (ed.), *Studies in Human Ecology* (New York: Harper & Row, 1961), pp. 175–86.

Research and Community Study

modern highways, Wagner concludes that "the more rapid the growth of the city's economy, the larger the city's size, the less will be the potential economic effect of a bypass highway on the sellers of highway-oriented goods on the old bypassed route." [43] Apparently the construction of a bypass does not in itself cause business reversals. However, if the local economy is already faltering then the bypass may indeed have an adverse effect on business. Similarly, in discussing the impact of highway relocation on Marysville, Washington, Garrison and his associates do not deny that some businesses may have suffered. However, they also point out that,

> the construction of the by-pass highway has made Marysville a somewhat more desirable place to live from the standpoint of residential amenities. It is presumed that this is largely related to the removal of traffic from downtown Marysville streets. This may also be related to the greater ease of access to Everett and other places because of the new highway facility. This should affect the competitive position of Marysville as a site for residential building and consequently the available market for businesses located in Marysville.[44]

There are many other questions that could be asked concerning the impact of new highways on community life. Some of these rather definitely fall into the bailiwick of the sociologist. For example, does the construction of freeways hasten the suburbanization of smaller communities that are located near large cities? One would presume that it does, but little research has been conducted along this line. Likewise, we can assume that many other changes, in both people and communities, result from changes in transportation networks. Indeed, transportation has always had a profound impact on community life.

[43] Hulse Wagner, *The Economic Effects of Bypass Highways on Selected Kansas Communities* (Lawrence, Kansas: The University of Kansas Center for Research in Business, n.d.), p. 44.

[44] William L. Garrison et al., *Studies of Highway Development and Geographic Change* (Seattle: University of Washington Press, 1959), p. 109.

Today most community-oriented research focuses on very specific problems. To be more precise, two aspects of community structure and process have been subjected to intensive investigation during recent years. First, research on community power, leadership, and decision making continues to be exceedingly popular. Secondly, there has been a rather striking resurgence of interest in human ecology, although many of the recent studies have little in common with earlier studies. At the same time, ethnographic studies are not as popular as they once were, even though some excellent work continues to be done. Thus, one study which has earned a great deal of favorable comment during recent years is Elliot Liebow's analysis of *Tally's Corner*.[45] In this study Liebow furnishes the reader with an in-depth picture of the lower-class Negro male and of the cycle of failure and frustration which entraps him. Liebow makes the nature of this cycle clear when he indicates that "the streetcorner man does not appear as a carrier of an independent cultural tradition. His behavior appears not so much as a way of realizing the distinctive goals and values of his own subculture, or of conforming to its models, but rather as his way of trying to achieve many of the goals and values of the larger society, of failing to do this, and of concealing his failure from others and from himself as best he can." [46]

Because many of the recent studies of community power, leadership, and decision making were considered in Chapter 6, anything further said at this point would be repetitious.[47] How-

[45] Elliot Liebow, *Tally's Corner: A Study of Negro Streetcorner Men* (Boston: Little, Brown and Company, 1967).

[46] Ibid., p. 222.

[47] Many of the recent articles on community power, leadership, and decision making have been reprinted and are readily available to the interested reader. For example, see Michael Aiken and Paul E. Mott, *The Structure of Community Power: An Anthology* (New York: Random House, 1970); Terry N. Clark (ed.), *Community Structure and Decision-Making: Comparative Analyses* (San Francisco: Chandler Publishing Company, 1968); and Willis D. Hawley and Frederick M. Wirt

ever, it might be well to review some of the more recent developments in human ecology inasmuch as modern ecological research differs in significant ways from that conducted during the 1930's. Specifically, modern ecologists do not spend as much time trying to isolate over-all patterns of urban spatial organization as did their forerunners. Rather, the tendency today seems to be to focus upon the spatial distribution of specific social or economic phenomena. A classic piece of research of this type is Otis Dudley Duncan and Beverly Duncan's study of residential segregation in the Chicago Metropolitan District.[48] Among other things, the Duncans found that persons of relatively high and relatively low socioeconomic status are more likely to be segregated from members of other socioeconomic groups than are persons of intermediate socioeconomic status, and that there is a direct relationship between socioeconomic status and the distance one lives from the center of the city. Of even greater importance is the fact that the Duncans develop several techniques for studying residential distribution and segregation which are simple but sophisticated.[49]

Another study along the same lines is Bahr and Gibbs' recent analysis of the relationship between residential segregation and other racial differences.[50] Although this is not an ecological study in the strictest sense of the word, Bahr and Gibbs do test the hypothesis that the greater the amount of residential segregation found in a metropolitan area, the greater will be the differences in the educational attainment of whites and Negroes. In turn, there should be a direct relationship between the de-

---

(eds.), *The Search for Community Power* (Englewood Cliffs, N.J.: Prentice-Hall, Inc., 1968). See also Richard A. Schermerhorn, *Society and Power* (New York: Random House, 1961), pp. 87–105.

[48] See Otis Dudley Duncan and Beverly Duncan, "Residential Distribution and Occupational Stratification," *The American Journal of Sociology,* **60** (March, 1955), pp. 493–503.

[49] Ibid., pp. 493–95.

[50] Howard M. Bahr and Jack P. Gibbs, "Racial Differentiation in American Metropolitan Areas," *Social Forces,* **45** (June, 1967), pp. 521–32.

gree of educational differentiation and the amount of occupational and economic differentiation between the two groups.
Surprisingly enough, this hypothesis cannot be confirmed and
Bahr and Gibbs are forced to conclude that "though subject to
various interpretations, the findings suggest that the elimination
of residential segregation by race would not bring about a decline (certainly not in a generation) in other forms of racial
differentiation, a most important point in analyzing race relations as a social problem." [51]

Cross-cultural studies of ecological phenomena have also retained their popularity. A recent study by Fernando Peñalosa,
for example, has suggested that the inverse-concentric-circle
model which purportedly characterizes Latin American cities
must be modified. In his study of three Mexican cities of moderate size (20,000 to 30,000 population) Peñalosa found that
proximity to major arterials has a much stronger influence upon
the location of middle- and upper-class residences than does
proximity to the central plaza. Since the two major arterials
commonly found in Latin American cities bisect each other at
the central plaza, the area inhabited by the elite therefore assumes the shape of a cross.[52] Similarly, Lois B. DeFleur has
recently published an ecological study of juvenile delinquency
in Cordoba, Argentina.[53] Basically, DeFleur finds that the
spatial distribution of juvenile delinquency in Cordoba is different from that found in the United States. Therefore, she
concludes that a number of ecological studies will have to be
performed before cross-cultural testing of social and cultural
theories of juvenile delinquency can occur. We cannot arrive at
adequate theories of juvenile delinquency until something is
known about the spatial context in which it occurs and which

[51] Ibid., p. 532.
[52] See Fernando Peñalosa, "Ecological Organization of the Transitional City: Some Mexican Evidence," *Social Forces,* **46** (December,
1967), pp. 221–29.
[53] Lois B. DeFleur, "Ecological Variables in the Cross-Cultural Study
of Delinquency," *Social Forces,* **45** (June, 1967), pp. 556–70.

groups have high rates of juvenile offenses. Ecological research provides us with this type of information.

Finally, social area analysis is the "hottest" thing in ecological research today. Because this approach was considered in Chapter 3, we shall not discuss it further. However, it should be pointed out that literally hundreds of cities, both in the United States and in other countries, have been subjected to study by this method. The reader who wishes to examine some of these studies should refer to the up-to-date bibliography appended to Janet L. Abu-Lughod's recent analysis of Cairo, Egypt.[54]

Summary

In this chapter we have considered the bearing of research on community study. It was suggested that research is essential if one is to arrive at adequate theories of community life and that it has a key role to play in any effort to solve community problems. Furthermore, we raised the possibility that findings derived from the study of specific communities can be generalized to other communities and to the larger society. The validity of the "community as sample" approach must, at this time, be left open to question.

More importantly, a tentative classification of community studies has been developed and the reader has been introduced to some of the outstanding studies of community life. The reader must have at least a passing acquaintance with these studies before our discussion of methods of community research will make much sense to him. At the same time, it should be clear that our review of community studies is by no means exhaustive. For every study we have cited, dozens more have gone unmentioned. Furthermore, it has been impossible to explore fully the few studies that have been reviewed. The only really satisfactory

[54] Janet L. Abu-Lughod, "Testing the Theory of Social Area Analysis: The Ecology of Cairo, Egypt," *American Sociological Review,* **34** (April, 1969), pp. 210–12.

way by which the reader can grasp the significance of these studies is by examining them himself.

It may be fitting to close this chapter with a few brief comments about the future of research on the community. Although the future cannot be predicted with accuracy, several things seem clear. First, sociologists and anthropologists will undoubtedly continue to do ethnographic studies, but perhaps less often than in the past. The research design which underlies the ethnographic approach is not easily applied to the analysis of modern urban communities with their huge populations. In order for an ethnographic study to be of great usefulness today, *it must shed light on problem-laden groups found within the urban milieu.* Secondly, there is also reason to suspect that studies which treat community size as an independent variable will decrease in popularity. In a society in which even rural people are quite urban in their ways, studies of this type are rather superfluous.

If these arguments are correct, research on communities will probably become increasingly focused upon specific aspects of community structure and process. This may be good, although somebody must always be on hand to remind us that the community is a whole and should be viewed as such. Likewise, sociologists must not throw up their hands in resignation when confronted with the task of studying the modern urban community with all its complexities. The student of community life has an inescapable responsibility to bring his finest research skills to bear on understanding communities of this type, because within them are harbored the greatest problems and the most exciting potentials of modern society.

Bibliography

Arensberg, Conrad M. "The Community as Object and as Sample," *American Anthropologist,* **63** (April, 1961), pp. 241–64.

Bahr, Howard M., and Jack P. Gibbs. "Racial Differentiation in American Metropolitan Areas," *Social Forces,* **45** (June, 1967), pp. 521–32.

Carr, Lowell Julliard, and James Edson Stermer. *Willow Run: A Study of Cultural Inadequacy*. New York: Harper & Row, 1952.

Davis, Allison, Burleigh B. Gardner, and Mary R. Gardner. *Deep South*. Chicago: University of Chicago Press, 1941.

Dollard, John. *Caste and Class in a Southern Town*. New Haven: Yale University Press, 1937.

Gans, Herbert J. *The Urban Villagers*. New York: The Free Press, 1962.

Gillette, Thomas L. "A Study of the Effects of Negro Invasion on Real Estate Values," *American Journal of Economics and Sociology*, **16** (January, 1957), pp. 151–62.

Haberle, Rudolf. "Social Consequences of the Industrialization of Southern Cities," *Social Forces*, **27** (October, 1948), pp. 29–37.

Havighurst, Robert J., and H. Gerthen Morgan. *The Social History of a War-Boom Community*. New York: Longmans, Green and Company, 1951.

Hollingshead, August B. "Community Research: Development and Present Condition," *American Sociological Review*, **13** (April, 1948), pp. 136–46.

————. *Elmtown's Youth*. New York: John Wiley & Sons, Inc., 1949.

Konig, Rene. *The Community*, translated by Edward Fitzgerald. New York: Schocken Books, 1968.

Liebow, Elliot. *Tally's Corner: A Study of Negro Streetcorner Men*. Boston: Little, Brown and Company, 1967.

Lynd, Robert S., and Helen Merrell Lynd. *Middletown: A Study of American Culture*. New York: Harcourt Brace Jovanovich, Inc., 1929.

————. *Middletown in Transition*. New York: Harcourt Brace Jovanovich, Inc., 1937.

Pfautz, Harold W. (ed.) *Charles Booth on the City: Pattern and Social Structure*. Chicago: University of Chicago Press, 1968.

Simpson, Richard L. "Sociology of the Community: Current Status and Prospects," *Rural Sociology*, **30** (June, 1965), pp. 127–49.

Sjoberg, Gideon, and Roger Nett. *A Methodology for Social Research*. New York: Harper & Row, 1968.

Stein, Maurice R. *The Eclipse of Community: An Interpretation of American Studies*. Princeton, N.J.: Princeton University Press, 1960.

Steward, Julian H. *Area Research: Theory and Practice*. New York: Social Science Research Council Bulletin 63, 1950.

Suttles, Gerald D. *The Social Order of the Slum: Ethnicity and Territory in the Inner City*. Chicago: University of Chicago Press, 1968.

Vidich, Arthur J., and Joseph Bensman. *Small Town in Mass Society*. Princeton, N.J.: Princeton University Press, 1953.

————, and Maurice R. Stein. *Reflections on Community Studies*. New York: John Wiley & Sons, Inc., 1964.

Warner, W. Lloyd, and associates. *Democracy in Jonesville*. New York: Harper & Row, 1949.

Warner, W. Lloyd, and Paul S. Lunt. *The Social Life of a Modern Community*. New Haven: Yale University Press, 1941.

————. *The Status System of a Modern Community*. New Haven: Yale University Press, 1941.

West, James. *Plainville, U.S.A.* New York: Columbia University Press, 1945.

Whyte, William Foote. *Street Corner Society*. Chicago: University of Chicago Press, 1955.

Methods of Community Study

There are several different methods by which communities can be studied. Among the most fruitful of these are participant observation, the social survey, and the use of documents. The applicability of these research methods to the study of community structure and process is the concern of this chapter.

In discussing the three major methods by which the community can be studied, we shall focus upon the type of data each method yields, upon what each demands of the investigator, and upon the advantages and limitations inherent in each. We shall not present a series of practical instructions relating to the use of each method,[1] nor will we argue that the student of community life must choose between participant observation, the social survey, or documentary analysis as his basic approach to research. A competent investigator can often use all three approaches to further his investigation.

---

[1] There are a number of textbooks which give the reader specific instructions on conducting research. For example, see William J. Goode and Paul K. Hatt, *Methods of Social Research* (New York: McGraw-Hill Book Company, 1952); Bernard S. Phillips, *Social Research* (New York: The Macmillan Company, 1966); John T. Doby (ed.), *An Introduction to Social Research,* 2nd ed. (New York: Appleton-Century-Crofts, 1967); Leon Festinger and Daniel Katz (eds.), *Research Methods in the Behavioral Sciences* (New York: Holt, Rinehart and Winston, 1953); and Claire Selltiz et al., *Research Methods in Social Relations,* rev. ed. (New York: Holt, Rinehart and Winston, 1959).

Participant Observation

It is appropriate to begin this chapter with a discussion of participant observation, because it is more closely identified with the study of communities than any other method of research. Not only has participant observation been the dominant methodological approach used by anthropologists to study primitive communities, but it has also been used by some of the most perceptive students of American community life. The popularity of participant observation as a method of studying the community lies in the fact that it can, when skillfully used, reveal aspects of community structure and process which cannot be uncovered in any other way.

Participant Observation: Definitions and Goals

There have been several good, relatively simple definitions of participant observation.[2] However, the nature of a rather complicated method of research cannot be explained in a few words. Rather, in explaining participant observation to the uninitiated, it would seem that three comments are in order.

1. Participant observation represents a particularly effective way to study units of social organization such as "primitive societies, deviant subcultures, complex organizations, social movements, communities, and informal groups."[3] On the other hand, it does not lend itself to the collection of large amounts of statistical data. Studies which demand this type of data are best carried out by means of a social survey.

2. In participant observation the investigator assumes a role within the group or community he seeks to study. It is through

[2] For example, see Morris S. Schwartz and Charlotte Green Schwartz, "Problems in Participant Observation," *American Journal of Sociology,* **60** (January, 1955), p. 344.

[3] George J. McCall and J. L. Simmons, *Issues in Participant Observation: A Text and Reader* (Reading, Mass.: Addison-Wesley Publishing Company, 1969), p. 1.

his participation in community life that the investigator collects data and gains insight into community structure and process. This means that the role of the participant observer can be extremely demanding. It may be literally years before the investigator has observed enough to render a valid analysis of the community. During this time he must carefully build and maintain rapport with community members, conscientiously scrutinize the effects of his presence on their behavior, and keep elaborate field notes. Furthermore, the participant observer uses a variety of specific techniques to collect his data. These include direct observation, interviewing, and the analysis of documents.[4]

3. In contrast to social surveys, studies which utilize participant observation are relatively unstructured. Indeed, one of the major advantages of this method of collecting data is that the investigator is free to capitalize upon unanticipated research opportunities as they present themselves and to make use of his informants in the most strategic way possible.[5] At the same time, the unstructured quality of participant observation increases the risk that the investigator will spend a great deal of time collecting superfluous data. Unless he keeps his ultimate goals in mind, he could painstakingly record a great many observations that are of little use to him or anyone else.

It is hoped that these comments make it clear that participant observation is that style of research in which the investigator collects his data by actually living, working, or otherwise interacting with the study group. If his study focuses upon the inner workings of a modern factory, he might well obtain a job as a factory worker. Similarly, in the course of studying a particular community, the investigator would take up residence in that community and observe it directly. There are some types of data which can only be collected in this way.

[4] For a brief discussion of the techniques used in participant observation see ibid., pp. 61–64.

[5] See John P. Dean, Robert L. Eichhorn, and Lois R. Dean, "Observation and Interviewing," in John T. Doby (ed.), *An Introduction to Social Research,* pp. 274–75.

Techniques of Participant Observation

We have already inferred that participant observation is one of several basic methodological approaches used by social scientists. Furthermore, we have also implied that participant observation involves the use of several highly specialized research techniques. Some of these techniques must now be examined.

Direct observation is obviously the core technique used in participant observation. Indeed, participant observation draws its strength from the fact that the investigator observes the community firsthand and witnesses the behavior of local residents in a variety of situations. Sometimes it is only because of his role as a direct observer that the investigator can gain a full appreciation of the subtleties of community life. This is especially true when an event occurs which is particularly dramatic but which cannot be anticipated in advance. When events of this type occur, local residents may not be able to describe what really happened. To expect them to put their deepest feelings into words is simply asking too much.

Direct participation is another basic technique used by the participant observer. The difference between direct participation and direct observation should be clear. In direct participation, the investigator assumes a role within the study group and becomes directly involved in its activities. For example, if the investigator seeks to study student activist groups, he would become a participating member of such a group. Similarly, if several local groups were at odds with each other over a highly significant issue (e.g., school integration), the investigator might become involved in the controversy as a means of getting an inside view of community conflict. That a research procedure of this type can entail several dangers is fairly obvious. Among other things, the investigator may well become so devoted to group purposes that he loses his scientific objectivity and detachment. Likewise, in conducting his research, he may become so closely identified with one group that he permanently jeopardizes his chances of studying other groups. Nonetheless, many proponents of direct participation maintain that these risks must be taken and that direct participation is the only way by which the sociologist can capture the full meaning and significance of group activities. It is hoped that participant observation helps us to see the truly human dimension of the phenomena we seek to understand.

There are several other research techniques used in participant observation. For example, the observer must do a great deal of interviewing. In this respect, McCall and Simmons draw a useful distinction between informant and respondent interviewing.[6] In informant interviewing, the investigator simply asks informed community members to tell him about events which have transpired and to interpret things he has observed himself. This type of interviewing is used with great frequency in participant observation simply because the investigator cannot directly observe everything which happens, nor can he always make sense out of what he does observe. The great challenge posed by informant interviewing is of course to get the informant "to report hard, particular facts so that the scientist can form his own, often quite different generalizations."[7] In respondent interviewing, on the other hand, the interviewee is not used as an assistant observer. Rather, the investigator seeks facts about the interviewee himself. This type of interviewing is similar to that used in social surveys.

Finally, the participant observer must use a wide variety of documents and unpublished records. This includes statistical material that has been compiled and/or published by federal, state, or local governments as well as newspapers, minutes of meetings, and even personal diaries. Data of this type are of significant value to the participant observer, and indeed to any student of community life. Among other things, the use of data of this type can save the investigator a great deal of time and often represent the participant observer's only source of information pertaining to certain types of events. This is par-

[6] McCall and Simmons, *Issues in Participant Observation,* p. 4.
[7] Ibid., p. 4.

ticularly true of events which happened so long ago that none of his informants can recall them.

Field Roles of the Participant Observer

One of the hallmarks of participant observation is that the investigator's behavior can have a profound impact on the type and quality of data he collects. Because of this a great deal of attention has been focused upon the types of roles the investigator can assume. Two of the most insightful analyses along these lines are those offered by Raymond Gold and Robert Janes.

A Typology of Field Roles: Raymond Gold. Raymond Gold argues that there are essentially four roles which can be adopted by the participant observer.[8] These roles seem to lie along a continuum with the *complete participant* at one end and the *complete observer* at the other. Intermediate role types are the *participant-as-observer* and the *observer-as-participant.*

The investigator who conceals his true identity and purposes from those whom he is observing is acting in the role of a *complete participant.* Rather than letting it be known that he is an investigator, he assumes the role behaviors appropriate to members of the group and becomes "one of the boys." The *complete observer,* on the other hand, refrains from interacting with group members and may not even make his presence known. Because members of the group are at most vaguely aware of the investigator's presence, he presumably has little influence upon their behavior. This research role is frequently used in studies of small-group behavior. In research of this type it is not uncommon for the investigator to observe a laboratory group through a one-way mirror or to eavesdrop systematically on group members in some other way. This role is not particularly useful when one is conducting a genuine field study. People

---

[8] See Raymond L. Gold, "Roles in Sociological Field Observations," *Social Forces,* **36** (March, 1958), pp. 217–23.

Research and Community Study

quickly become aware that there is a stranger in their midst and seek an explanation for his presence. This is all the more true when his activities are unique or unusual, as may be the case if the stranger is also a participant observer.

Once these two field roles are clearly understood, then the other two roles can be easily explained. Thus, the *participant-as-observer* role has much in common with the role played by the complete participant. The only major difference between the two roles is that in the participant-as-observer relationship "both field worker and informant are aware that theirs is a field relationship." [9] This role is used with great frequency in field studies of community life. It is very common for the investigator to announce his purposes and intentions, but then to blend into the fabric of local life as much as possible. On the other hand, the role played by the *observer-as-participant* has certain things in common with the role played by the complete observer. The investigator explains that he is conducting a field study but then tries, as much as possible, to remain aloof from direct participation in community events and activities. According to Gold, "the observer-as-participant role is used in studies involving one-visit interviews." [10] However, it is difficult to see why this has to be the case. A skilled investigator can explain his purposes to community members but still place his emphasis upon observation rather than participation.

The reasons that Gold and others have analyzed the roles that the participant observer can assume are more than purely academic. Rather, this type of analysis is of crucial importance, because the correlation between the role the investigator assumes and the type and quality of data he collects may be strong. For example, the "complete participant" is less likely to have a lasting influence upon the behavior of community members than is the investigator who makes it known that he is conducting research. The reason for this is simple. On the

[9] Ibid., p. 220.
[10] Ibid., p. 221.

whole, people feel more threatened by a person who, in effect, announces that he has come to observe them than by a person whom they think is a new colleague, neighbor, or whatever. The same advantage is inherent in the complete observer role, but for a different reason. In this case community members may not even be aware that there is a new person in their midst. At the same time, both of these roles do pose certain dangers. The complete participant, for example, can easily become so closely identified with the community and its members that he completely loses his scientific objectivity and detachment. The complete observer, on the other hand, may remain so aloof and detached that he completely misses many of the subtleties of community life. But more serious than this are the ethical questions which are brought to the forefront by the practice of concealing one's identity from persons who are being studied. Most of us will say and do things in the presence of a person whom we think to be a new group member that we would not say or do if we knew that our behavior was to be the subject of a research report. The question of whether the investigator has a right to use information he obtains by keeping his identity concealed is a difficult one indeed.

Many of these problems are avoided if the investigator reveals his identity and purposes to community members. If nothing else he cannot be accused of being a spy or prying into other people's lives. At the same time, we have already hinted that the knowledge that they are being observed and studied may cause some people to modify their behavior. The tendency for community members to put their best foot forward and to conceal the less desirable aspects of their collective existence from the investigator would seem to be great.

The Community Role of the Participant Observer: Robert W. Janes. We have argued that the way in which he enacts his role as an investigator is one variable which affects the type and quality of data which the participant observer collects. Another writer, Robert W. Janes, has suggested that the manner in which community members define the investigator's place in the community also affects his ability to collect meaningful, accurate data. Because of this we now turn our attention to the "community role" of the participant observer.

To be more specific, in reporting on his field study of Riverville, a small Midwestern town, Janes observed that "the community role of the author and his family apparently underwent a progressive redefinition in the course of their residence." [11] When the Janes first arrived in Riverville they were treated of course as *newcomers*. During their tenure in this role the investigators were given general information about Riverville and were subjected to careful scrutiny by community members. After spending a period of time in Riverville, Janes was finally "graduated" from his role as a newcomer. At this point local residents defined him as a *provisional member* and then as a *categorical member* of the community. In his role as a provisional member, Janes' occupation was examined very closely, as were his associational memberships and interests (i.e., church affiliation, club memberships, recreational interests, and so on). During this phase of his relationship with the community, local residents voluntarily supplied him with information about people and issues but "without any of the invidious intimations of later statements." [12] By the time that Janes had become accepted as a categorical member of the community, apparently local residents had concluded that his reasons for studying Riverville were legitimate and that it was safe to give him the "inside story" on local people and issues. However, it was not until Janes became defined as a *personalized member* of the community that he was able to establish "a continuing sense of rapport" with community members.[13] In this role, Janes was able to get community members to discuss their personal thoughts, feelings, and attitudes with him. Finally, when Janes

[11] Robert W. Janes, "A Note on Phases of the Community Role of the Participant-Observer," *American Sociological Review,* **26** (June, 1961), p. 448.

[12] Ibid., p. 448.

[13] Ibid., p. 449.

indicated that he had completed his research and would soon be leaving Riverville, he was assigned the role of *imminent migrant*. In this, the concluding stage of his relationship with the community, Janes found that his informants would offer him no new information about Riverville and its people. Rather, they were more interested in what he thought about the community. Indeed, the residents of Riverville appeared to be somewhat threatened by Janes' departure, perhaps because they knew that the die had been cast. Once Janes and his family left Riverville, nothing that they could do would have any influence on his conclusions.

Advantages and Limitations

The advantages and limitations of participant observation have been vigorously debated. Some investigators view it as the only method by which meaningful, valid data can be collected. To others its potentially subjective quality and the fact that it yields largely nonquantifiable data disqualify it as a respectable means of gathering data. Because the merits and deficiencies of participant observation have been so hotly contested, they must be spelled out.

The primary advantage of participant observation as a basic methodological approach is rather obvious: there are certain types of data which can only be unearthed by the investigator who enters into close and continuous interaction with his informants. Some advocates of participant observation, for example, would argue that it is only through the field study that one can gain insight into the subtleties of human thought, action, and emotion. A long and highly structured interview is not a satisfactory way of uncovering these types of data, nor is such information available in census materials, courthouse records, or newspapers. Indeed, participant observation does allow the investigator to bring the truly human dimension into his study. It is this fact which apparently prompted Becker and Geer to state that "participant observation can . . . provide us with a yardstick against which to measure the completeness of data gathered in other ways, a model which can serve to let us know what orders of information escape us when we use other methods." [14] Some of the remarks that were made earlier in this chapter should make it clear that the present writer tends to concur with this statement, but with a few qualifications.

There are of course other advantages inherent in participant observation. Many of these have been spelled out by Dean, Eichhorn, and Dean.[15] Certainly one of the cardinal advantages of participant observation lies in the fact that as the investigator conducts his research, he is not wedded to a specific set of questions. Rather, he is free to pursue his quest for knowledge in any seemingly profitable direction. He can assume that different informants know different things and can tailor his questions to take these "knowledge differentials" into account.[16] This cannot be done when the interviewer is required to ask the same questions of everyone he contacts, as is almost always the case in survey research.

At the same time, participant observation has its limitations as a methodological tool. These limitations are indeed serious in that they have a direct bearing on the validity of the data collected. Specifically, two objections to participant observation have been raised. These may be summarized as follows.

1. Several writers have noted the hazards which center around the fact that the participant observer becomes a part of the situation he is observing.[17] Among other things, the investigator may unavoidably influence the behavior of group members because his presence is a reality with which members

[14] Howard S. Becker and Blanche Geer, "Participant Observation and Interviewing: A Comparison," *Human Organization,* 16 (1957), p. 28.

[15] See John P. Dean, Robert L. Eichhorn, and Lois R. Dean, "Observations and Interviewing," pp. 276–79.

[16] See ibid., p. 275.

[17] For further discussion of this and similar problems see Morris S. Schwartz and Charlotte Green Schwartz, "Problems in Participant Observation," *American Journal of Sociology,* 60 (January, 1955), pp. 343–53.

of the group must cope. They may do this by restricting their conversation when he is present, by "showing off" for him, or by otherwise tailoring their behavior to fit the fact that they are being observed. Similarly, the investigator's close relationship with the study group increases the likelihood that his findings and conclusions will reflect a variety of biases. The investigator may identify more closely with one informant than he does with another and unintentionally may give undue weight to things told him by informants he personally likes. Furthermore, because the investigator assumes a role within the study group, he eventually may grow blind to many of its unique features. The student of community life, for example, can easily lull himself into believing that "the way things are done here is the way in which they are done everywhere." If and when this happens, the investigator has ceased to view the community from the vantage point of a disinterested and objective scientist and has come instead to view it as a community member. Finally, the very nature of participant observation makes it almost impossible to check the original investigator's conclusions by replicating the study. Another investigator may be accustomed to looking for different things than the original observer and will relate to informants in different ways. These problems are compounded by the considerable amount of time which may elapse between the original and the replicatory study.

2. Participant observation has also been criticized on the grounds that it usually does not yield quantifiable data. In a sense, these criticisms are well taken. Data which can be expressed in quantitative form are more easily presented than qualitative data, and they can be manipulated in such a way that the relationships between two or more variables are revealed. Furthermore, once such a relationship is established, its strength can be measured statistically (for example, by means of correlational analysis). This is usually not the case with data gathered by the participant observer. When the participant observer does manage to quantify his observations, it is usually in the form of qualitative statements such as *more than* and *less than, above average* and *below average,* and so on.

Both of these criticisms of participant observation are of course valid. However, participant observation must be evaluated in terms of the uses to which it is put. Although many things can adversely affect the quality of data gathered by this method, at the present time it seems to be the only way by which one can get an *in-depth picture* of communities, subcultures, and complex organizations. Furthermore, it must be hoped that an unbridgeable chasm does not develop between those who favor participant observation and those who prefer the survey approach. As a matter of fact, participant observation can and should supply the investigator with the preliminary information and insight that he must have before he can begin to test relationships by means of a social survey.

The Social Survey

When professional sociologists refer to a research project, they often mean a study in which data are gathered by systematically interviewing a large number of people. This is essentially what we mean by a social survey. Needless to say, the social survey represents the most common method by which sociologists collect data. Hence, we must examine the survey approach and its applicability to the study of communities.

Characteristics of the Survey Approach

There are several ways by which the characteristics of a social survey could be explained. However, because we have just discussed participant observation, perhaps we can learn the most about the social survey by comparing it with participant observation. Our previous discussion should make it clear that three characteristics of participant observation stand out above all others in importance. First, in participant observation the investigator uses a small number of informants. These informants are hand-picked in terms of their ability to shed light on the research problem of interest to the investigator. Second, the investigator tailors his questions to fit each informant. This is because he recognizes that each informant can make a unique contribution to his understanding of the problem. Finally, the data collected by the participant observer are usually non-quantitative: they consist of a series of more or less factual statements made by both the informants and the investigator. The characteristics of a social survey are rather different. They may be summarized as follows.

1. In survey research the investigator collects his data through interviews with a very large number of people. Sometimes this includes every member of the study population (e.g., all residents of Lubbock, Texas), but it is more common for him to draw a sample representative of the larger population (e.g., every tenth resident). This is done because conclusions based on interviews with a relatively small number of respondents can be just as valid as conclusions based on interviews with all members of the study population, assuming that the sample is carefully chosen. This means a considerable savings in both time and money. Furthermore, the survey researcher never hand-picks his respondents. Rather, his goal is to determine what characteristics are typical of the study population; therefore he chooses his respondents at random. Hence, at the completion of his field work the survey researcher has normally interviewed a rather large number of people. His sample presumably mirrors the larger population and therefore provides him with a picture of that population. This is in distinct contrast to the method used by the participant observer. The participant observer frequently collects his data from a small number of exceptionally well-informed, articulate people.

2. In survey research each respondent is asked the same question and must answer these questions in terms of a few clearly defined categories. If this is not the case (i.e., if the questions are open-ended), then the investigator classifies the respondent's answers after the interview has been completed. The advantages of this procedure are obvious.[18] Among other things,

18 The so-called structured interview also has some serious disadvantages. For a discussion of both its advantages and disadvantages see Clair Selltiz et al., *Research Methods in Social Relations*, pp. 257–63.

Research and Community Study

it greatly simplifies the task of processing and analyzing the raw data. The investigator does not have to decide what the respondent "really said," nor does he have to comb through a wide variety of statements relating to a number of diverse subjects. Rather, he simply counts the number of responses which fall into each category and presents his findings in tabular form. This again is a much different procedure than that used by the participant observer. In analyzing his findings, the participant observer is faced with the enormous task of sorting through a wide variety of statements and personal observations and of organizing them in such a way as to support his argument. Most of the time it is impossible for him to present his data in tabular form.

3. Finally, the survey approach is particularly suitable for testing hypotheses and theories. There are two reasons for this. First, we have already indicated that survey data are easily converted into quantitative form: one simply counts the number of respondents who are male or female, who favor or who are against a particular policy, or whatever. Secondly, in the social sciences most hypotheses either consist of a simple proposition or state a relationship between two or more variables.[10] In a study of attitudes toward local government, for example, we might hypothesize that people who live in small communities tend to disapprove of the city manager form of government. Likewise, we might also hypothesize that people of high socioeconomic status have more favorable attitudes toward city managers than do people of low socioeconomic status. If the survey researcher asks the right questions, he can easily test both of these hypotheses. To be more specific, the percentage of the total population which disapproves of the city manager form of government can easily be determined and the investigator can use correlational analysis to measure the relationship between socioeconomic status and attitudes toward city managers. Operations of this type cannot be performed with data collected by the participant observer. At most, the participant observer can

[10] See Phillips, *Social Research,* p. 219.

report that it was his impression that most people disapprove of the city manager form of government. Likewise, he may be convinced that people of high socioeconomic status have more favorable attitudes toward city managers than do people of low socioeconomic status, but he usually cannot calculate statistics and construct tables to show that this is the case.

It should be clear that our purpose is not to criticize participant observation. Rather, we seek only to acquaint the reader with some of the basic properties of the social survey. To be more specific, we have indicated that the survey researcher collects his data from a large number of randomly selected respondents, that all respondents are asked about the same questions, and that data collected by means of a survey lend themselves to the testing of hypotheses. That this method of collecting data has many advantages should be obvious.

The Outlines of Social Survey

We must examine the applicability of the survey approach to the study of territorial communities. Before doing this, however, it might be helpful to trace the steps entailed in conducting a social survey. This review will be superfluous for the reader who is experienced in social research, but it may help the inexperienced person to understand the methodological procedures involved in conducting a social survey.

Delineating the Problem. The first step in any scientific investigation is to delineate a research problem. The investigator must decide what it is that he wishes to investigate and clearly indicate the nature of his study. When he first becomes interested in doing research he will have of course only a vague idea concerning the direction his research might take. As time passes, however, his preliminary "ideas must be translated into a precise statement of the research problem: preferably the investigator will before he begins his fieldwork, be able to specify one or more hypotheses which will guide his research." [20] If his

[20] The characteristics of a good hypothesis are discussed in William J. Goode and Paul K. Hatt, *Methods of Social Research,* pp. 68–73.

research problem is not delimited in this manner, the investigator may find that he makes little progress toward completing his study.

There are several things which influence the investigator's choice of research problems. One of these is the availability of research funds. Although most agencies which support research do allow the investigator a considerable amount of freedom in defining his problem, they also insist that the research be relevant to their needs. In addition to funding, however, there are other things which should be considered in choosing a research problem. Some of these can make or break a study.

1. The investigator must carefully appraise the potential value of his research. The value of a study of course can be measured in several ways. For example, the student of community life might well ask himself whether the proposed research will fill a gap in our understanding of communities and/or whether it will test some of our theories of community structure and process. Phillips puts the case well when he states that "a wise choice of a scientific problem differs from an unwise choice in that it advances the goals of science; an unwise choice does not." [21] Similarly, the investigator might also consider whether his study will enhance our ability to solve community problems. If both of these questions can be answered in the affirmative, then the investigator is undoubtedly on the right track in terms of choosing a good research problem.

2. The investigator must also ask himself whether the proposed research is technically feasible. Is the problem suitable for study by means of a social survey? Can data be collected which will enable the investigator to test his hypotheses? It is one thing to jot down a list of hypotheses which capture one's interest and enthusiasm. It can be much more difficult to devise rigorous means to test them.

3. The investigator should always consider whether he has sufficient resources to carry out the research. If a social survey is the only feasible means by which the study can be conducted,

[21] Phillips, *Social Research,* p. 75.

then the investigator must recognize that the survey approach normally requires that interviewers be hired and trained. Likewise, the investigator must be well versed in questionnaire construction and statistical and computer analysis, and above all, he most possess a good amount of patience. If the investigator cannot provide these things, he might be well advised to try another type of research.

4. Finally, the investigator must be thoroughly dedicated to his research and firmly convinced that his problem is worth pursuing. It must be remembered that any type of research is difficult and demanding. If the problem and the research it entails do not ignite the investigator's enthusiasm and imagination, the research project will soon become a nightmare for him.

Research Design. Once the research problem has been delineated, the investigator must develop his research design. A research design simply specifies the procedures that he will follow in conducting his study. In survey research, for example, the research design must delineate the study population and indicate the methods that will be used in selecting a sample of respondents from this population. In addition, it should indicate the type of data collection instrument that will be used and how the raw data will be analyzed.[22] A good research design is one which is both thorough and detailed. That careful attention to matters of research design is essential if one's study is to be successfully completed should be obvious. Bernard S. Phillips, for example, tells us that "the attempt to formulate a research design very early in the development of the investigation can aid the scientist in achieving a more focused approach. In moving from problem definition to research design, the implications of the general research goals must be outlined in order to make decisions on specific procedures." [23]

Data Collection. After a research problem has been selected

---

[22] The things which should go into a good statement of research design are outlined in Delbert C. Miller, *Handbook of Research Design and Social Measurement* (New York: David McKay Company, Inc., 1964), pp. 3–6.
[23] Phillips, *Social Research,* pp. 77–78.

and the research design has been developed, the investigator must focus on the technicalities of conducting the survey. He usually begins by identifying the persons he intends to interview. As has already been indicated, he may decide to interview all members of the study population. In conducting most surveys, however, this is both impractical and unnecessary because a sample can be chosen which accurately reflects the entire population.

It is beyond the scope of this book to offer a detailed discussion of sampling procedures.[24] In most social surveys the investigator uses a random sample or some variation thereof. By this we mean that each member of the study population has an equal chance of being included in the sample. If this procedure is followed and if the sample is of the correct size, then the members of the sample should closely parallel the members of the study population in their characteristics and attributes. For example, if nonwhite females make up 20 per cent of the study population, then approximately 20 per cent of a carefully drawn sample will consist of nonwhite females. The same relationship between the sample and the study population should hold in terms of the variables upon which the investigator wishes to collect data. It is only because of the tendency for a random sample to mirror the larger population that a sample survey can yield results as trustworthy as those obtained by a complete enumeration of the population.

At about the same time that a sample is drawn, the investigator must also decide what information he will obtain from his respondents. We shall not deal with the technicalities of constructing and administering a satisfactory interview schedule.[25] However, as the investigator embarks on this phase of his

[24] There are a number of good discussions of types of samples and of sampling procedures. See Russell L. Ackoff, *The Design of Social Research* (Chicago: University of Chicago Press, 1953), pp. 83–126; and Leslie Kish, *Survey Sampling* (New York: John Wiley & Sons, Inc., 1965).

[25] Again, several good discussions are available. See Charles F. Cannell and Robert L. Kahn, "Interviewing" in Gardner Lindsey and Elliott

research, there are several things he might keep in mind. In the first place, he should remember that the interview schedule is a tool which helps him to gather data which bear directly upon his problem or hypotheses. Each time the investigator adds a question to his interview schedule he might well ask himself how it will contribute to his study. Secondly, the investigator must also give some thought to how his respondents will react to the questions he proposes to ask them.[26] It is foolish to ask questions that respondents cannot or will not answer. In this regard, attention must be paid to questions which require the respondent to recall something (e.g., a previous year's income) and to those which touch upon particularly sensitive topics (e.g., personal deviance, sexual behavior, and so on). Lastly, we might point out that there are a variety of norms which guide the experienced investigator in constructing an interview schedule.[27] These norms relate to the way in which questions are worded, the order in which they are presented to the respondent, and so forth.

Assuming that data are to be collected by means of an interview, the last step in the data collection phase is to administer the interview to all members of the sample. Needless to say, it is essential that the interviewer be highly skilled if valid, reliable data are to be obtained. Undoubtedly the most important skill the interviewer must possess is the ability to communicate. Indeed, Dean, Eichhorn, and Dean remind us that "the crux of a successful survey is the communication process that takes place in the interview." [28] This means that interviewers must be well trained and highly motivated. If these conditions are met and if the interview schedule has been care-

---

Aronson, *The Handbook of Social Psychology,* 2nd ed., Vol. II (Reading, Mass.: Addison-Wesley Publishing Company, 1968), pp. 526–90.

[26] See Leon Festinger and Daniel Katz, *Research Methods in Behavioral Sciences,* pp. 16–17.

[27] See Gideon Sjoberg and Roger Nett, *A Methodology for Social Research* (New York: Harper & Row, 1968), pp. 199–202.

[28] John P. Dean, Robert L. Eichhorn, and Lois R. Dean, "The Survey," in John T. Doby (ed.), *An Introduction to Social Research,* 2nd ed., p. 251.

fully designed, then the investigator can have confidence in his findings. If they are not met, then his data may be worthless.

Analysis and Presentation of Data. The analysis and presentation of one's findings constitute the final step in any research project. With the development of modern statistical techniques and of high-speed computers, the analysis of survey data has become rather complicated. However, the person who is new to survey research may find his task easier if he realizes that the logic of survey analysis is very simple: the investigator tries to determine what factors (independent variables) cause variation in the phenomena (dependent variables) he is observing (e.g., the factors that cause some people to look askance at the city manager form of government). Sometimes this can only be done by controlling other factors which might cause a spurious relationship between the independent and dependent variables.

The way in which the investigator presents his findings depends partly upon his publication plans. Every publisher has its own expectations concerning the length of the manuscript and the amount of technical detail included in it. Furthermore, the way the investigator prepares his report depends partly upon whether he intends to disseminate his findings to his professional colleagues or to the general public. On the whole, reports prepared for consumption by a professional audience deal more thoroughly with technical and methodological details than those that are to have a wider readership. This does not mean that the investigator can cut corners in preparing material for presentation to the general public. Anyone who is willing to wade through a research report has the right to know how and why the investigator arrived at his conclusions.

Social Surveys and Community Study

Little has been written during recent years concerning the use of social surveys in studying community life. Nonetheless, many of the earliest social surveys were essentially community studies. One thinks immediately, for example, of Charles

Booth's monumental studies of London and its people.[29] Booth's seventeen-volume work was published between 1892 and 1896 and has been hailed by Sidney and Beatrice Webb as "the greatest statistical enterprise ever attempted by a private investigator at his own expense." [30] Likewise, B. S. Rowntree's almost equally famous surveys of York, England (circa 1900 and 1936) should not be forgotten, nor should the Pittsburgh Survey (1909–1914) conducted by Paul Kellogg.[31] The most noteworthy feature of these early community studies was their broad scope and richness of detail.

Today there is a tendency to use the survey approach to investigate very specialized problems. Needless to say, we cannot possibly discuss all the ways in which the survey approach can be used to study community life. However, some of the more important problems which can be investigated by means of a survey are the following:

1. A social survey is the only practical means by which quantitative data on the characteristics of the study population can be collected. It might be noted in passing that the U.S. Census is essentially a survey, the precision and richness of which make it an outstanding source of social, economic, and demographic data. It is also appropriate to use the survey approach to collect data on socioeconomic status, standards of living, and innumerable other characteristics of community members. When data of this type are collected, it is usually cross-tabulated with data pertaining to the respondent's behavior, attitudes, or values.

2. A social survey also lends itself to the collection of data relating to social participation and the use of community services. Data on associational membership, church attendance, use

---

[29] Charles Booth, *Life and Labour of the People in London* (London: Macmillan Company, Limited, 1902).

[30] Cited in Pauline V. Young, *Scientific Social Surveys and Research,* 3rd ed. (Englewood Cliffs, N.J.: Prentice-Hall, Inc., 1956), p. 13.

[31] Dates in parentheses indicate the year in which the surveys were conducted. All of these studies are discussed in ibid., pp. 9–24.

Research and Community Study

of public facilities, and involvement in local politics can all be gathered by means of a survey. To cite one example, Babchuk and Booth have recently collected data pertaining to the membership of Nebraska's adult population in voluntary associations.[32] Likewise, the University of Kentucky's Bureau of Community Services has published data on reading and library use in Lexington, Kentucky. These data, taken from interviews with a sample of 484 respondents, reveal that the residents of this city read more than one might expect [33] but that many of them never use the public library.[34] Needless to say, data of this type are usually collected in order to test hypotheses, some of which can be rather significant. It could be hypothesized, for example, that there is a relationship between community size and participation in voluntary associations, the use of libraries and other public facilities, or attitudes toward community improvement projects. The significance that can be attached to studies of this type depends of course on the degree to which they shed light on theories of community or help us in finding solutions to community problems.

3. The social survey is a useful tool for collecting data on patterns of interaction. For example, several surveys have been conducted which shed light on patterns of neighboring in cities and metropolitan areas.[35] Generally speaking, these studies indicate that nonfamilial, primary-group ties are stronger and more viable in large communities than we once thought. The survey approach can also be used to determine the amount of

[32] See Nicholas Babchuk and Alan Booth, "Voluntary Association Membership: A Longitudinal Analysis," *American Sociological Review,* **34** (February, 1969), pp. 31–45.

[33] Dennis E. Poplin, *Reading and Library Use In Lexington, Kentucky* (University of Kentucky: Kentucky Community Series Number 30, November, 1964), p. 9.

[34] Ibid., Tables 29 and 30.

[35] For example, see Wendell Bell and Marion D. Boat, "Urban Neighborhoods and Informal Social Relations," *American Journal of Sociology,* **62** (January, 1957), pp. 391–98; and Joel Smith, William H. Form, and Gregory P. Stone, "Local Intimacy in a Middle-sized City," *American Journal of Sociology,* **60** (November, 1964), pp. 176–84.

interaction between the various racial, ethnic, religious, and status groups found in the modern community.

4. Perhaps the most important value of the survey approach is that it enables us to collect data on the attitudes and perceptions of community members. Among other things, surveys can be designed which shed light on people's attitudes toward local government, local schools, local welfare agencies, or any other group, institution, or program. Likewise, ways have been developed to measure a person's attitude toward the community in which he lives. Especially to be noted in this regard are Claud A. Bosworth's *Community Attitude Scale* and Donald R. Fessler's *Community Solidarity Index.*[36] The latter scale is particularly interesting in that it measures a person's opinion of his own community. Finally, the survey approach can be used to collect data pertaining to the perceptions held by community members. In doing research on community power structure, for example, we often ask our respondents who, in their opinion, holds power and makes the key decisions in their community.

Other facets of community life can be studied by the survey researcher. However, the preceding discussion gives the reader some idea of the type and range of data which can be collected by this method. It should be remembered, of course, that relatively few surveys are of interest to the student of community life. All too often we fail to distinguish between research *on* communities and research that is only tangentially related to community study.

Documents as Data

The use of participant observation and/or the survey approach allows the investigator to collect data on many different

[36] Both scales are reproduced in Delbert C. Miller, *Handbook of Research Design and Social Measurement,* pp. 193–201. Bosworth's scale was originally presented in his Ph.D. dissertation (University of Michigan, 1954), whereas Fessler's scale was first published in his article "The Development of a Scale for Measuring Community Solidarity," *Rural Sociology,* **17** (June, 1952), pp. 144–52.

research problems. The only limitation on the topics that the investigator can explore are those imposed by social norms. There are some things which people think and do which are simply not revealed to a stranger. However, the investigator should also realize that he can often unearth a wealth of *data compiled by other people*. The use of documents as sources of data is of paramount importance in social research.

In most communities these type of data are available in abundance. One thinks immediately, for example, of documents of a historical nature. With a little searching, the investigator can frequently locate histories of the community, of some of its organizations, and of some of its leading families. These histories may be compiled by private citizens, or their compilation may be an official function of the mayor's office, a club secretary, or someone else. In some research projects the use of historical materials is absolutely essential if one is to understand the community and its present configurations. The present grows out of the past. At the same time, the investigator who has little or no training in the use of historical documents should proceed with care. Historical documents range all the way from those whose credibility and authenticity are beyond question to those that are completely fraudulent. There are a number of books and articles which spell out guidelines for determining the value of historical materials.[37]

In addition to formal histories, a host of official and semi-official records is usually available to the student of community life. This includes records relating to vital events (births, deaths, marriages, and divorces), school attendance, property transactions, arrests, and so forth, as well as governmental budgets, the annual reports of social agencies, and the minutes of various meetings. Sometimes records of this type are kept for years so that the investigator can study changes in the variables of in-

---

[37] See especially Louis Gottschalk, "The Historian and the Historical Document," in Louis Gottschalk, Clyde Kluckhohn, and Robert Angell, *The Use of Personal Documents in History, Anthropology and Sociology* (New York: Social Science Research Council Bulletin 53, 1945), pp. 28–47.

terest to him. Likewise, the local newspaper is a potentially valuable source of data. The uses to which its articles, editorials, letters to the editor, and even advertisements can be put is limited only by the investigator's creativity. This does not mean, however, that there are no hazards inherent in the use of newspapers as sources of scientific insight. The contents of the typical newspaper are carefully selected and the publisher's primary goal is to produce a document which will be widely read. This means that some community relevant activities and events do not get newspaper coverage whereas other events and activities are overdramatized.

Finally, the U.S. census of population is an invaluable source of information for the student of community life. Perhaps the only way for an inexperienced investigator to familiarize himself with its contents is by browsing through its many volumes. If he is interested in the Lubbock, Texas, Standard Metropolitan Statistical Area, for example, some of the more important items of information he will undoubtedly be able to obtain from the 1970 census of population are as follows:

1. The total population of the Lubbock SMSA as of April 1, 1970, cross-classified by age, sex, and race.

2. Number of persons in the labor force, classified by employment status (employed, unemployed) and cross-classified by race and sex.

3. Occupational composition of the labor force (number of persons in professional, technical, and managerial occupations, in clerical and sales occupations, etc.), by sex and race.

4. Median number of years of schooling completed by persons twenty-five years of age and over, cross-classified by sex and race.

5. Median income of families and unrelated individuals.

These data are published for all communities which have a population of 2,500 or more. The U.S. Bureau of the Census publishes more detailed data for Standard Metropolitan Statistical Areas (including Lubbock, Texas). Furthermore, for the SMSA's these data are not only available for the metropolitan area as a whole but for each of its census tracts. These, according to the Bureau of the Census, are "small, permanently established, geographical areas into which large cities and their environs have been divided for statistical purposes." [38] Normally, census tracts have a population of 4,000 or more and are relatively homogeneous in terms of their demographic, social, and economic characteristics. Thus, the investigator who knows how to use the U.S. census of population has a wealth of information at his fingertips. This information can serve as background data for a social survey or a field study or as the raw data for a demographic analysis of the community. Materials taken from the U.S. census of population can often be supplemented by those contained in the U.S. censuses of housing, business, manufactures, and even agriculture.

The competent investigator must be able to locate data of the type we have just described. These data can reduce greatly the amount of time and money required to conduct certain types of studies. Similarly, if the event being studied occurred in the distant past, historical documents are the investigator's only source of information. It is, however, not enough simply to locate such data. The investigator must also know how to make correct use of them. Among other things, this requires that he know how to assess the authenticity and credibility of the record or document. Many records and documents are not compiled for scientific purposes and the compiler may or may not be motivated to produce a record that is accurate and unbiased. Thus, the U.S. Bureau of the Census is staffed by highly trained specialists who seek to gather and compile data which accurately reflect the demographic, economic, and social characteristics of the U.S. population. On the other hand, the writer of a history may have a variety of motives in addition to that of presenting an unbiased account of past events. He may write his book in order to justify the position of some individual or group with

[38] U.S. Bureau of the Census, *Census Tract Manual,* 5th ed. (Washington, D.C.: U.S. Government Printing Office, 1966), p. i.

which he is identified or he may "spice" up his work so that it will have a wide readership.

To determine the degree of authenticity and credibility which can be accorded a document is no easy task. However, Louis Gottschalk suggests four general rules which might be kept in mind as the investigator attempts to assess the validity of a historical document.[39] First, if the documentarian or recorder made his report immediately after the event occurred, it may be more accurate than one which was recorded after a considerable amount of time had elapsed. With the passage of time one's memory fades and facts get distorted. Secondly, one should also consider the motives of the person who compiled the document. If the writer compiled the document in order to aid his own memory, it may be more accurate than if he compiled it to impress a superior (e.g., his commanding officer) or to propagandize a particular group. Thirdly, Gottschalk advances the proposition that "the fewer the number for whose eyes the document was meant (i.e., the greater its *confidential nature*) the more 'naked' its contents are likely to be."[40] This means in effect that if the documentarian's goal was to reach a mass audience, then he may have been forced to embellish his report with drama, to draw conclusions which appealed to his audience, and so forth. The value of the document as an objective source of data may therefore be decreased. Finally, documents compiled by experts on the matter under investigation are generally superior to those compiled by laymen. The expert is likely to see more things and to be able to interpret more accurately what he does see than is the person with an untrained eye.

It is important to note that Gottschalk is a historian and that his primary goal is to provide us with guidelines for determining the credibility of historical documents. However, he maintains that "the same four rules would seem to hold true for human documents exploited by any of the social studies."[41]

[39] Louis Gottschalk, "The Historian and the Historical Document," p. 16.
[40] Ibid., p. 16. Italics in original.
[41] Ibid., p. 16.

Summary

Research on community life has always been a vital part of sociology. Indeed, some of the community studies which were cited in Chapter 8 have become classics and are among the richest documents produced by sociologists. At the same time, the methods by which we study community life are not inherently different than those by which we study other forms of social organization. The three major ways by which sociologists can collect data are through participant observation, the survey approach, and the analysis of documents and records.

A question may arise as to which of these methods should be used to conduct a community study. However, Bernard S. Phillips makes it clear that this is probably a meaningless question. Thus,

> Not all of the beliefs surrounding social research have their origins in popular culture. In fact, some of the erroneous ones are propounded by social researchers themselves. One of these is that one given method of research is *ipso facto* better than other methods, regardless of the problem under investigation.[42]

In short, one's choice of method should be governed by his choice of a research topic. Certainly each method yields a different type of data and is uniquely suited for the investigation of particular types of problems. We have seen that participant observation allows the investigator to get an in-depth view of groups, institutions, and communities, that the survey approach lends itself to the collection of quantitative data on the characteristics and attitudes of community members, and that documents and records are often the investigator's only source of information about the past. If the investigator wishes to conduct an in-depth, statistically rigorous study, the use of all three methodological approaches may be necessary.

Be this as it may, it is entirely appropriate that the last section of this book deals with methods of research. A backward glance will reveal that our chief concern has been with theories

---

[42] Phillips, *Social Research,* p. 5.

of community. On more than one occasion, however, it has been pointed out that good theories are a product of good research, and vice versa. Thus, during the past few decades students of community life have developed a number of theoretical systems which potentially help us to understand communal phenomena. During the same period of time an untold number of community studies have been conducted. Yet those of us who regard the community as a worthy object for study still face the challenge of bringing theoretical relevance to our research and of subjecting our theories to rigorous testing. If students of the community do not meet this challenge, then they can expect some rather devastating criticism to be aimed in their direction.

Bibliography

Dean, John P., Robert L. Eichhorn, and Lois R. Dean. "Observation and Interviewing," in John T. Doby (ed.), *An Introduction to Social Research,* 2nd ed. New York: Appleton-Century-Crofts, 1967.

Fessler, Donald R. "The Development of a Scale for Measuring Community Solidarity," *Rural Sociology,* **17** (June, 1952), pp. 144–52.

Gibbs, Jack P. *Urban Research Methods.* Princeton, N.J.: D. Van Nostrand Company, Inc., 1961.

Gold, Raymond L. "Roles in Sociological Field Observations," *Social Forces,* **36** (March, 1958), pp. 217–23.

Janes, Robert W. "A Note on Phases of the Community Role of the Participant-Observer," *American Sociological Review,* **26** (June, 1961), pp. 446–50.

McCall, George J., and J. L. Simmons. *Issues in Participant Observation: A Text and Reader.* Reading, Mass.: Addison-Wesley Publishing Company, 1969.

Phillips, Bernard S. *Social Research: Strategy and Tactics,* 2nd ed. New York: Macmillan Company, 1971.

Schwartz, Morris S., and Charlotte Green Schwartz. "Problems in Participant Observation," *American Journal of Sociology,* **60** (January, 1955), pp. 343–53.

Name Index

Abu-Lughod, Janet L., 103n., 271
Ackoff, Russell L., 293n.
Adrian, Charles R., 221n.
Agger, Robert E., 203–204
Aiken, Michael, 268n.
Alihan, Milla A., 87–88
Alinsky, Saul, 233–34
Allen, Francis R., 215n., 217n.
Anderson, Nels, 213–14
Angell, Robert, 299n.
Arensberg, Conrad M., 15n., 254–56
Arenson, Eliott, 293–94n.

Babchuk, Nicholas, 205n., 297
Babcock, Richard F., 227n.
Bahr, Howard M., 269–70
Baker, George W., 184n.
Bales, Robert F., 161n.
Banfield, Edward C., 50–51
Bebout, John E., 148n., 156–58
Becker, Howard, 108, 110, 114
Becker, Howard S., 284
Beegle, J. Allen, 219
Bell, Wendell, 100n., 101, 102–103,
   297n.
Bello, Francis, 226n.
Bensman, Joseph, 43n., 260–61
Berger, Bennett M., 56n.
Beynon, Erdmann Deane, 90n.
Bierstedt, Robert, 150–51, 170n.
Bloomberg, Warner, Jr., 193n.
Blumenfeld, Hans, 47, 54n.
Boat, Marion D., 297n.
Bonjean, Charles M., 197n., 199
Booth, Alan, 205n., 297
Booth, Charles, 66, 296
Boskoff, Alvin, 55, 56
Bosworth, Claud A., 298
Bredmeier, Harry C., 148n., 156–58
Broom, Leonard, 156n.
Brown, A. Theodore, 223n.
Brownell, Baker, 8–9, 21, 25
Buckley, Walter, 162n.
Burgess, Ernest W., 18, 68, 76–81,
   104

Cannell, Charles F., 293n.
Caplow, Theodore, 90n.
Carr, Lowell Julliard, 265–66
Chapin, F. Stuart, Jr., 196n.
Chapman, Dwight W., 184n.
Clark, S. D., 56n.
Clark, Terry N., 202n., 268n.

Cole, William E., 213–14
Conkin, Paul K., 221n.
Cooley, Charles Horton, 108
Cottrell, Leonard S., Jr., 156n.
Coulter, Phillip B., 229n.
Cowgill, Donald O., 215n.
Cristaller, Walter, 36
Cumming, Elaine, 187n.
Cumming, John, 187n.

Dahl, Robert H., 193–94, 196n.
Danielson, Michael N., 215n., 229n.
Dansereau, H. Kirk, 266n.
D'Antonio, William V., 20n., 196n.
Danzgar, M. Herbert, 20n.
Davie, Maurice R., 89–90
Davis, Allison, 20n., 259n.
Davis, Kingsley, 11, 33, 41, 161, 168n.,
   170n., 173n., 175n., 178
Dean, John P., 277n., 285, 294–95
Dean, Lois R., 277n., 285, 294–95
DeFleur, Lois B., 270
de Guarry de Champnouf, M., 66
Dentler, Robert A., 210, 233n.
de Tocqueville, Alexis, 205
Dewey, Richard, 31n., 37, 39–40, 43,
   49
Dobriner, William M., 54
Doby, John T., 275n., 277n., 294n.
Dollard, John, 20n., 261
Douglas, Harlan Paul, 54
Duncan, Beverly, 269
Duncan, Otis Dudley, 31n., 66n.,
   218n., 260n., 269
Dunham, Arthur, 230n.
Durkheim, Emile, 66, 108, 114

Eels, Kenneth, 260n.
Eichhorn, Robert L., 277n., 285, 294–
   95
Ensminger, Douglas, 43n.
Elmer, M. C., 66n.
Ericksen, Eugene C., 20n.

Fararo, Thomas J., 193n.
Fessler, Donald A., 298
Festinger, Leon, 275n., 294n.
Firey, Walter, 57n., 65, 97, 104, 219
Form, William R., 184n., 197n.
Forman, Louis A., 237n.
Freeman, Linton C., 193n.
Frieden, Bernard J., 236n.
Friedlander, Walter A., 235n.

Friedman, Lawrence M., 224n.

Galpin, Charles J., 12n.
Gans, Herbert J., 4, 224n., 227n., 259
Gardner, Burleigh B., 20n., 259n.
Gardner, Mary R., 259n.
Garrison, William L., 267
Gee, Wilson, 69n., 248
Geer, Blanche, 284
Gettys, Warner E., 87
Gibbs, Jack P., 31, 33n., 41, 269
Gillette, Thomas L., 250
Gilmore, Harlan W., 218n., 219n.
Glabb, Charles N., 233
Goffman, Erving, 5, 139
Gold, Raymond L., 280–82
Goldrich, Daniel, 203–204
Goldschmidt, Walter, 12n.
Goode, William J., 275n., 290n.
Gordon, Chad, 202
Gottschalk, Louis, 299n., 302
Green, James, 191n.
Greer, Scott, 3, 5n., 53
Gregg, Dorothy, 177n.
Grossman, David A., 236n.

Haberle, Rudolf, 266
Haer, John L., 264
Halbwachs, Maurice, 66
Hall, Oswall, 260n.
Haller, Archie O., 264n.
Halpern, Joel M., 33n., 42
Hansen, Asael T., 90n.
Harper, Ernest B., 230n.
Harris, Chauncey D., 83–84
Hatt, Paul K., 31n., 90, 275n., 290n.
Hauser, Philip M., 31n., 34n., 42, 50, 54n.
Havighurst, Robert J., 266
Hawley, Amos H., 35, 48, 75n., 88, 91, 95–96, 104
Hawley, Willis D., 198, 268n.
Hield, Wayne, 177n.
Hiller, E. T., 13–14
Hillery, George A., Jr., 3n., 9, 64, 133–34, 138–41, 143, 145–46
Hillman, Arthur, 221n.
Hoiberg, Otto G., 189n.
Holland, John B., 190, 191n., 192n.
Hollingshead, August B., 20n., 88, 257, 260
Homans, George C., 158, 159n.
Hoyt, Homer, 82–83
Hunter, Floyd, 20n., 188n., 196n., 197
Hyman, Herbert H., 205n., 264n.

Janes, Robert, 280, 282–84
Janowitz, Morris, 55n.
Johnson, Lyndon B., 235, 236n.

Kahn, Robert L., 293n.
Katz, Daniel, 275n., 294n.
Kaufman, Harold F., 17n., 181, 191n., 207
Kellogg, Paul, 296
Keyes, Fenton, 42, 45n.
Kimball, Solon T., 188
Kinsey, Alfred C., 264
Kish, Leslie, 293n.
Kluckhohn, Clyde, 299n.
Kluckhohn, Florence, 22
Kolaja, Jiri, 182–83, 207
Kornhauser, William, 196

Labutut, Jean, 219n.
Lane, Wheaton J., 219n.
Lasswell, T. E., 40
Lebeaux, Charles N., 38–39, 40
L'Enfant, Major Pierre Charles, 223
Levin, Yale, 66n.
Levy, Marion J., Jr., 167n.
Liebow, Elliot, 268
Lindesmith, Alfred, 66n.
Lindsey, Gardner, 293n.
Lockwood, David, 177n.
Loomis, Charles P., 108n., 114n., 116n., 149, 154, 162, 219
Lunt, Paul S., 20n., 259n.
Lynd, Helen M., 20n., 196n., 258
Lynd, Robert S., 20n., 196n., 258

McCall, George J., 276n., 297n.
McEntire, Davis, 215n.
MacIver, Robert M., 15, 16n., 21, 64, 121–22, 143
McKenzie, Roderick D., 51, 52n., 68, 71–76
McKinney, John C., 108n., 110, 116
McNeil, C. F., 230
Mair, Harry W., 194n.
Malinowski, Bronislaw, 166
Mangus, A. R., 264n.
Martin, Clyde E., 264n.
Martin, Walter T., 55
Mayo, Selz C., 190, 191n., 196n.
Meeker, Marchia, 260n.
Merton, Robert K., 156n., 164n., 166, 200–201, 250–51
Meier, Richard L., 229
Mial, Curtis, 239
Mial, Dorothy, 239
Miller, Delbert C., 196n., 216, 292n., 298n.
Miller, Paul A., 191, 192n., 197
Miner, David W., 3, 5
Monane, Joseph H., 148n.
Morgan, H. Gerthen, 266
Mott, Paul, 268n.
Mumford, Lewis, 223n., 226n.

Name Index

Murdock, George P., 90n.
Murphy, Raymond E., 36, 47n., 57

National Advisory Commission on Civil Disorders, 185–86, 206
Nelson, Lowery, 12n., 46
Nett, Roger, 250, 294n.
Nisbet, Robert A., 7, 8, 9, 21, 25
Nosow, Sigmund, 184n.
Nuttall, Ronald L., 202

Ogburn, William F., 215n., 218
Olson, David M., 197n., 199

Page, Charles H., 21
Park, Robert E., 18, 66–69, 85, 86n., 104
Parsons, Talcott, 108, 114n., 156n., 161
Pearsall, Marion, 188–89
Peñalosa, Fernando, 90n., 270
Perloff, Harvey S., 222n.
Pfautz, Harold W., 66n., 260n.
Phillips, Bernard S., 275n., 289n., 292, 303
Polsby, Nelson W., 21n.
Pomeroy, Wardell B., 264n.
Poplin, Dennis E., 297n.
Pryor, Robin J., 57n.

Quinn, James A., 68, 74n., 91–95, 104

Radcliffe-Brown, A. R., 164, 165n.
Ramsey, Charles E., 12n.
Reckless, Walter C., 78–79
Redfield, Robert, 40, 64, 114, 121, 125–33, 143, 144, 259n.
Reiss, Albert J., 14, 31n.
Reps, John W., 22n.
Reuter, E. B., 90n.
Robson, William A., 47
Rodwin, Lloyd, 221n.
Rose, Arnold, 72
Ross, Murray G., 230n.
Rothman, Jack, 230n.
Rowntree, B. S., 296

Sanders, Irwin T., 15, 21, 43n., 148n., 212n., 228, 239n.
Schermerhorn, Richard A., 269n.
Scheuch, Erwin K., 202
Schnore, Leo F., 31n., 34n., 42n., 54n., 55n.
Schwartz, Charlotte Green, 276n., 285n.
Schwartz, Morris S., 276n., 285n.
Seeman, Albert L., 99n.
Selltiz, Claire, 275n., 288n.
Sewell, William H., 264n.

Shevky, Eshref, 100, 101n., 102–103
Silberman, Charles E., 234
Sills, David, 227n.
Simmons, J. L., 276n., 279
Simpson, Richard L., 257
Sjoberg, Gideon, 31, 64, 133, 134–37, 143, 145, 250, 294n.
Smith, Joel, 297n.
Smith, T. Lynn, 32, 39n., 45n.
Smith, T. V., 80n.
Sorokin, Pitirim A., 114
Sower, Christopher, 188n.
Stein, Maurice R., 4n., 86n., 262
Stermer, James, 265–66
Steward, Julian H., 254, 257
Stone, Gregory P., 297n.
Strange, John H., 215n.
Strodtbeck, Fred, 22
Sunshine, Morris H., 193n.
Sussman, Marvin B., 189n.
Sutton, Willis A., Jr., 16n., 182–83, 186, 187n., 207
Swanson, Bert E., 203–204

Taggert, Glen, 12n.
Taylor, Carl C., 12n.
Theodorson, George A., 67n., 266n.
Tiedke, Kenneth E., 191n., 192n.
Tonnies, Ferdinand, 114–121, 144, 202
Turbeville, Gus, 174n.

Ullman, L., 83
Underwood, Kenneth W., 174n.
U.S. Bureau of the Census, 41, 46, 52, 301
U.S. Department of Housing and Urban Development, p. 225

Verner, Coolie, 12n.
Vidich, Arthur J., 43n., 260–61

Wagner, Hulse, 267
Walter, Benjamin, 196n.
Walton, John, 21n.
Warner, W. Lloyd, 20n., 259–60
Warren, Roland L., 14, 18n., 64, 133, 134, 141–43, 145, 148n., 156, 160, 212n.
Webb, Beatrice, 296
Webb, Sidney, 296
Webber, Melvin M., 221–22
Weber, Max, 108
Weiss, Shirley F., 196n.
West, James, 259
Wheelis, Alan, 24–25
White, L. D., 80n.
Whyte, William Foote, 259n.
Whyte, William H., Jr., 226

Wildavsky, Aaron, 196n.
Wilensky, Harold L., 38, 40
Williams, Elgin, 177n.
Williams, Marilyn, 100, 101n.
Wirt, Frederick M., 198, 268n.
Wirth, Lewis, 32, 36–38, 259n.
Wolfinger, Raymond E., 21n., 198
Wright, Charles R., 205n., 264n.

Yinger, J. Milton, 173n.
Young, Pauline V., 296n.

Zelditch, Morris, 161n.
Zimmerman, Carle C., 64, 123–25, 143–45, 201
Zopf, Paul E., 32, 39n., 45n.
Zorbaugh, Harvey W., 85n., 87n.

Subject Index

Agricultural technology, 216–18
  and the emergence of cities and metropolitan areas, 216
  modernization of, 216–18
Associations, MacIver's concept of, 122

Basic social processes, see Interaction
Boston, Massachusetts, ecological structure of, 97–98
Boundary maintenance, 162–63; see also Types of community boundaries
Building codes, 227

Case studies, as sources of data, 138
Census tracts, defined, 301
Central cities, 52–54
  changes in, 54
  and the metropolitan community, 52
  occupants of, 52–53
  and social system theory, 157–58
Centralization, as an ecological process, 71–73
Citizen involvement
  in the Community Action Program, 236
  in episodes of community action, 206
City planning, 221–29, 360–79
  and building codes, 227
  and the Demonstration Cities and Metropolitan Development Act, 224–25
  and direct action, 227–28
  history of, 222–25
  and the Housing Act of 1949, 224
  and the master plan, 226–27
  obstacles to, 228–29

City planning (Cont.)
  problems and procedures in, 225–28
  traditional assumptions of, 221–22
  and vested interest groups, 228–29
Classical ecology, 67–90
  basic assumptions of, 67–69
  and the biotic level of social organization, 67–68, 87–88
  the central role of competition in, 69–71, 88–89; see also competition
  and the concentric zone hypothesis, 76–81
  criticisms of, 87–90
  and the ecological processes, 71–76
  and natural areas, see Natural areas
  and the principle of dominance, 70
  and the social level of organization, 67–68, 69
  structural features of, 152–53
  as a territorial unit, 9–13
  as a unit of social organization, 13–25
  as a variable in research, 262–67
  a word of many uses, 3–5
Community action, see also Initiated community action, universe of community action
  routinized, 186
  spontaneous, 184–86
  types of, 184–92
Community action and community development, 233–39; see also Community development in foreign countries
  Saul Alinsky and the power bloc approach, 233–34
Community Action Program, 235–38
  maximum feasible participation of the poor in, 236

Community Action Program (*Cont.*)
and national emphasis programs, 237
principle components of, 236
purposes and philosophy of, 235–36
success of, 237–38
Community action theory, 16–17
Community areas, 35–36
Community autonomy, Warren's concept of, 142–43
Communal and associational relations, MacIver's typology of, 121–22
Communal organizations, Hillery's concept of, 140–41
Communication facilities, and the fusion of rural and urban, 219–20
Communities
classification by type, 29–30
demographic differences between, 30–33
ecological differences between, 33–36
and the extra-communal (or societal) level, 141–42
functional analysis of, 168–75
sociocultural differences between, 36–40
Community
defined, 3, 8, 9, 14, 122
input-output relations within, 156–58
and mass society, 5–7
as a moral or spiritual phenomenon, 5–9
as a network of interaction, 16–20
as a psycho-cultural unit, 21–25
quest for, 7
as a sample, 253–57
as a social group, 13–14
in sociological perspective, 9–25
Community change, *see also* City planning; Community action and community development; Community organization
planned, 211, 220–39
unplanned, 24
and urbanization, 212
Community development in foreign countries, 238–39
Community leadership, *see* Leaders; Power elite; Influentials
Community life
future of research on, 272
studies of, 257–71
Community of limited liability, 55
Community organization, 230–33
defined, 230
goals and objectives of, 231–33

Community organization (*Cont.*)
public involvement in, 232
Community power structure,
and the pluralistic thesis, 198
reputational approach to the analysis of, 198–99
ruling elite model of, 197–98
studies of, 20
types of, 203–204
Community problems, of concern to city planners, 225–26
Community sentiment
consequences and implications of, 23–25
defined, 21
elements of, 22–23
and social control, 24–25
Community size, as a research variable, 263–65
Community structure, defined, 95
Community structure and dynamics
ethnographic studies of, 258–59, 268
research on, 258–62
Commuter's Zone, 80
Competition, and the spatial organization of cities, 68–71
Complete observer, 280
ethical questions concerning, 282
Complete participant, 280
Concentration, as an ecological process, 73–74
Concentric zone hypothesis, 76–81
criticisms of, 81
empirical tests of, 89–90
Constructed types
and the clarification of concepts, 134
defined, 109
nature of, 108–110
utility of, 110–13
Constructed type theories of community
major criticism of, 144–45
significance of, 144
Cosmopolitan communities, 124–25
Cultural disorganization
Redfield's concept of, 129–30

Demonstration Cities and Metropolitan Development Act, 224–25
Dependent variable, the community as a, 265–67
Documents
authenticity and credibility of, 301–302
historical, 299
local newspapers as, 300

Documents (*Cont.*)
use of in community research, 298–302

Economic Opportunity Act, 235
Economic systems, at the community level, 171–72
Education, as a communal subsystem, 172–73
Elmtown, 260
Eminent domain, right of, 228
Equilibrium, *see also* Social systems
criticisms of the concept, 162
defined, 161
Expressive activities, 159
External pattern (or system), 158–60

Family
as a component of the modern community, 174–75
functions of the, 175
in modern urban society, 39
in the preindustrial city, 136–37
Folk communities, Redfield's concept of, 132
Folk-urban continuum, 125–33
and community change, 129–31
and cultural disorganization, 129–30
and individualism, 131
and secularization, 131
Functionalism (or functional theory), 163–75
criticisms of, 177
and functional alternatives, 168
and functional requisites, 166–68
and latent functions, 168
and manifest functions, 168
and the modern community, 168–75
nature and purposes of, 164–66
and the postulate of indispensability, 167
and the postulate of universal functionalism, 166
and social system theory, 164

Gemeinschaft and *gesellschaft,* 114–21
and the analysis of communities, 114
as ideal types, 119
and social and cultural change, 119–21
and the types of law, 118–19
and the types of will, 115–16
Gemeinschaft-like relationships, 116–17, 118
Gesellschaft-like relationships, 117–18, 187
Groups, *see* Social groups

Highways, impact upon community life, 266–67
Hinterlands
and community areas, 35–36
conceptualization of, 34
and the rural community, 34, 43
and the urbanite, 34
Horizontal axis (or pattern), 17, 143, 160
Housing Act of 1949, 224
Human ecology, *see also* Classical ecology; Concentric zone hypothesis; Natural areas; Neo-orthodox ecology; Social area analysis; Sociocultural ecology
concentric zone theory of, *see* Urban spatial organization
criticisms of, 87–90
cross-cultural studies of, 270–71
defined, 95
foremost goal of, 65
historical development of, 66–67
multiple-nuclei theory of, *see* Urban spatial organization
recent developments in, 269–71
sector theory of, *see* Urban spatial organization
tasks of, 65, 69

Independent variable, the community as an, 263–65
Influentials
and community decision making, 202–203
cosmopolitan, 200–201
local, 200–201
Informant interviewing, 279
Initiated community action, 186–92, 304–13
characteristics of, 187–89
and community leadership and involvement, 193
main purpose of, 187
role of professional persons in, 189
stages in, 190–92
Institutions
and community structure, 151–52
properties of, 152
Instrumental activities, 159
Interaction
and the basic social processes, 18–20
defined, 17, 153–54
Internal pattern (or system), 158–60
Interview schedules, 293–94
Invasion, as an ecological process, 75–76

Juvenile delinquency, ecological study of, 270–71

Land settlement, *see* Patterns of land settlement
Latter-day Saints (Mormon), 12, 99
Leaders
 grassroots, 196–97
 institutional, 194–96
Local government, 169–71
 functions of, 170–71
Localistic communities, 123–24
Localistic and cosmopolitan communities, Zimmerman's typology of, 123–25

Marysville, Washington, 267
Mass society, *see also* Community characteristics of, 6
Master plans, 226–27
Methods of community study, *see* Documents; Participant observation; Social surveys
Metropolitan communities
 characteristics of, 51–52
 definitions of, 47
 emergence and growth of, 50–51
 population densities of, 48
 structure of, 51–58
Metropolitan government, 229
Middletown, 258
Moral communities, *see* Community

Natural areas, 84–87
 and the concentric zone hypothesis, 84–85, 135
 cultural distinctiveness of, 85–86
 and the efficient administration of city government, 86–87
 as a geographic concept, 85
 research on, 90
Natural will, 115–16
Neo-orthodox ecology, 91–96
 Amos H. Hawley's theory of, 95–96
 and classical ecology, 91
 and the concept of ecological structure, 92–93
 criticisms of, 96
 and ecological interaction, 92
 as an economic interpretation of ecological structure, 94–95
 and the hypothesis of intensiveness of utilization, 94
 and the hypothesis of median location, 94
 and the hypothesis of minimum cost, 93
 and the hypothesis of minimum ecological distance, 93
 James A. Quinn's theory of, 91–95

Observer-as-participant, 281

Participant-as-observer, 281
Participant observation, 276–87
 advantages of, 284–85
 characteristics of, 287–88
 dangers in, 278
 definition and nature of, 276–77
 limitations of, 285–86
 techniques of, 278–80
Participant observer
 community roles of, 282–84
 field roles of, 280–82
 roles of and the quality of data, 281–82
Participation, in community action episodes, 204–206
Patterns of land settlement, 11–12
Population density
 and community size, 33
 as a measure of urbanity, 33
 and types of communities, 32–33
Population size
 and cross-cultural research, 30, 31–32
 and types of communities, 30–32
 and urbanism, 42
Power elite
 characteristics of the, 197
 occupations of, 197
Power structure, *see* Community power structure
Preindustrial cities
 ecological organization of, 135
 economic organization of, 136
 Sjoberg's typology of, 134–37
 social organization of, 136–37
 technological base of, 137
Primary community area, 35

Race relations, research on, 261–62
Rational will, 116
Religion
 as a communal subsystem, 173–74
 and community conflict, 173–74
 functional theory of, 173–74
Research
 choice of methods of, 303
 and the clarification of concepts, 251
 and community problems, 251–53
 on community structure and dynamics, 258–62
 and community study, 247–57
 functions of, 249–52
 on highways and community life, 266–67
 nature of, 248–49
 on race relations, 261–62

Research (*Cont.*)
and school integration, 252–53
on selected aspects of community life, 268–71
on social stratification, 259–61
and the U.S. Census of Population, 300–301
Research design, 292
Research problems, choice of, 291–92
Respondent interviewing, 279
Riots, as a type of community action, 185–86
Riverville, 283–84
Roles, of the participant observer, 280–84
Roles and community structure, 150
Rural communities
demographic characteristics of, 41–43
homogeneity of, 44–45
low division of labor in, 45
patterns of action in, 112–13
population densities of, 42–43
population size of, 41–42
primary relationships in, 44
social rank in, 44
sociocultural characteristics of, 43–45
subtypes, 45–46, 74–75
and their hinterlands, 43
Rural-urban fringe, 56–58
nature of, 57
problems of, 57

Salt Lake City, Utah, 98–99
Sample, the community as, 253–57
criteria for selecting, 254–56
Sampling procedures, in social surveys, 293
Satellite cities, characteristics of, 55
Secondary community area, 35
Segregation
in the Chicago Metropolitan District, 269
as an ecological process, 74–75
and natural areas, 74, 85
and property values, 250
and other racial differences, 269–70
Seneca, Illinois, 266
Social area, defined, 101
Social area analysis, 100–103
utility of, 101–103
variables used in, 100–101
Social change
and community problem solving, 210–11
and initiated community action, 187–88
Ogburn's approach to, 218

Social change (*Cont.*)
and social problems, 210–11, 341–42
Social classes
at the community level, 20
in the preindustrial city, 136
Warner's analysis of, 259–60
Social control, and local government, 170
Social groups, *see also* Community
Bierstedt's classification of, 150–51
communities as, 13–14
as a component of community structure, 150–51
properties of, 13
Social stratification, research on, 259–61
Social surveys, 287–98; *see also* Interview schedules; Research design
analysis and presentation of data from, 295
characteristics of, 287–90
data collection in, 292–95
steps entailed in, 290–95
and testing hypotheses and theories, 289–90
use of in community study, 295–98
Social systems
and boundary maintenance, 162–63
characteristics of, 15
defined, 148–49, 161
and equilibrium, 161–62
and input-output relationships, 156–58
and the instrumental-expressive dichotomy, 159
interaction in, 153–58
interrelatedness in, 158–62
and locality relevant functions, 14–15
Social system theory
and community structure, 149–53
criticisms of, 177
summary of basic principles of, 176
Sociocultural ecology, 96–100
crucial implications of, 99–100
and rational adaption, 97
and sentiment and symbolism, 97–99
Springdale, 260–61
Standard metropolitan statistical area, defined, 32, 47
Statuses, and community structure, 150
Suburban ring, 54–56
components of, 54–55
and the metropolitan community, 54

312

Subject Index

Suburbs (or suburban communities)
  defined, 55
  types of residential, 56
Succession, as an ecological process, 76
Symbiosis, 70
Systemic linkage, 154

Talladega, Alabama, 188
Tally's Corner, 268
Technology, and the preindustrial city, 137
Territorial variables, *see also* Territory
  academic approaches to, 12, 13
Territory, *see also* Community
  as a dependent variable, 11–12
  as an independent variable, 10–11
Tertiary community area, 35
Theories of community, classification of, 63–64
Theory
  defined, 250
  function of, 247
  and research, 249–51
Total institutions, 5, 139, 140
Transportation facilities, and the fusion of rural and urban, 219
Types of community boundaries, 168
Typological tradition, 114

Universe of community actions
  and communal phenomena, 181–84
  criteria for the delineation of the, 182–84
  and degress of "community-ness," 182
Urban areas, characteristics of, 36–40
Urban communities
  anonymity of, 40
  class structure of, 49
  heterogeneity of, 40, 49
  high division of labor in, 40
  hinterland relationships of, 48
  impersonal relationships in, 40
  and overt symbols of status, 40, 49
  patterns of action in, 112–13
  population densities of, 47–48
  population size of, 46–47

Urban communities (*Cont.*)
  Redfield's concept of, 132
  and social control, 48
  sociocultural characteristics of, 48–49
Urban places, defined, 46–47
Urban populations, heterogeneity of, 37
Urban spatial organization
  concentric zone theory of, 76–81
  multiple-nuclei theory of, 83–84
  sector theory of, 82–83
Urban sprawl, 226
Urbanism, as a trait associated with entire societies, 39
Urbanism and the urban personality
  specific traits of, 37–38
  the traditional view of, 38–39
Urbanization
  defined, 212–13
  and improvements in agricultural technology, 216–18
  and improvements in transportation and communication, 218–20
  and its derivations, 220
  of rural areas, 219–20, 357–59
U.S. Bureau of the Census, 31, 32, 300–301
Utah cities, ecological structure of, 98–99

Vertical axis (or pattern), 18, 143, 160
  and community autonomy, 143
Vill, 138–40
  elements of, 139–40
  Hillery's definition of, 139, 140

Washington, D.C., plans for, 223
Willow Run, Michigan, 265–66

Yucatan Peninsula, 126–27, communities on the, 127–29, 205–209

Zone of better residences, 79–80
Zone of independent workingmen's homes, 79
Zone of transition, 78–79
Zoning ordinances, 227